A HISTORY OF MEDIEVAL
POLITICAL THOUGHT

'A splendid book ... The best short guide to medieval political thought to date.'

Ken Pennington, *Syracuse University*

Joseph Canning's survey of medieval political thought is grounded in a wide range of primary source material. He has also brought together the latest research, much of which is now made available in English for the first time. The result is a comprehensive yet accessible one-volume account of medieval political thought from around 300 to 1450.

The book covers four periods, each with a different focus. From 300 to 750 Canning examines Christian ideas of rulership. The often neglected centuries from 750 to 1050, the Carolingian period and its aftermath, are given special attention. From 1050 to 1290 the conflict between temporal and spiritual power and the revived legacy of antiquity comes to the fore. Finally, in the period from 1290 to 1450, Canning focuses on the confrontation with political reality in ideas of church and state, and in juristic thought.

Joseph Canning is Senior Lecturer in History at the University of Wales, Bangor. He is the author of *The Political Thought of Baldus de Ubaldis* (1987).

A HISTORY OF MEDIEVAL POLITICAL THOUGHT

300–1450

Joseph Canning

London and New York

First published 1996
by Routledge
11 New Fetter Lane, London EC4P 4EE

Simultaneously published in the USA and Canada
by Routledge
29 West 35th Street, New York, NY 10001

Reprinted 1998

Typeset in Palatino by
Poole Typesetting (Wessex) Limited
Bournemouth, Dorset

Printed and bound in Great Britain by
Clays Ltd, St Ives plc

British Library Cataloguing in Publication Data
A catalogue record for this book is available from the British Library

Library of Congress Cataloguing in Publication Data
Canning, Joseph.
A history of medieval political thought, 300–1450 / Joseph Canning.
p. cm.
Includes bibliographical references and index.
1. Political science–History.   I. Title.
JC111.C33   1996
320'.01–dc20 96–10821

ISBN 0–415–01349–6
ISBN 0–415–01350–X (pbk)

For Roberta

CONTENTS

PREFACE

The completion of this book marks the end of a long journey which I began, when, as an undergraduate at Cambridge, I attended the lectures and seminars of Walter Ullmann. I owe a considerable debt to him for inspiring me to study the political thought of the Middle Ages and for supervising me as his research student.

I should like to thank the University of Wales, Bangor, for two periods of study leave to finish this work, and its School of History and Welsh History for research grants. Without Ann Illsley's efficiency in obtaining inter-library loans, my task would have been much more difficult. I also wish to express my gratitude to the British Academy for financial support for necessary research. The resources of Cambridge University Library and the Warburg Institute have also been of very great assistance. I wish to record my gratitude to my original editor at Routledge, Janice Price, for her encouragement while this book was being written.

I should like to thank Professor Dr Otto Gerhard Oexle for inviting me for two research visits as a *Stipendiat* at the Max-Planck-Institut für Geschichte at Göttingen, a paradise for historical research. I should also like to thank my good friend there, Dieter Girgensohn, for arranging my original invitation: he and his wife Bettina helped make my stays extremely happy and fruitful.

I owe my greatest debt of gratitude to my wife, to whom this book is dedicated, for sustaining me throughout the time of preparation and writing, and to my children who put up with having an author as a father.

INTRODUCTION

This study seeks to interpret the history of the political ideas of medieval western, that is Latin, Europe and covers the period between the early fourth and the mid-fifteenth century. This starting-point, still within late antiquity, has been chosen because it marks the public acceptance and then dominance of Christianity, a development which was to provide the fundamental context for the political ideas of the Middle Ages proper. The concluding date is more problematical, because it can well be argued that the period from the thirteenth to the mid-seventeenth century forms a coherent whole in terms of political thought. The problem is that there is no clear end to the Middle Ages because of the diversity of cultural development in different parts of Europe and the survival of medieval ideas and attitudes well into the seventeenth century. It would, however, prove far too unwieldy to prolong this book to 1650 or thereabouts. A division in about the middle of the fifteenth century has been accepted because it reflects the effective end of the medieval papacy and the beginnings of early modern territorial monarchies, and because the development of Renaissance humanism increasingly created a new world of political discourse.

The first and fundamental problem, however, in treating medieval European political thought is to define clearly the nature of the subject. In this study a broad definition will be used: ideas concerning the nature, organisation, government and ends of society. This wide approach is dictated by the characteristics of medieval political thought and of the sources from which the historian may reconstruct it. The most obvious omission from this definition is any mention of the state, which would have to be included in any examination of post-medieval political ideas.

The reason for this absence helps characterise a large part of the Middle Ages: although the term 'state', being in content historically fluid, can have medieval as distinct from a variety of modern connotations, it is difficult to see that it can be meaningfully employed to describe aspects of politically organised society in the medieval west before the twelfth century. The whole question of the state in the Middle Ages is, however, a very vexed one: there are, for instance, scholars who would locate an idea of the state in as early a period as the Carolingian. The disagreements hinge around the degree of rigour employed in the application of the term 'state' and illustrate a profound difficulty concerning the interpretation of western medieval political thought: so much of its content does not fit into modern preconceptions about what comprises political thought.

This difficulty is also apparent in the nature of the sources for this enquiry. Medieval political thought cannot be adequately treated by considering the works of a string of political thinkers: such writings were largely lacking in the Middle Ages, and in so far as they existed, were products only of the period from the twelfth century onwards. Most medieval writers relevant to this study were primarily theologians, philosophers or jurists: political ideas formed only a minor part of their concerns. The basic intellectual orientation of these thinkers must be borne in mind when interpreting them. Similarly, the works of publicists involved in the disputes between the papacy and secular rulers have to be understood within the context of each conflict and according to the intentions of the writer: such men were not professedly political thinkers. The importance of legal, and especially juristic, sources was paramount, and because of the role of the church, ecclesiological questions assumed a political significance which they would have lacked in a more secular age. Furthermore, throughout the medieval period, and certainly in its earlier part, a range of other kinds of source has to be considered: coronation orders, for instance, and histories. The sources of medieval political thought, therefore, consist both of writings directly or indirectly concerned with political matters, and other forms of material which permit the elucidation of political assumptions, attitudes and mentalities.

Such considerations lead the student of medieval political thought to treat it within its historical context. This method will be followed here, because the historical meaning of the whole range of medieval political ideas can only be discerned, when the sources, in all their variety, are viewed against the background of the societies, institutions, conflicts and intellectual *milieux* in which they were produced and with which they were concerned. This is in any case very much a historian's attitude, and of course it is perfectly possible to approach, where relevant, the sources of medieval political thought from a purely philosophical or jurisprudential stand-point. Differing kinds of meaning would thereby be gleaned from the material, but not that which was originally contained in the source, or which, in the case of a writer, he sought to express.

Given the nature of the sources to be considered and the method to be followed, it has seemed best to combine in this book a thematic with a chronological approach, thereby enabling the integrity of every historical stage to be preserved and the longer-term connections to be made. The focus is on the west; Byzantine political thought is only considered for purposes of comparison and in so far as it affected the west, because the Byzantine empire had a very different history: there the state endured as a continuation of the Roman empire of antiquity, and the position of the church in relation to the secular power increasingly diverged from that existing in the west, where ecclesiastical claims to independence developed to an extent unknown in the east. Although the church and secular rulers normally worked in harmony throughout the Middle Ages in the west, the opportunity for conflict was ever-present from the mid-eleventh century onwards, when the papacy substantially enlarged its jurisdictional claims. There was thereafter an underlying tension between secular and ecclesiastical power, which on occasion broke out into full-scale conflicts. The existence of such disputes in the west and their virtual absence in the more static east had the most profound long-term implications for the political ideas of both parts of Christendom. The conflicts between the church and secular power, reflecting the divided loyalties of those involved, provided so much of the dynamism of western medieval political thought, and prevented the emergence of the idea of a monolithic society. Writers engaged in these disputes radically disagreed about the ordering of society, its government and the public obligations of its members. Fundamental enquiries concerning the nature and purpose of rulership were exhaustively pursued precisely because of this disagreement. As a result, profound contributions were

made to perennially important political questions, but contributions which were characteristically medieval in content. The
modern enquirer into medieval political thought is first struck by
the prominence of religious aspects; but, as we shall see, therein lies
only part of the story.

LIST OF ABBREVIATIONS

Auth.	*Authentica ad Codicem*
C.	*Codex Iustinianus*
c.	*capitulum*
Clem.	*Clementinae constitutiones*
col.	column
Coll.	*Collationes Authentici*
Cons.	*Consilium*
Const.	*Constitutio*
D.	*Digesta Iustiniani*
Decr. Grat.	*Decretum Gratiani*
Dist	*Distinctio*
DM	Marsilius of Padua, *Defensor minor*
DP	Marsilius of Padua, *Defensor pacis*
Ep.	*Epistola*
Extrav. comm.	*Extravagantes communes*
Feud.	*Libri feudorum*
gl.	*glossa*
Inst.	*Institutiones Iustiniani*
l.	*lex*
MGH	*Monumenta Germaniae Historica*
Cap.	*Capitularia regum Francorum*
Conc.	*Concilia*
Const.	*Constitutiones*
DH II	*Heinrici II. diploma*
DO III	*Ottonis III. diploma*
Epp.	*Epistolae*
L de L	*Libelli de lite*
SS	*Scriptores*
Nov.	*Novellae Iustiniani*

xiv

LIST OF ABBREVIATIONS

PL	J.P. Migne, *Patrologia latina*
Reg.	*Registrum*
Sext.	*Liber sextus Decretalium Bonifacii P. VIII*
ST	Thomas Aquinas, *Summa Theologiae*
X.	*Decretales Gregorii P. IX seu Liber extra*

1

THE ORIGINS OF MEDIEVAL POLITICAL IDEAS, *c.* 300–*c.* 750

The political ideas of the ancient world largely conditioned the development of those of the Middle Ages. This process was, however, a highly complex one involving reinterpretation and innovation as these ideas were applied in the context of medieval conditions radically different from those which prevailed in ancient Greece, Rome or Israel. Antiquity provided so much of the intellectual raw material which was worked into peculiarly medieval structures of thought. Furthermore, the history of political ideas reflected the vicissitudes of the classical heritage in the medieval Latin west. In the early Middle Ages that inheritance was severely attenuated, whereas it was deeply enriched from the late eleventh century by the rediscovery of the whole of Justinian's codification of the Roman law, the *Corpus iuris civilis*,[1] and from the mid-twelfth by the growing body of Aristotelian works available in Latin translations. This is not to suggest, however, that the whole content of medieval political ideas rested on concepts derived from the ancient world. Some areas, such as, for instance, feudal notions, were specifically medieval developments. The rich texture of political ideas in the Middle Ages was provided by the way in which the medieval versions of ultimately Greco-Roman and biblical concepts coexisted and interacted with purely medieval modes of thinking. In the Byzantine empire the integration of classical and biblical ideas into a structure of political thought followed a path markedly different from that which the west pursued, but one which directly influenced the west in certain crucial phases.

The immediate foundations of early medieval political thought lay in the lengthy period of transition between the ancient world and the Middle Ages proper, that is to say between the reign of the Emperor Constantine (306–37) and the early eighth century, which in the west saw the rise to power of the Carolingians and in the east the existence of a thoroughly Greek Byzantine empire. It is necessary to begin our enquiry with this period of transition because it produced ideas basic not only to the whole thought-structure of the early Middle Ages but ones which were pervasive throughout the medieval period. A complete survey of intellectual life in these transitional centuries will not be attempted here: only those aspects important for the Middle Ages will be considered.

This period witnessed the conversion of Constantine, his foundation of Constantinople as the first predominantly Christian city and the reception of Christianity as the official religion of the Roman empire in 380; thus was provided the Christian context fundamental to the development of political ideas in the Middle Ages. In the west, Roman life became gradually barbarised with the settlement of Germanic peoples within the frontiers of the empire. With the gradual collapse of Roman administration as barbarian kingdoms emerged in the fifth and sixth centuries, regionalism developed leading ultimately to territorial kingship which became the characteristically medieval form of rulership. Yet within these kingdoms, notably in Gaul, Spain and Italy, increasingly diluted elements of Roman civilisation persisted into the seventh century. In the east, the Roman empire survived and became more and more Greek in outlook. Although the bases of Byzantine political thought had already been laid down in the fourth century, when the Roman empire remained intact, the eastern empire – despite its continuing universalist claims – had by the second half of the seventh century become clearly Byzantine, possessing control over only a part even of the original eastern portion of the empire: despite the attempted reconquests of Justinian the west had been lost apart from a remnant of power in Italy, and the advance of Islam in the seventh century had conquered Syria, Palestine and North Africa. Indeed it was the seventh century which really marked the end of antiquity and the beginning of the Middle Ages. The west in reality was left to its own resources; its regionalism crystallised into kingdoms: the Visigothic in Spain, the Frankish in Gaul, the Lombard in Italy and the Anglo-Saxon and Celtic ones in the British Isles. Byzantium, despite its grandiloquent universalist claims, turned inwards into its Greek culture and destiny. Much of the future lay with Islam which through its conquests largely destroyed what remained of the unity of Mediterranean civilisation. By 713 Islam had conquered the Visigothic kingdom, and by 720 Septimania in southern France, although its control there proved to be only short lived. Indeed, in 732/3 the Frankish leader Charles Martel halted any further Moslem advance northwards in a battle which took place at Tours or Poitiers. In a western Latin Europe limited, in effect, to Gaul, parts of western Germany, Italy and the British Isles, the stage was set for the Carolingian Renaissance, the flowering of a purely medieval western culture, in which were elaborated concepts of rulership which remained fundamental for the rest of the Middle Ages.

BYZANTIUM: THE CHRISTIAN EMPIRE

The conversion of Constantine, and Christianity's later status as the official religion of the Roman empire, produced in the long term a radical change in Christian attitudes to political life and the state. It was, however, a development which came about gradually: the immediate effects of Constantine's conversion itself can be exaggerated. Previously, there had been a range of Christian reactions to the Roman state. At one pole there existed negative alienation reinforced by sporadic persecutions largely caused by Christian unwillingness to participate in the pagan cult of the divinity of the emperor. A form of indifferentism resulting in political quietism was also prevalent. Following Christ's words, 'My kingdom is not of this world',[2] Christians considered this life but a passing preparation for the next, where in heaven they would find their true home. Amongst Christians, there was also a more positive attitude recognising the necessity of the Roman state and indeed its divinely sanctioned existence which justly claimed their submission in all that was not sin: 'Render unto Caesar the things that are Caesar's and to God the things that are God's.'[3] This message was supported by the words of St Peter, 'Fear God, and honour the emperor',[4] and of St Paul,

> You must all obey the governing authorities. Since all government comes from God, the civil authorities were appointed by God, and so anyone who resists authority is rebelling against God's decision, and such an act is bound to be punished.[5]

3

Indeed many Christians in the third century served the Roman state as soldiers. The transformed public position of Christianity in the fourth century did not result in the disappearance of the negative and indifferentist attitudes: these coexisted in tension with wholehearted Christian acceptance of the validity of the state. The change which did occur was a fundamental one: Christian theory of government and rulership was developed to accommodate an imperial power which was itself Christian. The results were of the greatest long-term significance, because from this point onwards into the Middle Ages there grew a theory and practice of government understood and justified in Christian terms. In itself Christianity advocated no particular form of government, but because the church was confronted with monarchy as the only form of rule existing in late antiquity and the early Middle Ages, Christian political thought emerged as monarchical.

The fundamental structure of Byzantine political thought was established in essence during the reign of Constantine himself, and remained largely unchanged throughout the existence of the empire. The father of this theory was Eusebius of Caesarea (263–339) whose interpretation of the significance of Constantine's reign exerted the widest influence. Eusebius believed that Constantine's establishment of the Christian empire marked a crucial turning-point in human history, nothing less than the fulfilment of God's promise to Abraham. This view interpreted Roman history as being determined by divine providence: that the empire was founded under Augustus, in whose reign Christ was born, in order to facilitate the spread of the Christian religion, a development culminating in the conversion of the emperor himself.

Eusebius also adapted Hellenistic ideas of kingship which by the third century had markedly influenced the development of Roman concepts of emperorship. According to Hellenistic theory the ruler was the image of God and his vicegerent on earth ruling a kingdom which was an imitation (*mimesis*) of that of heaven. Under the influence of Neoplatonic ideas the kingdom could thus be seen as a microcosm reflecting the order of the macrocosm of the universe itself. The ruler was understood as being himself divine: the Roman emperor was indeed 'lord and God' (*dominus et deus*). Eusebius, following the intention of Constantine, was able with ease to Christianise this pagan view. All that was necessary was to claim not a form of divinity for the emperor, but simply divine appointment confirmed by Constantine's closeness to God as shown by the special revelations to him and his military success. Thus the emperor was God's human vicegerent on earth ruling over an empire which was the reflection of the kingdom of heaven. Monotheism infused this cosmic order: just as there was one God in the universe there was one emperor (*Basileus*) in this world.

In relief at the end of recent severe persecution the bulk of the Christian church, like Eusebius, was only too willing to accept Constantine's close supervision of ecclesiastical matters. Constantine took it upon himself to summon ecclesiastical councils. Shortly after the decree of toleration known as the Edict of Milan (313) he called the Council of Arles in 314 to attempt to resolve the Donatist question;[6] in 325 he convoked the first ecumenical council itself at Nicaea. Constantine had brought the Christian church within the structure of the Roman state and thereby subjected it to his authority. He claimed jurisdiction over all the external aspects of Christianity, that is to say ecclesiastical organisation and administration, whereas bishops, he accepted, had authority over purely spiritual matters, such as the formulation of doctrine and the administration of sacraments. He also considered that as emperor he had religious responsibility for the pagans in his empire: thus the *Vita Constantini* (Life of Constantine) records that in a dinner speech given to the fathers of the Council of Nicaea he described himself as 'bishop of those without [i.e. pagans]' (*episkopos ton ektos*).[7] In Christian terms Constantine was not a bishop or priest in any sacramental sense, although he was accorded liturgical honours not given to any other layman. When he died, as a mark of special reverence he was declared a Christian saint, the equal of the apostles (*isapostolos*): so much had he done for his adopted religion.

After the death of Constantine, apart from the interlude of the Emperor Julian's (361–3) brief favouring of paganism, the view which understood the Roman empire as a Christian one gained in strength. The culmination of this process was the decree, *Cunctos populos*, whereby in 380 the emperors Valentinian II and Theodosius I made Catholic Christianity the official religion of the empire. From now on paganism went into further decline and the equation between Roman and Christian was consolidated.

From the point of view of the history of political ideas, the classic expression of Christian Roman emperorship is found in the *Corpus iuris civilis*. This was begun at Justinian's command in 527 and completed in 534 by a committee chaired by Tribonian. The codification consisted of three main parts. The largest was the *Digest* (or *Pandects*), divided into fifty books and comprising selections from thirty-nine classical jurists ranging from the second to the fourth centuries. A short introductory textbook for students, the *Institutes* (in four books), was added. The third part was the *Code* in twelve books containing imperial constitutions including many by Justinian himself. By the act of codification, the emperor made all parts of this *Corpus iuris* his law deriving efficacy from his will and thus possessing equal validity. The language of this compilation was Latin: there were very few Greek passages. Justinian forbade any commentaries on his codification but found he had to supplement it by issuing further constitutions, known as *Novels*, until his death in 565. These were mainly written in Greek, and in *c.* 580 a collection of 168 of them was made for general use. In the medieval west the *Novels* became known in two versions: the *Epitome Iuliani*, a Latin abridgement of 124 constitutions, and the *Authenticum* comprising 134 in either the original Latin or a translation from the Greek. By the twelfth century the *Authenticum* was considered part of the *Corpus iuris* as a whole.

The *Corpus iuris* contains the fundamental Roman law distinction between public and private law (*ius publicum* and *ius privatum*). The vast bulk of the compilation is private law. Its public law content, which is directly related to matters of politics and government, although it is restricted in extent and unsystematically presented, contains statements of enduring importance for political thought. There are, however, major problems of interpretation. Because of the speed of codification there are contradictions resulting from the diversity of the sources consulted. Thus, for instance, statements produced under the principate exist side by side with laws reflecting conditions under the dominate and Byzantine emperorship. Yet all laws in the *Corpus iuris* are accorded equal weight by the will of Justinian. The historian has to consider what each text meant when it was originally produced, how it was understood in the sixth century and what it was thought to signify in later periods of European history. Although the overall tenor of the *Corpus iuris* reflects a monarchical form of government, it also contains material echoing constitutional and legal ideas deriving ultimately from republican Rome: this is notably the case in the *Digest* and

6

Institutes. Because of such inconsistencies and irreconcilable elements in the text, it thus proved possible in the late Middle Ages to ransack the *Corpus iuris* for statements to support theories of both monarchy and government by the people. Furthermore the opening titles of the *Digest*, especially, contain principles of general relevance to any system of law or government. The destiny of the *Corpus iuris* was to serve as a vast treasure-house of legal and political ideas for medieval and early modern Europe.

However, its influence in the west was long delayed until the revival of scientific jurisprudence at the university of Bologna from the end of the eleventh century and the beginning of the twelfth. Before that period in the west, some Roman law was known primarily through the barbarian codes, the *Lex Romana Visigothorum* and the *Lex Romana Burgundionum*. In the east, the influence of the *Corpus iuris* was also problematic. Because of the decline in the knowledge of Latin, Greek translations and commentaries were produced. In *c.* 741[8] a short official summary of the law based on the *Corpus iuris* and the novels of subsequent emperors was produced by the emperors Leo III and Constantine V: this was known as the *Ecloga Isauriorum*. The great Greek version of the *Corpus iuris* known as the *Basilica* was issued by Leo VI (886–912) continuing the work of his father, Basil I. The original text of the *Corpus iuris* retained legal effect, although by the twelfth century Justinian's legislation was known to all intents and purposes only through the medium of the *Basilica*, a development culminating in the decision made by the imperial Court of Justice in 1169 whereby a law included in the *Corpus iuris* but not the *Basilica* was held to be invalid.

The dominant political message of the *Corpus iuris* is a theocratic one. The emperor derives his power from God: in the constitution *Deo auctore* at the beginning of the *Digest* Justinian describes himself as 'at God's command governing our empire, which has been entrusted to us by heavenly majesty'.[9] The divine source of imperial authority is constantly reiterated in the *Code* and *Novels*. 'At divine command we took up the imperial insignia.'[10] The emperor's laws are sacred (*sacrae* or *sacratissimae*),[11] thus reflecting the Christianising of his pagan role as *pontifex maximus*. They are, furthermore, of everlasting effect: Justinian decreed that his codification was to be valid 'forever' (*in omne aevum*).[12] His divine office is a universal one: he is 'lord of the world' (*dominus mundi*).[13] It is, therefore, his will alone which constitutes law: 'what has pleased the *princeps* has the force of law' (*quod principi placuit legis habet vigorem*).[14] He is thus no less than the 'living law' (*lex animata*), an application of the Hellenistic concept of the ruler as *nomos empsychos*: 'Let the imperial rank be exempted from all our provisions [in this constitution], because God has subjected the laws themselves to the emperor, by sending him as a living law to men.'[15] He is in short not bound by the law, but 'freed from the laws' (*legibus solutus*).[16] This famous phrase indicates that the emperor is above human law: he is not subjected to the laws which derive from his own universal authority. This formulation laid the foundation for the elaboration of the concept of absolute power in the late Middle Ages.[17]

On the other hand there are also in the *Corpus iuris* statements which indicate the possession of authority by the Roman people. The historical outline of Roman law in D.1.2.2 includes a brief sketch of the republican period, and republican sources of law are treated in D.1.1.7 and Inst. 1.2, 3–5. The most fundamental question however concerns the origin of the imperial power itself: reference is made to the so-called *lex regia* or 'royal law', whereby the Roman people transferred its power and authority to the emperor. The meaning of these references to the *lex regia* has been hotly debated by historians. One school of thought has seen it as an *ex post facto* legal construction to justify the transition from the republic to the empire. Such a law in fact never existed, but was postulated by later classical jurists to explain the transfer of sovereignty from the Roman people to the first *princeps*, Augustus, a device, in short, to legitimise the imperial power.[18] The other view identifies the *lex regia* with the *leges de imperio* by which the popular assembly gave power to each emperor at the beginning of his reign.[19] Justinian himself clearly considered that the *lex regia* established the empire: 'By an ancient law (*lege antiqua*) which was called "royal", all the authority and all the power of the Roman people were transferred to the power of the emperor.'[20] For Ulpian, what has pleased the *princeps* has the force of law, 'since by the royal law, which was passed concerning his imperial authority, the people confers on him all its authority and power',[21] a statement which can be understood to refer either to an original *lex regia* or to a *lex de imperio*. The problem with this interpretation is that only one such *lex de imperio* survives: that for Vespasian. In the form in which we have it, only part of the text remains and does not conform with the description of the *lex regia*: it is not a general transfer of power but confers specific powers and exemptions. It is pure speculation to consider that the missing first part would have contained such a general transfer; the existence of other *leges de imperio* is also hypothetical. The most likely interpretation is that the *lex regia* was indeed a later and classical juristic construction adopted by Justinian as having been genuinely enacted as a law. The name *lex regia* is itself strange. The nomenclature 'royal' would be at home in a Byzantine context but utterly alien to that of the principate. It has been suggested that the word is a Byzantine interpolation into Ulpian's text; Theodor Mommsen considered it more likely that it reflected the jurist's Syrian background.[22]

Whatever the truth about the *lex regia*, its significance for political thought was that it expressed the idea that the emperor's power derived from the people, and thus provided a model for the popular source of governmental power to be elaborated later in the Middle Ages and the early modern period. The *lex regia* raised a fundamental problem concerning the origins of authority, because its inclusion in the *Corpus iuris* meant that both divine and popular sources of rulership coexisted. These two sources could be seen as being mutually exclusive, and the *Corpus iuris* itself does nothing to solve this problem. At the time of Justinian the conception of the divine origin of imperial power overwhelmed any idea that the people was in any meaningful sense the source of authority; the only echo of such an ultimately republican idea was to be found in the acclamation of a new emperor by the senate, army and people. Such acclamation either sufficed as a form of election after the death of an emperor or, as was more normal in Byzantine history, confirmed the already co-opted choice of the previous incumbent. Either way, popular acclamation only served to declare the divine choice of emperor whose power came from God directly. With the revival of Roman law studies in the high Middle Ages the mutual implications of the two sources of authority were to be more thoroughly explored together with the question of whether the *lex regia* had been revocable or irrevocable.

The question of the people's authority also arises in the treatment of customary law in the *Corpus iuris*. This was a relatively unimportant area in Justinian's time but one which was to be crucial for the Middle Ages. In its general classification of custom, Roman law, following Greek terminology, was not profound, describing it as *ius non scriptum* (unwritten law) as opposed to *ius scriptum* (written law) – a superficial distinction based on outward form. There is, however, in the *Digest*, one passage which goes to the heart of the matter by isolating the will of the people as the constitutive element in custom. It considers that the popular will makes both written laws (*leges*) and custom, and therefore holds that custom can abrogate a *lex*:

> What does it matter whether the people declares its will by a vote or by its actions? It is, therefore, most correctly accepted that laws are abrogated not only by the vote of the legislator, but also by the tacit consent of all through disuse.[23]

This was written by the second-century jurist, Julian, and reflects the survival of republican ideas into the principate. A constitution of Constantine, however, directly contradicts this text by maintaining that a custom cannot abrogate a *lex*, a sign of the diminished importance of custom by the fourth century.[24] There is thus no suggestion in the *Corpus iuris* that custom can revoke imperial law: indeed, Justinian maintains that the emperor, being through his will the sole source of law, is also its unique interpreter.[25] When in the late Middle Ages juristic theories of the authority of the people were developed, however, this passage from Julian through its understanding of the power of consent provided ammunition for the elaboration of theories of the autonomy, and indeed sovereignty of the people.

The *Corpus iuris* can thus appear ambiguous about the ultimate source of legal and political authority. Although in the sixth century it was meant to be the comprehensive enactment of a divinely appointed emperor, it provided sufficient material for later medieval and early modern theories both of monarchy and of government by the people. It was especially possible for such later jurists and political thinkers to take passages out of context. A notorious example is the statement, 'what touches all should be approved by all' (*quod omnes tangit, ab omnibus comprobetur*).[26] This occurs in a constitution of Justinian concerning the relationship between guardian and ward, and means that where there are several guardians of the one ward, certain acts require the agreement of all the guardians, because their interests are at stake. Clearly this law has nothing to do with political matters. Nevertheless, medieval jurists employed this famous dictum in a political sense as part of the development of theories of consent.[27]

There might also appear to be ambiguity about whether the emperor was limited by law. As regards positive law – that is, human enacted law – there were statements which tended to modify the starkness of the claim that the emperor was *legibus solutus*. Although the *Corpus iuris* derived its legal force from Justinian's will, the imperial power existed within the context of the body of the Roman law itself. The Roman tradition of government was essentially a legal one, and Justinian's motivation in codifying classical juristic opinion and imperial decrees was born out of reverence for the law and a desire to preserve and revivify it. Precisely because the emperor's power was derived from the law (in the form of the *lex regia*) it was thought fitting that he should obey the laws.[28] There was however no obligation on him to do so and thus ultimately his freedom was preserved: obedience to the laws would be purely voluntary on his part.

At the beginning of the *Digest* and the *Institutes* the discussion of general jurisprudential principles goes beyond questions of positive law. Distinctions are drawn between *ius civile*, the provisions of a particular legal system such as the Roman; natural law (*ius naturale*); and the law common to all peoples (*ius gentium*). The treatment of the relationship between natural law and the *ius gentium* is contradictory. Ulpian considers natural law to be that which mankind shares with the animals, and to cover mating and the procreation and education of children: it is therefore different from the *ius gentium* which concerns only human beings.[29] Gaius, however, connects both laws by presenting the *ius gentium* as the product of natural reason (*naturalis ratio*): this view appears to have been the general opinion among Roman jurists.[30] Indeed Inst. 1.2, 11 maintains that, 'Natural law, which is uniformly observed by all peoples, was established by a kind of divine providence and remains always constant and unchanging.'[31] Yet elsewhere the Stoic idea of the original natural liberty of mankind is contrasted with the introduction of slavery by the *ius gentium*.[32] Clearly, the treatment of the natural law and the *ius gentium* is incoherent and sparse; but the few statements dealing with them enjoyed an enormous influence in the Middle Ages simply because they were included in the *Corpus iuris*. From the twelfth century onwards the discrepancy between the approaches of Ulpian and Gaius was to provoke among jurists fundamental discussion which explored the meaning of nature itself, and thereby involved profound implications for their theories of government and society. The crucial point is, however, that the *Corpus iuris* presented positive law as existing within a normative context, thus providing at least some of the seeds of full-blown medieval natural law theories. There was nevertheless a fundamental difference of approach. The *Corpus iuris* did not maintain that positive law contrary to natural law was in any sense invalid: as Ulpian says, 'The civil law is that which neither wholly departs from the law of nature or peoples, nor follows it in everything.'[33] The emperor was certainly not considered to be obliged to obey natural law. Later in the Middle Ages, in contrast, jurists commenting on the Roman law contributed to the theory that positive law and governmental measures contrary to the natural law and the *ius gentium* were invalid: the relevant passages were thus woven into a theory going far beyond anything contained in the *Corpus iuris* itself.

As regards the emperor's relationship with the Christian church the *Corpus iuris* gives a great deal of information, which, however, must be seen in a wider context for its correct evaluation. This relationship, despite its central importance for Byzantine political and religious life, remained somewhat ill-defined. To try and understand it an interpretative distinction needs to be drawn between two meanings of the term 'church'. The empire itself (the *Basileia*), being Christian, was understood as the church in the wider sense of the body of Christians; of this body the emperor, as God's vicegerent, was the head on earth. It was not possible for Byzantines to conceive of the empire without the church and *vice versa*. In a narrower sense, however, the church was understood to be an ecclesiastical body with a sacerdotal hierarchy. The problems arose concerning the emperor's relations with this institution.

In the preface to Nov. 6, Justinian sets out the relationship between the emperor and the clergy. A distinction is made between the emperorship (*imperium*) and the priesthood (*sacerdotium*). Both derive directly from God:

> Amongst men God's greatest gifts, conferred by his mercy from on high, are the priesthood and the emperorship. The former's ministry is in divine matters; the latter presides over and cares for human ones. Both, deriving from one and the same origin, regulate human life.[34]

The emperor's main responsibility (*sollicitudo*), he continues, is to preserve true Christian doctrine and the integrity of the clergy. With these aims attained, the state (*respublica*) will be correctly governed, due harmony (*consonantia*) achieved, and God's favour obtained through the prayers of a faithful priesthood.[35] The moral and doctrinal well-being of the clergy is essential for the health of the Christian empire, and thus demands imperial supervision.

This imperial role was expressed in permanent form by the legislation of Justinian and his predecessors. The first thirteen titles of the *Code* were concerned with the clergy and religious questions, as were many of the *Novels*. The emperor's capability to legislate in this way was a Christian application of the traditional Roman view that public law included matters relating to religion and the priesthood, which were thus perceived as the concern of the state.[36] Although Justinian preserved the crucial distinction between the *imperium* and the *sacerdotium*, he also maintained that there was not much difference between them. This view, which was formulated with ecclesiastical property specifically in mind, expressly reflected the public status of the clergy in a Christian empire.[37] In essence Justinian's position represented the long-standing Byzantine compromise between the imperial and priestly powers. Emperors had indeed called church councils, presided over them and participated in their discussions. Yet the authoritative formulation of doctrine remained the concern of the *sacerdotium*. Nevertheless, Justinian, in launching his anti-Nestorian attack against the Three Chapters without first convoking a church council, provoked the accusation of undue interference in ecclesiastical matters, and then had to call the Fifth Ecumenical Council which proceeded to endorse his views. The accepted role of the emperor was to make canons issued by the church and synodal decrees into laws of the empire. Thus Justinian reiterated that the canons of the four ecumenical councils be considered to be imperial *leges*.[38] Furthermore, as a professed example of the desired *consonantia* between imperial and ecclesiastical authority, he gave legal effect to the deposition of Patriarch Anthimus by a synod chaired by Pope Agapetus and the new patriarch, Menas.[39] Similarly, the emperors since Constantine had permitted both secular and clerical suitors to bring cases before the bishops' courts, and Justinian confirmed that only church judges could deal with purely ecclesiastical matters.

Justinian certainly exercised very considerable power over ecclesiastical affairs and was personally extremely interested in theology. It used to be conventional to describe the image of the emperor in the *Corpus iuris* as Caesaropapist, indicating thereby that he possessed divinely instituted supreme power within a unified entity of church and empire.[40] More recent scholarship has questioned the aptness of the term 'Caesaropapism' in the Byzantine context.[41] Although the emperor was commonly called 'priest and emperor' (*hiereus kai basileus*),[42] he remained a layman throughout the Byzantine period. He was not a priest in that he did not possess the sacramental power of orders: he had not been ordained. He was only a priest in the sense of possessing jurisdictional powers in ecclesiastical matters.[43] Although the emperor was the head of the church understood as the empire, he was definitely not the head of the church conceived as an ecclesiastical body. Justinian accepted the primacy of the pope and the second place of the patriarch of Constantinople.[44] Whatever the vicissitudes in the long historical relationship between Constantinople and the papacy, the head of the church at Constantinople was recognised to be the patriarch. Normally there was harmony between church and emperor, in the interests of which the clergy would practice 'economy' (*oikonomia*) involving the avoidance of disputes on relatively unimportant matters. Nevertheless, when a major clash could not be avoided the clergy adhered to its claim to be the interpreter of doctrine. Thus in the eighth and ninth centuries, although the church was divided over iconoclasm, the anti-iconoclastic party among the clergy was able in the end successfully to resist those emperors who wished to forbid the veneration of icons and religious images. It even happened that a patriarch excommunicated an emperor, as Nicholas Mysticus did Leo VI because of his fourth marriage. Furthermore, from 491 the patriarch received the confession of faith of the newly appointed emperor. Canon law existed side by side with secular law (*nomos*) and the church in interpreting and augmenting the canons, provided the spiritual and moral context within which the emperor ruled. Since the relationship between the two kinds of law, in so far as both concerned religious matters, was ill-defined, collections setting out parallel texts of first the ecclesiastical and then the relevant secular law were developed and known as *nomocanones*, of which the most well known was the seventh-century one in fourteen titles. These compilations facilitated considerable independence on the part of the patriarch and his synod in the interpretation of the law. A development of this trend is found in the ninth-century *Epanagoge* of Basil I, in which, under the influence of Patriarch Photius, the freedom of the church is stressed.

Yet the power of the patriarch of Constantinople should not be exaggerated. His coronation of the emperor, which first occurred in 457, was in no sense constitutive but purely part of the declaration of the divine choice. Indeed, initially the patriarch acted as representative of the Roman people; it was only gradually that the coronation became more ecclesiastical in character. As a guarantee of orthodoxy a coronation oath to uphold the faith and the position of the church can be discerned in the ninth century. The purely ecclesiastical rite of anointing was only introduced into the inauguration ritual in the twelfth century. Furthermore, the procedure for creating the patriarch himself was subject to considerable imperial control beneath the appearance of preserving ecclesiastical freedom. Three candidates were canonically elected by synod. It was then the emperor's prerogative to choose one of these three. If he did not favour any of them, he could then nominate a man of his own choice, in whose appointment the synod would have to aquiesce. Likewise, emperors forced at least 36 of the 122 patriarchs elected between 379 and 1451 to resign or be deposed.[45] Most telling of all were the traditional words which made it clear that the emperor instituted a patriarch at the latter's consecration by divine grace and the imperial power proceeding therefrom.

Although the structure of Byzantine political thought was largely fixed from the time of Constantine and Eusebius there were clearly some developments in it, as the increasingly ecclesiastical aspect of imperial consecration shows. Similarly the legislation of Leo VI, through depriving the senate and *curiae* of their little remaining authority, and also confirming the trend since Justinian whereby the consulate was reserved to the emperor, consolidated the imperial monarchy by removing these purely theoretical vestiges of republican institutions. Nevertheless, it has been justifiable to concentrate here on the *Corpus iuris* which, containing the expression of Byzantine political ideas in permanent legal form, was the prime means of transmission of these to the high and late Middle Ages. As we shall see, however, the influence of Byzantine forms of rulership was also important in the early medieval west: the emperor provided the model of the Christian ruler both as legislator and monarch of a universal empire.

THE WEST

Christian kingship

During the gradual disintegration of the Roman empire in the west the most widespread form of rulership which emerged was Christian kingship. The long-term historical significance of this development can hardly be exaggerated because it laid the foundations of the theory of monarchy which survived into modern times.

In the fourth and fifth centuries the earlier Roman suspicion of kingship had become eroded under the influence first of Hellenistic and then of Christian ideas. The Bible provided the images both of kingship in Israel and of Christ the King.[46] In the west it became common to refer to the empire as a kingdom (*regnum*) and the emperor as king (*rex*), whereas in the east the emperor's title *Basileus* simply meant 'king'. This change facilitated the development of a Roman–Christian form of kingship in the barbarian kingdoms.

The nature of barbarian kingship after entry into the Roman empire has provoked intense debate among modern scholars. The centre of the problem concerns the question of Germanic kingship. In the nineteenth century German historians produced a theory which maintained that the Germanic tribes had a form of rulership based on popular election, and, furthermore, that this kind of popular kingship persisted as a fundamental element in barbarian and early medieval monarchy in the west. Such rulership, because it derived from the people, was, therefore, limited and answerable to a popular assembly. Indeed, within the German tradition of historical writing the theme of Germanic kingship has provided a model for the interpretation of the political conceptions of the Middle Ages. One has only to look at the seminal studies of Otto Gierke, Fritz Kern and Walter Ullmann to find this.[47] Yet there is a growing opinion in recent scholarship that this whole great intellectual structure of Germanic kingship is a myth. There is very little evidence indeed for the nature of Germanic kingship before entry into the Roman empire. Such evidence as there is derives from non-Germanic sources, notably Caesar, Tacitus' *Germania* and Ammianus Marcellinus. Enormous and misplaced scholarly industry has been devoted to trying to elucidate the meaning of the few relevant phrases in these works.

Thus for instance we cannot be sure of what Tacitus meant in his famous statement that the Germans 'choose kings for their nobility, and war-commanders for their valor'.[48] Furthermore, it is methodologically unsound to generalise about supposedly common 'Germanic' features in the rulership of tribes diverse in kind, space and time.[49]

The form of kingship which in fact emerged in the post-entry barbarian kingdoms was overwhelmingly Roman and Christian in character and stressed the power and authority of the monarch. Initially Roman influence was strong and direct, reflecting the way in which barbarian kingship was assimilated into the decaying Roman governmental system. These kings ruled largely with the co-operation of the surviving Roman senatorial class, and certain of them accepted imperial legitimisation of their rule through receiving Roman offices. Thus in fifth-century Italy, for instance, the Ostrogoth, Odovacer, ruled with imperial sanction and his successor, Theoderic, gained the Emperor Anastasius' recognition of his kingship in 497. Likewise in Francia the emperor conferred on Clovis in 508 an honorary consulate and permitted him to wear regalia. According to Gregory of Tours Clovis thereafter employed the title 'consul or Augustus' (*consul aut augustus*).[50] A turning-point came, however, with Justinian's Gothic War to reconquer the west (535–55): thereafter it seems that no western kings sought imperial confirmation of their rule. The west increasingly went its own way.

In the barbarian kingdoms God was understood to be the ultimate source of royal authority. This notion, which was widely prevalent in the sixth century, became focused into the formula that such a ruler was 'king by the grace of God' (*rex dei gratia*) – that he ruled by God's favour. This formulation became fundamental to medieval conceptions of kingship and was the distant ancestor of early modern divine right monarchy. The earliest known use of the formula itself in the west apparently dates from the reign of the Lombard king, Agilulf (590–616); Isidore of Seville also applied it to the Visigothic king, Svinthila (621–31); by the end of the seventh century the Anglo-Saxon kings were employing it or similar titles; and in the second half of the eighth century it became part of Charlemagne's royal title.[51] The idea of kingship by divine favour was, however, older than the formula itself and can be discerned as early as the reign of the Vandal king, Huniric

(d. 484).[52] In the east the idea that the emperor ruled by God's grace had been prevalent from the fifth century, but appears not to have been the source of the western concept.

The origins of the idea of kingship by divine grace lay in interpretations of the Bible. Certain texts in the New Testament were directly relevant. Two in particular had a general application to the relationship between God and the individual Christian, but were applied in this context specifically to that between God and the king: 'By God's grace this is what I am' (1 Corinthians 15:10),[53] and 'A man can lay claim only to what is given him from heaven' (John 3:27).[54] Two other texts applied overtly to governmental and jurisdictional power: as we have seen, Romans 13:1 stated that all government came from God, and in John 19:11 Christ said to Pilate, 'You would have no power over me if it had not been given you from above.'[55] None of these passages mentioned kings as such, but taken together, and understood in a *milieu* in which kingship was the current form of government, they provided a mental context for perceiving royal power as being derived from God's goodwill or favour. The Old Testament also provided ample evidence for the divine source of the power of the kings of Israel, beginning with the account of Samuel's anointing of Saul. The identification of the people of the Franks with Israel in the Merovingian period encouraged the application of Old Testament imagery to Frankish kingship, an interpretation which was developed further under the Carolingians. Yet the Old Testament was ambivalent about kingship. Samuel was reluctant to institute the monarchy and pointed out the disadvantages of having a king (1 Samuel 8:6–18), and the wickedness of Israel in wanting one, since its only true king was Yahweh (1 Samuel 12:12–20). Similarly Hosea 8:4 declares, 'They have set up kings, but not with my consent, and appointed princes, but without my knowledge.'[56] These reservations were, however, generally ignored in the spread of divine grace monarchy and only resurfaced infrequently in medieval discussions of the role of kings.

The implications of this theocratic form of kingship were profound for the relationship between ruler and ruled. The king was understood to derive his authority directly from God: he was God's vicegerent on earth, and was as such often described as his vicar (*vicarius dei*). The people he ruled were not considered to be the source of his power, but were instead thought to have been divinely conceded to the royal care. The ruler in turn by virtue of his divinely granted authority conceded offices and powers to those he governed. The members of the people were, in short, subject (*subditi*) to their king, and lacked a right of resistance to him. In this hierarchical structure the monarch, as the superior instituted over his subjects who were his inferiors, was a true earthly sovereign. This model of kingship was in essence established in the period of the barbarian kingdoms but developed as the Middle Ages progressed. Nevertheless, as we shall see, it was only one aspect of the complex phenomenon of medieval monarchy.

The classic treatment of the model of theocratic kingship has in modern times been given by Walter Ullmann. The core of his interpretation of medieval political ideas has been in terms of what he described as the 'ascending' and 'descending' theses: the antithesis between the derivation of power downwards, as it were, from God, or upwards from the people. This analysis is based essentially on the question of the *origin* of governmental power and authority. Yet in interpreting medieval political thought quite as much weight, if not more, should be given to the *purpose* of such power. This is not, of course, to deny that Ullmann did consider teleological aspects; but if these are accorded a more central role somewhat different conclusions can be reached.[57]

When theocratic kingship is seen in terms of its purpose the seemingly absolute nature of such monarchy appears modified. Precisely because rulership was understood to have been instituted by God it was considered to exist for a divinely willed end. Kingship was viewed as an office existing within a Christian normative structure: there was no place for the arbitrary exercise of the monarch's will. The king's role was that of Christian service for the common good of his people. As St Paul said, 'The state is there to serve God for your benefit ... The authorities are there to serve God ... All government officials are God's officers.'[58] Gregory the Great, whose works were fundamental to the development of medieval thought, writing in the late sixth century, classically described this royal role in terms of the established theme of Christian ministry,[59] a formulation which was to have a determining influence on medieval conceptions of kingship. The king in performing this function was to observe a characteristically Christian *humilitas*,[60] a notion alien to Greek or Roman political thought. Isidore of Seville, writing in the Visigothic kingdom of Spain in the first part of the seventh century, also made this idea of ministry a fundamental part of his treatment of kingship. Not only were Isidore's works the most important literary products of Visigothic Spain, the most culturally precocious of the barbarian kingdoms, but many of his statements exerted a disproportionate effect on the development of thought in the Middle Ages themselves. This is particularly true of his ideas concerning kingship and political life. This is not to claim any originality or great depth for his thought; it is just that his formulations proved peculiarly long lived. Indeed, many of the basic concepts of medieval theocratic kingship are to be found in his works.[61] The moral purpose of kingship is summed up in Isidore's retailing of the ancient axiom, 'You will be a king if you act rightly, if you do not, you will not be', based on a play on the words *rex* and *recte* (rightly), a trite but effective observation which for him assumed a Christian value-system.[62] He stressed the king's duty to aim at justice (*iustitia*), the virtue which in the Middle Ages was to come to encapsulate the duties of a Christian ruler. Similarly, the king should observe clemency, humility and patience, and in general serve the Christian religion which characterised the community which he governed.[63] In sum the king must rule for his subjects' benefit and was answerable to God for the way in which he ruled them, an idea which echoed Hebrews 13:17, 'Obey your leaders and do as they tell you, because they must give an account of the way they look after your souls.'[64] Isidore was attempting to integrate Roman, biblical and patristic moral criteria into his theory of kingship, thus illustrating that according to both Greco-Roman and Judaeo-Christian political ideas rulership should have the moral aim of achieving the common good. Indeed, this shared teleological orientation facilitated the fusion of ancient and Christian ideas throughout the Middle Ages.

The fundamental duty of the Christian ruler to care for his subjects' well-being was also understood in terms of his role as their protector or preserver. The Roman source for this idea can be found in the model of a tutor who must act in the interests of the minor committed to his guardianship. Indeed, Cicero, for instance, had described government as a *tutela*,[65] and this notion in the form of the monarch's *tuitio* of the Christians whom he ruled also appeared in Isidore.[66] Furthermore, there existed the similar Germanic conception of *Munt* (*mundeburdium*) which as early as the reign of the Merovingian king Childebert I (511–58) was rendered into Latin as *tuitio*.[67] The concept of *Munt* (in Anglo-Saxon *mundbora*) remained fundamental to kingship and received prominent treatment, for instance, in the important late seventh-century Merovingian royal formulary of Marculf.[68] The king's tutorial role is a large theme which runs throughout medieval political thought. The seeds of it are to be found in this early period, although its main development appears to be from the Carolingian period onwards. The thesis of the king as tutor and the people which he rules as being in the position of a minor under age in relation to him, has been integrated by Walter Ullmann into his model of theocratic monarchy: the king acts for the people which has been committed to his care by God and which cannot act for itself.[69] As we shall see, care must be taken with this interpretation, not least because the royal tutorial role limits the king's freedom of action in that it recognises by implication the existence of the people or *regnum* as an entity independent of its ruler because he has to protect its inherent rights. The minority-thesis is the logical corollary of the tutorial theme but it is only clearly enunciated in the twelfth century with the renaissance of the scientific study of Roman law. In that law the minor does not receive his rights from his tutor. This problem illustrates the difficulties involved in elaborating such a thesis over a lengthy period of time. Certainly, in the sixth and seventh centuries the king's duty to provide *tutela* or *Munt* should be seen as a defining limitation on his monarchical powers in terms of their purpose, and as modifying Ullmann's dubious argument that the people derived all its public rights from its divinely appointed ruler. The king had the responsibility to provide protection for his people.

The whole theme of the common good reveals the inherent rights of the people and its existence as an entity separate from its ruler. Indeed, throughout the early development of theocratic monarchy the role of the people should not be underestimated. The people, in the sense of the great men of the realm, participated in the making of the king. In the barbarian kingdoms the mechanisms of king-making varied: although, for instance, actual election was widespread it does not appear to have been universal, and the Merovingians themselves seem to have lacked a fixed ritual for transferring royal power.[70] Certainly the magnates had to signify their acceptance of the new monarch, if only by acclamation. True choice could be highly restricted, sometimes within the limits of a legitimate blood line (*stirps regia*), as in the case of the Merovingians. Nevertheless, there remains very little hard evidence concerning royal inauguration rituals in this early period. The popular involvement in the making of a king did not conflict with the divine source of his authority once chosen, but was rather a necessary part of the process of legitimisation of his rule whereby one individual was designated as king. The monarch accepted by the people was favoured by God and ruled by his grace.

Similarly, the popular element in the creation of law in the barbarian kingdoms was compatible with theocratic monarchy; customary law coexisted with royal law as it was to do throughout the Middle Ages. As regards the codes of barbarian law produced in this period, modern scholarship considers that they did not display any distinction between people's law (*Volksrecht*) and king's law (*Königsrecht*).[71] They consisted of both custom and innovation, but since they were written and given authority by the ruler's will, they were royal legislation. In issuing these codes the barbarian kings were seeking to act out the role of the Romanised Christian ruler as legislator according to the model of Roman emperorship. This function served both to buttress the royal authority and to dignify and legally define the people itself. The barbarian kingdoms were composed of different peoples (*gentes*), and these codes each applied to a specific *gens* – they were not therefore territorial. Thus the law to which an individual person was subject was not that of the land but that applicable to his *gens*, and was thus to this extent personal. Those of Roman descent were subject to Roman law. In 506 the Visigothic king, Alaric II, enacted what was to become the most important barbarian code of Roman law: the *Lex Romana Visigothorum* (also known as the *Breviarium Alarici*). This was to maintain its influence, in southern France at least, until the thirteenth century. There was also a *Lex Romana Burgundionum* issued by King Gunobad in *c.* 517 for the Romans living in his Burgundian kingdom. Of the Germanic codes the Visigothic ones were the most impressive. The earliest was the *Codex Euricianus* issued in *c.* 476; this showed a mixture of Roman and purely Germanic elements. Euric's code was revised by Leovigild (572–80) in the *Codex revisus*, which retained the separate legal regimes for Romans and Goths. The most innovatory development of Visigothic law, however, was the emergence of a territorial code. This appears to have been the work of Chindasvind in 643/4, and to have been consolidated by the *Lex Visigothorum* of Reccesvind (*c.* 654).[72] The culmination of Visigothic codification was that of Ervig in 681. The Frankish code, the *Lex Salica*, whose first recension dated probably from 507–11, was also royal law.[73] Similarly, the Lombard codes from the Edict of Rothari in 643 onwards were clearly issued by a theocratic monarchy.[74] Almost all the barbarian codes were written in Latin which, because of the example of Roman law, was considered to be the proper medium for Christian legislation. The only exceptions were the Anglo-Saxon laws, written in the vernacular but none the less the expression of Christian monarchy, as the codes beginning with that of Aethelberht (602–3) made clear.

Yet the nature of these barbarian codes did show that the theocratic king worked within limitations. Even though he issued the codes and could revise those of his predecessors, he was legislating within a legal tradition largely based ultimately on custom. There was a strong generally held sense that he should himself observe his laws once made, a view which had also been clearly expressed by Augustine and Isidore.[75] Both the Germanic and, as we have seen, the Roman traditions were opposed to any arbitrariness on the part of the ruler: he governed within a legal structure. Thus quite apart from the higher norms which hedged in any Christian ruler, the theocratic king was considered to be limited by human law. This raises a fundamental problem concerning the interpretation of theocratic monarchy. According to the model initially outlined it would appear that such a king through deriving his power from God was in such a position of sovereignty that he could not be limited by any law created by the people or indeed by any law he or his predecessors had made: he was as it were a law unto himself and answerable only to God. However, conceptions of theocratic monarchy changed during the Middle Ages, and the strict application of the abstract thesis to any particular period can be misleading. In reality the theocratic aspect of medieval kingship was never as clear-cut as the model might suggest. The model applies to the barbarian codes in the sense that the king gives them legal force, yet they remain in a profound sense the people's law. At a deep level there is co-operation between ruler and people. This can be seen as an ambiguity or a discrepancy within this conception of monarchy; but to view it this way is really to impose too rigid an interpretative structure on the complexity of medieval ideas of rulership and to complain when apparent inconsistencies result. The theocratic thesis is attractive as a means for understanding medieval kingship because of its simplicity, but if applied too rigorously it has the defect that it is precisely that – too simple. The problems involved in the theocratic ruler's relationship to existing positive law only received overt and detailed attention far later in the Middle Ages with the development of scientific jurisprudence, when difficulties were clearly perceived.

The importance of custom as a legal norm in the barbarian kingdoms and then the early Middle Ages has raised fundamental problems of interpretation concerning the creation of law. Fritz Kern argued that law-making as such was alien to this period, that instead the law was held to be something eternally valid and unchanging which was 'found' or 'discovered' by rulers, judges and those expert in the law. This thesis of 'the good old law' proved peculiarly tenacious.[76] Its implications were to deny the possibility of true legislation, and certainly of innovative legislation, and thus to preclude legislative sovereignty on the part of rulers. Instead Kern saw the law itself as being the true sovereign in the Middle Ages. In opposition to this view Walter Ullmann, for instance, structured his whole understanding of medieval law-creation around the argument that all human law was ultimately the product of human will: of the people's in the case of the 'ascending' thesis and of the ruler's in that of the 'descending'. The nature both of custom, as the expression of popular implicit consent, and of legislation, as the embodiment of the will of the monarch or the consent of the people, was understood within this model.[77] This view demanded the existence of sovereignty and illuminated its location.

The notion of a 'good old law' which is 'found' is a modern mental construct, which Janet Nelson has called a myth;[78] indeed, terms directly indicating 'law-finding' appear to be absent from the sources.[79] Above all, the Kern theory creates problems because it introduces concepts which are unnecessary for the comprehension of medieval political ideas. Law in this early period can be divided simply into the great mass of popular custom; that small part of custom included in royal codes; and royal decrees. Where law did not exist in a written form, law was what experienced men declared it to be.[80] There is no need to go beyond these categories. In point of fact we have very little hard evidence for custom other than that included in written codes.[81] The most useful definition of custom sees it as being in some sense created by the people and those who declare what it is. Where barbarian and medieval customs were not written down there was infinite scope for unconscious innovation: they of their nature evolved. Custom did not cease to be such through the mere fact of being written down; but if it was included in a royally issued code it took on, as we have seen, the character of legislation. Sophisticated analysis, however, of the constitutive elements of custom, in terms of the tacit consent of the people, usage, lapse of time and the relationship between written and unwritten law, only emerged with later medieval scientific jurisprudence.

The limitations imposed on theocratic kingship by popular elements, higher norms and the demands of the common good were accepted in the barbarian kingdoms and ensured that there was no arbitrary royal absolutism. Normally kings ruled within these constraints. But what happened if they ceased to observe them? Could these limitations be enforced and, if so, by whom? This was to be a problem which was to be inherited by the Middle Ages. In reality, if a king refused to be bound by such limitations, there existed no legal right of resistance to him. A crucial distinction was involved: the king was limited but not controlled. If these limitations could not be enforced, did this mean that they did not really exist? To argue in this way is to adopt a view which only accepts the validity of power. In barbarian kingdoms and the Middle Ages such limitations were considered to have validity, whatever the actions of individual monarchs. Although the lack of a right of resistance is certainly consistent with the logic of the theocratic model, it is not necessarily solely derived from it. Contrary to the myth of Germanic popular monarchy there is only one dubious piece of evidence (concerning the Burgundians) for any right of resistance amongst pre-entry Germans.[82] It may be that barbarian theocratic monarchy was in this respect built upon older Germanic foundations.

Kingship and priesthood

Theocratic monarchy only made sense as a form of government over Christians. The society in which it existed could therefore be seen as being identified with the church in the wide sense of those baptised into membership of it. Because of the fundamental division into clergy and laity, the relationships between secular rulers and the church as a purely ecclesiastical and clerical body were to assume central importance in the political ideas of the medieval west: indeed, the very designation of monarchs as secular reflected this religious context. Although the main developments occurred in the Middle Ages proper, some of the seeds were sown in the period of the barbarian kingdoms and some of the basic questions raised.

Yet precisely because the king held theocratic power in such a society, was he in any sense a priest or could he be fully categorised as a layman? The answer is not an easy one. The king in that he did not exercise sacramental functions was not a priest, and was never, either in the barbarian kingdoms or at any time in the Middle Ages, understood to be a priest in such a sense. To this extent the division between clergy and laity was maintained. But there were other aspects to priesthood than the purely sacramental, and it was in these areas that the king could be considered as a priest. If one considers the Visigothic kingdom, for instance, the king exercised a jurisdictional control over the clergy and one which they accepted. Certainly from the time of the Third Council of Toledo called by Reccared in 589, church councils were either summoned directly by the king or held with his permission: indeed, the notable series of Councils of Toledo, which by their decrees contributed to the development of a territorial law for Visigothic Spain, are clear evidence for the identity of church and society. The king legislated in ecclesiastical matters, nominated bishops and even excommunicated.[83] The role of the clergy was to formulate and teach the norms of Christian society, and that of the king to enforce them: as Isidore said, it was the role of the temporal ruler to accomplish 'through the terror of discipline' what the priest has failed to bring about 'through the preaching of doctrine'.[84] Although the monarch himself was subject to the norms set forth by the episcopacy this did not result in any right of resistance or deposition on the part of the clergy. Svinthila, for instance, had fallen before he was condemned in 633 as an unjust and faithless king by the Fourth Council of Toledo, which held that he had already deprived himself of the kingship.[85] The sense in which the Visigoths were priest-kings can be understood according to the distinction between two forms of sacerdotal power, the sacramental one of orders (*potestas ordinis*) and that of jurisdiction (*potestas jurisdictionis*), although this terminology only became current in the twelfth century.[86] Isidore stressed the responsibility of this lofty royal vocation by holding that the king was answerable before God for the church in his care.[87] Similarly, the Merovingians were likened to priests, but not in a sacramental sense: thus Gregory of Tours, for instance, referred to Guntram as 'king like a good priest'.[88] The identification of the Franks with Israel permitted Venantius Fortunatus to call Childebert I by the name of Melchisedech, who at the time of Abraham had combined the offices of 'king of Salem' and 'priest of God most high', a model which in the Middle Ages was to be of continuing importance for the idea of the combination of royal and sacerdotal power.[89] The foundations of the more highly developed Carolingian conception of priest-kingship were laid in the Merovingian period.

In the Visigothic kingdom, but nowhere else before the Carolingian period, the practice of the clerical anointing of kings emerged. There is dispute about its first appearance. It is possible that Svinthila's successor may have been anointed in 631 in order to legitimise his rule by thus raising him above the level of his people.[90] From the consecration of Wamba in 672 no unanointed king ruled in Spain. The origins of this rite remain obscure. It most likely derived from post-baptismal chrismation which provided an indirect link with Old Testament royal anointing: the liturgy referred to 'the oil wherewith thou hast anointed priests, kings and prophets'.[91] There is no evidence of episcopal unction in Visigothic Spain to serve as a model, nor do the fragmentary remains of the royal consecration liturgy (surviving from the late seventh century) refer to the anointings of Saul and David.[92] The rite had to be administered by the clergy; but they did not gain any control over the monarch as a result.[93] This Visigothic anointing had no long-term historical influence because of the Islamic conquest. It was to be the Carolingian royal unction that was to initiate the true western tradition of the consecration of kings with all its implications for the nature of royal priestly powers and a changing relationship between the clergy and the secular ruler.

There still, however, remains the question of whether any form of Germanic sacral kingship underlay Christian theocratic monarchy in the barbarian kingdoms. A sacral king combined royal and priestly functions in that he was a cult-king embodying his people's good luck which he maintained through his link with divinity. This is a very obscure subject which has provoked radical disagreements among scholars. J.M. Wallace-Hadrill, for instance, has supported the argument that the Germanic tribes brought a form of sacral kingship with them into the empire, although he admits that by the first half of the seventh century Christian concepts of kingship had ousted heathen ones amongst the Merovingians.[94] Furthermore, William A. Chaney has stressed the interaction of Germanic and Scandinavian sacral kingship with Christian theocratic conceptions throughout the whole Anglo-Saxon period.[95] There is a broad stream of scholarship, especially German, which supports the thesis of Germanic sacral kingship.[96] Yet there are serious problems in accepting this idea. As already noted, there are extreme difficulties in determining the beliefs of pre-entry Germans. The earliest Roman evidence for German sacral kingship is provided by Ammianus Marcellinus' treatment of the Burgundians. Yet the value of his testimony for conditions just before the migrations is questionable.[97] His famous statement that the Burgundian king 'by ancient custom, after having laid down his power, is removed, if under him the fortune of war shall have wavered, or the land denied a full harvest', could indicate either sacrality or, equally well, simply the attempt to obviate the effects of supposed divine displeasure.[98] Furthermore, anthropological comparisons with similar tribal societies in which war leaders are dedicated to the cult of a war god do not provide historical evidence for conditions amongst the Germans. The crucial question, however, is concerned not with any pre-entry notions, but with whether sacrality underlay barbarian and then medieval theocratic monarchy in any sense. Here the problem is a conceptual one. Once such rulership was firmly established, it is very difficult to isolate reliably any sacral elements within it since any which might qualify can be understood in a purely Christian sense – that is, as being simply the signs of God's favour. The evidence for the divine origin of Germanic royal families is also ambiguous. Although Jordanes, for instance, refers to the demigods called Anses as the ancestors of the Amals, Theoderic's dynasty, there is apparently no hard evidence that either he or the Ostrogoths themselves considered that the royal family in fact participated in divinity through descent.[99] Similarly, the insertion of Woden in the genealogies of Anglo-Saxon kings, whereas it may indicate a sacral monarchy at some early stage, by the time of Bede at least becomes purely conventional and lacks any real content derived from a pagan past.[100] What seems to have happened generally is that any originally sacral elements, which there may have been, were transformed by the development of theocratic monarchy in such a way that they ceased to exist in any identifiable sense. The long hair of the Merovingians has often been seen as a sign of their sacrality. This interpretation may be relevant to their early years, but with the increasing Christianisation of their kingship their hair was most likely seen only as indicating legitimacy, which may indeed have been its function all along.[101] Barbarian and medieval theocratic kings nevertheless possessed one supposed royal power which may have preserved a faint remnant of sacrality: that of healing (of touching for the king's evil), which went back at least as far as the Merovingian Guntram, and is evidence of a charisma which appeared to go beyond divine favour. It is, however, outside Christendom that one must look for clear proof for the existence of sacral kingship in the early Middle Ages: to the Scandinavian and Icelandic sagas.

The claims of the papacy

In the west the division between clergy and laity had results which went far beyond just preventing the emergence of any monolithic form of priest-kingship. From the late fourth and above all the fifth century there is clear evidence that the papacy was emerging as a governmental institution. This development was to have profound effects both within the church conceived as a purely ecclesiastical body and for the relationship between secular and spiritual power in the Christian world as a whole. It was in this early period that certain crucial characteristics of the papacy were formed, the seeds which grew into the papal monarchy of the Middle Ages.

It became increasingly apparent that the papacy possessed two aspects: the popes had both a purely spiritual role as pastors and teachers, and also a strictly jurisdictional one. The two were inter-related as different facets of the same office, but the dominant characteristic of the medieval papacy was to be its growth as a jurisdictional and hence governmental institution. The reason was that the church was perceived in corporational terms: it was the body of the faithful (*corpus fidelium*) which needed to be governed; it was not a purely spiritual communion of believers. Papal government was exercised by means of the law: it was jurisdiction in the fundamental sense of laying down the law. That it should take this form was largely the result of the Roman context of the papacy's development: Roman governmental and legal concepts heavily influenced papal ideas of government. The die was cast when popes began to imitate imperial rescripts by issuing decretals (that is, letters which determined matters authoritatively), the first surviving one being that sent in 385 by Siricius to the Spanish bishop Himerius of Tarragona.[102]

The understanding of the nature of papal authority became more closely defined in legal form. The foundation of that authority was understood to lie in Christ's commission to St Peter in Matthew 16:18–19:

> You are Peter and on this rock I will build my Church. And the gates of the underworld can never hold out against it. I will give you the keys of the kingdom of heaven: whatever you bind on earth shall be considered bound in heaven; whatever you loose on earth shall be considered loosed in heaven.[103]

From the 380s this passage was increasingly used by the papacy. Together with Christ's injunction to Peter in John 21:15–17: 'Feed my lambs ... Feed my sheep',[104] it was destined to provide the scriptural base of papal jurisdictional and pastoral claims in the Middle Ages. On the face of it the Matthean passage is not clear, as is witnessed by its tortured history in Christian exegesis. Who is the 'rock', St Peter or Christ himself? The papacy, of course, identified the 'rock' with Peter.[105] The 'rock' could also be the truth of Christ's divinity or Peter's faith. Furthermore, what is the meaning of 'binding and loosing'? The phrase could have a purely spiritual sense relating to sin. Yet the papacy interpreted it in a jurisdictional manner, and in so doing reflected rabbinic practice which used the terms in connection with decisions in regard to the law, although the main influence would have been the Roman law employment of 'to bind' (*ligare*) and 'to loose' (*solvere*). Christ, in short, was understood in this passage to have instituted a church and to have imparted jurisdiction to Peter within it as a response to the latter's recognition of his master's divinity. Even the Johannine passage, which appears quite literally pastoral, was also given a legal interpretation as fulfilling the Matthean one.

But was Peter to have a successor or was this a purely personal commission in response to his faith? This was the crucial question regarding the claims of the papacy. How could a link be established between each pope and Peter? The assumption behind the papal view was that Christ had established a visible church, which if it was to survive needed a continuing government, and therefore a succession of popes. There was, however, no documentary evidence that St Peter had instituted a successor. Towards the end of the fourth century this deficiency was remedied for the papacy. Rufinus translated into Latin, with elaborations, a spurious letter attributed to Pope Clement I and which had been written in Greek in the late second century. According to this St Peter passed on to Clement the powers of binding and loosing contained in Matthew 16:18–19 thus making him the heir to his authority.[106] Already in the decretal of Siricius mentioned above the pope had been called the heir of St Peter.[107] This theme received an epoch-making development at the hands of Leo I (440–61), who building on the work of his predecessors made the most important contribution to the expression of papal claims in late antiquity.[108] Leo produced the formula that the pope was the unworthy heir of St Peter (*indignus haeres beati Petri*).[109] Leo's view was coloured by Roman law ideas of inheritance whereby the heir was considered to be legally identical with the deceased. Thus Leo sought to show that the pope succeeded to the same legal powers as St Peter, but that because of each pope's personal unworthiness there was involved no claim to St Peter's personal merits in response to which the original commission had been made. This was the basis of the fundamental distinction between the office and the man which the papacy was to insist upon throughout the Middle Ages and beyond. However depraved or unsuitable an individual incumbent might be, he still retained his full legal authority as pope. Indeed, as Leo said of his office, 'We are in St Peter's place' (*vice Petri fungimur*)[110] – the first pope overtly to claim this vicariate.

The pontificate of Leo showed the developed monarchical form of papal government with emphasis on the pope's primacy (*primatus*) and headship (*principatus*) of the church. Certainly from the time of Siricius' decretal onwards that headship had been interpreted within a corporational context. The church, on the basis of St Paul's image of it as the body of Christ (*corpus Christi*),[111] was considered to have as its head (*caput*) the Roman church (whose head was the pope) and the other churches as its members (*membra*). This organic or organological theme, which ordered those comprising the whole according to their various functions, was to be fundamental for papal theory in the Middle Ages. Leo interpreted his jurisdictional role of headship in a specifically judicial fashion by seeking to encourage the papacy's existing claim to be the supreme court of appeal in ecclesiastical cases. Walter Ullmann held that Leo's vision of the pope's role in the Christian *corpus* culminated in the possession of plenitude of power (*plenitudo potestatis*) – that is, the fullness of Christ's jurisdictional powers given to St Peter.[112] This view should, however, be assessed with caution. Although *plenitudo potestatis* did come to have this sense in the thirteenth century, Leo I used it in a far more restricted manner: to indicate how the delegated and therefore partial authority of a papal vicar, that is legate, differed from the pope's, which was full in relation to it.[113] The fulfilment of the early development of papal monarchy should rather be seen as emerging after Leo's pontificate. By the end of the fifth century the constitutional formula, 'the pope is judged by no one' (*papa a nemine iudicatur*) was established. This expressed what amounted to sovereignty in jurisdictional terms.[114]

In the early sixth century the organological theme received further elaboration in a non-papal source which was to have immense influence on ecclesiological and political thought in the Middle Ages, and was to be of especial assistance to the papacy. An anonymous writer in Greek, who purported to be St Paul's disciple, Denis (Dionysius) the Areopagite, and is thus known as Pseudo-Denis, produced amongst other works two on the theme of hierarchy, *On the Celestial Hierarchy* and *On the Ecclesiastical Hierarchy*.[115] These soon found their way into the papal library, although they were translated into Latin only much later (by 835). The author had the distinction of coining the term 'hierarchy', by which he meant an ordering of inferior ranks depending on superior ones and culminating in God the 'principle of unity' (*principium unitatis*). This Christian view of the order of the world showed strong Neoplatonist influence and owed much to the works of Proclus (410–85). Neoplatonic ideas, according to which man the microcosm mirrored the structure of the macrocosm, the universe itself, were to supplement the Pauline view as another main source of medieval organological ideas, notably through Chalcidius' commentary on Plato's *Timaeus*.[116]

The development of the papacy as a governmental institution within the Christian *corpus*, conceived as a public body, is obviously that aspect which is directly relevant to the history of political ideas. Yet to overstress this particular process would be to neglect other parts of the papacy's role. Its jurisdictional function was at heart but the legal expression of its spiritual mission, which also found more direct doctrinal and pastoral realisation. Most dramatically, Leo I's definition through his legates at the Council of Chalcedon in 451 ensured that the papal solution to the long-standing debate concerning the relationship between the divine and human natures of Christ was accepted as the definition of orthodoxy in both east and west. The pastoral function of the pope received perhaps its most influential elaboration in the pontificate of Gregory I (590–604). He stressed the pope's primacy within a structure of hierarchy and obedience, yet in an overall context of service to his flock. It is no accident that he adopted as the pope's official title, 'servant of the servants of God' (*servus servorum dei*). His attitude is summed up by his claim that he had the 'care and headship' (*cura et principatus*) of the church committed to him by God. For him the powers of papal primacy existed to defend the faith and to secure ultimate appellate jurisdiction in ecclesiastical cases. The coexistence of the jurisdictional and pastoral roles of the pope was indeed highlighted in Gregory's reign. As a result diametrically opposed interpretations have been reached by modern historians. For instance, whereas Walter Ullmann stressed Gregory's place within the growth of papal monarchy in the west, Jeffrey Richards considers that the emphasis was on humility in the exercise of jurisdiction.[117]

Since the pope's jurisdictional powers were inherited from St Peter, each pontiff on election was understood to succeed St Peter directly, rather than succeeding the previous pope. The pope however only received his sacramental powers on consecration as bishop of Rome; he derived these through normal episcopal apostolic succession and thus succeeded his predecessor in this respect. Whereas papal jurisdictional powers were complete on his election by (in theory) the clergy and people of Rome, the full complement of papal powers was only reached on his consecration. It would be misleading to employ the developed categories of *potestas jurisdictionis* and *potestas ordinis* to elucidate the position of the pope at this time, but his emerging claims were that he possessed a general jurisdictional power by virtue of his papal office; that he enjoyed a pre-eminent sacramental, pastoral and teaching role as the bishop of the pre-eminent see; and that as the bishop of Rome he had specific local spiritual and jurisdictional functions. The question of the relationship of the powers of the pope and those of bishops was to be a particularly thorny one in the Middle Ages: there was to be a history of tension between the bishops' pretensions to local autonomy and the centralising tendency of the papacy. Certainly at this time, although Rome was stressing its appellate jurisdiction, local jurisdiction was understood to form part of the powers which a bishop derived from apostolic succession; it would be much later that the competing idea that bishops derived their jurisdiction from the pope would be developed. The fifth century was indeed a crucial moment in history because the predominantly legal direction which the papacy then took was to be a fateful one for the Middle Ages and beyond. This trend was to a considerable extent historically conditioned both by the retreat of imperial authority in the west and the papacy's Roman environment. From the theological point of view the history of the medieval papacy could have been different with a central emphasis, not on the legally interpreted passages from Matthew 16:18–19 and John 21:15–17, but on Peter's role as first Easter witness: 'The Lord has risen and has appeared to Simon' (Luke 24:34).[118] Because the papal office encompassed a range of possibilities, there was to be an enduring problem in the Middle Ages concerning the nature and limits of papal authority.

As regards the specific question of the relationship between secular and spiritual power the claims of the fifth-century papacy were to provide the seeds of developments central to the political ideas of the Middle Ages. Although the papacy operated within the context of a Christian world (*mundus*) identified with the Roman empire, imperial claims were undermined by the consistent papal treatment of the emperor as a son (*filius*) of the church, on the grounds that he was a Christian and thus subject to ecclesiastical authority in religious and moral matters. In this way the first fracture in the structure of imperial sovereignty was produced. Although it was not perceived at the time, the road was opened in the west for the medieval conflicts between the two powers. In 390 St Ambrose had already, in his censuring of the Emperor Theodosius I, expressly treated him as a son of the church. Ambrose had thereby laid an important part of the foundations of the medieval papacy, but unintentionally so because he himself did not accept the jurisdictional primacy of Rome, attributing to St Peter only 'a primacy of confession not of honour' (*primatus confessionis non honoris*).[119] The hierarchical view of clerical superiority over the laity was expressed by Ambrose and the papacy in the form that the role of the clergy was to teach (*docere*) and of lay people to learn (*discere*). As Pope Celestine I (422–32) said, 'The people is to be taught, not followed' (*docendus est populus, non sequendus*).[120] Theological knowledge (*scientia*), the preserve of the clergy, was perceived as the basis of authority in a Christian society: the stage was set for the move which the church was to make from its teaching to its governmental or jurisdictional role.

However, the Acacian Schism – the first full-scale conflict between the churches of Rome and Constantinople, and thus also between the papacy and an emperor – encouraged Pope Gelasius I (492–6) to define more closely the relative powers of the empire and the priesthood. In so doing he produced classic formulations which both drew on existing papal ideas and also innovated. The schism's ostensible cause was a dispute over conflicting Monophysite and Chalcedonian Christological interpretations. The Emperor Zeno (474–91), who sheltered Patriarch Acacius, had intervened in 482 through issuing an edict, known as the *Henoticon*, which contained a formula of faith aimed at achieving unity but which infringed the definition of the Council of Chalcedon. Thus Zeno, solely on his own authority, was laying down the law in a purely religious matter. In doing so he was acting in the traditional Roman fashion by treating *res sacrae* as matters of public law subject to imperial rulership – a reflection of the sacral nature of the state. Furthermore, he then, quite logically, laid the charge of *laesa majestas* against some of the bishops who opposed him. This attitude was unacceptable to the papacy under Felix III (483–92), and his head of chancery and successor, Gelasius himself, who denied the imperial claim to legislate in religious matters.

Gelasius, in a letter of 494 addressed to Zeno's successor, Anastasius I, maintains that 'there are indeed two things, emperor *augustus*, by which this world is principally ruled: the consecrated authority of bishops (*auctoritas sacrata pontificum*) and the royal power (*regalis potestas*)'.[121] 'Royal' here both applies to monarchs in general, and the emperor in particular, as the context makes clear.[122] Gelasius innovates in arguing that the government of Christendom is divided between the secular and the spiritual power, a logical extension of existing papal governmental claims. As he explains in his *Tractatus* IV, or *Tomus*, c. 11, this division was decreed by Christ to avoid the effects of human pride (*superbia*).[123] The two powers are to exist in parallel and observe the limits assigned to them.

In religious matters the clergy are in control. Indeed, the emperor 'is the son, not the director of the church, and in so far as religion is concerned, it befits him to learn, not teach':[124] he is to this extent subject to the clergy.[125] Within the clerical body itself primacy and pre-eminence lie with the pope.[126] In secular affairs, however, the clergy obey and use imperial laws because the emperor's power was instituted by God.[127] Yet even so the advantage lies with the clergy: bishops cannot be tried in lay courts even for treason, an aspect of their claim to the prerogative of independent jurisdiction (*privilegium fori*), to which they had been aspiring since the fourth century.[128] Although the two powers are distinct, they are not equal. Because the clergy alone define the content of religious matters, they, not the emperor, in effect determine the relative boundaries of both powers in a Christian society. Indeed, 'of the two [powers] that of the priesthood is a greater burden, in so far as they must also render account before God for the very kings of men',[129] a responsibility implying that of a superior answerable for the actions of an inferior. Walter Ullmann, however, offered the more thorough-going interpretation that Gelasius was deliberately employing terminology from Roman constitutional law to convey that episcopal *auctoritas* was so much higher than mere royal *potestas* that it directed the imperial power, which had a purely auxiliary function.[130] This reading, however, places more weight on Gelasius' words than they can bear. The pope showed no sign of intending a technically exact usage because he was not consistent: elsewhere he referred to each as a *potestas* (as in *Tomus*, c. 11) and in fact also reversed the application of the terms.[131]

Even so, Gelasius' thesis amounted to a definite denial of Roman imperial priest-kingship. The irony was that *Cunctos populos* had itself contributed to this development.[132] Since Christianity had thereby been made the official religion of the empire and thus its government and doctrine the subject of public law, a Christian character had been given to the emperor's existing roles as priest and king, which were but two aspects of the one function of rulership. Gelasius' interpretation of papal governmental ideas, since it had effect at this very level of public law, purported seriously to limit the Christian emperor's jurisdiction by claiming that bishops shared the rulership of the Roman world. If Christianity had remained but a sect in Roman terms, the whole question would never have arisen in this form. Gelasius, obviously, did not derive his arguments from Roman law; but their effect, because the church was legally a public corporation, was to challenge the emperor's legal position. The imperial court, as Justinian's Nov. 6 was to make clear, never accepted the Gelasian view.[133]

It is important, however, not to exaggerate the immediate effect of Gelasius' ideas even in the west. In the sixth century the papacy appears to have retreated from his position in its dealings with the emperor who, it accepted, was in some sense king and priest. This marked a return to the situation under Pope Leo I, who had, for instance, referred to the Emperor Leo I's 'sacerdotal and apostolic mind' in combating heresy.[134] Indeed, the papal chancery seems to have forgotten about Gelasius' formulations concerning the relationship between spiritual and secular power until the Carolingian period.[135] From that time onwards, however, his statements were central to any discussion of this subject. Yet, as we shall see, his words were to be interpreted in radically different ways. Gelasius' clearly expressed view that the secular and spiritual powers were distinct was a seminal contribution to the theme of dualism which was to run through medieval political thought: that there were two parallel jurisdictions, the existence of which involved a division of ultimate authority and thus, possibly, of loyalties. Indeed, he expressly denied secular governmental power to the clergy, and his argument in the *Tomus* about the effects of pride certainly applied to any such encroachment by the *sacerdotium* quite as much as to any on the part of the emperors. Yet through stressing the superiority of the clergy in religious matters he also provided ammunition for those who in the Middle Ages sought radically to expand the scope of what could be considered the due concern of spiritual jurisdiction in a Christian society, and thus seriously to limit the freedom of action of the secular ruler. Such was not Gelasius' own intention: he sought primarily to protect the doctrinal independence of the church and the judicial freedom of the clergy.

Gregory I's views on the relationships between spiritual and secular power were very different from those of Gelasius and reflected the changed circumstances of the papacy after the Gothic Wars. Whereas Gelasius' ideas had been sharpened through confrontation, Gregory worked in an atmosphere of deliberate co-operation with Constantinople and the imperial Exarchate of Ravenna, and accepted that the emperor could validly involve himself in religious affairs and indeed legislate for them. To this extent he abandoned Gelasius' sharp distinction between the two powers. Being, like all popes, legally a subject of the emperor, Gregory sought to respect his sovereign's rights while at the same time fulfilling his own duties as pontiff: to preserve the faith, the pre-eminence of the Roman church, and the privileges of the clergy. Whenever he found himself in opposition to the emperor, he sought to avoid open conflict. As regards Gregory's attitude to western kings, however, there has been serious disagreement among modern scholars. Walter Ullmann argued that Gregory's pontificate marked a fundamental turning-point for the development of the early medieval papacy and, indeed, the history of Europe, in that the pope deliberately turned to the Germanic nations of western Europe as the proper theatre for his extension of papal monarchic primacy (*principatus*), since the way was blocked by the empire in the east. Ullmann found it highly significant that, whereas Gregory consistently called the emperor 'lord' (*dominus*), he addressed western kings as his 'sons' (*filii*). As Robert Markus and Jeffrey Richards have shown, however, this grand interpretation is not supported by the evidence: Gregory viewed the western barbarian nations from an essentially Byzantine perspective, whereby they were considered to be ultimately subject to the universal Roman emperor. As pope, his prime interest was pastoral – to encourage the spread of Catholic Christianity and deepen the faith of those nations already converted: he was not seeking to extend papal power as such over the west.[136] He did however claim the right to impose the purely spiritual sanction of excommunication on secular rulers as well as clergy.[137]

Gregory's pontificate belonged to the end of the world of late antiquity. As that world crumbled in the course of the seventh century the papacy and the emperors drifted further apart as imperial authority diminished in Italy with the growth of Lombard power. The popes remained subjects of the empire, and, indeed, continued to have to obtain imperial confirmation of their election before they could be consecrated.[138] Yet this subjection became progressively out of tune with the realities of power in the west. Furthermore, there was papal resistance against imperial involvement in doctrinal matters. Pope Martin I (649–55), in defence of Chalcedonian christological orthodoxy, fought against the Emperor Constans II's attempt to impose monotheletism,[139] and paid for his bravery by being arrested, taken to Constantinople, and there condemned for treason. He was deposed and died in exile. In contrast, after the brief reconciliation between Rome and Constantinople achieved by the Sixth Oecumenical Council (680-1), which condemned monotheletism, Pope Sergius I (687–701) was able successfully to resist the Emperor Justinian II's attempt to impose the decrees of the Quini-Sext Council (692) by force.[140] The emperor no longer had any real power over the papacy. Indeed, Pope Constantine I (708–15), on the last medieval papal visit to Constantinople in 711, successfully demanded a safe-conduct and received the emperor's ritual prostration before him (*proskunesis*). Although a form of paper agreement over the Quini-Sext decrees was reached, they were never enforced in the west. Constantine also felt strong enough to refuse to recognise Justinian II's successor, Philippikos Bardanes (711–13) who officially reverted to monotheletism. In the 720s and 730s Byzantine power in Italy was further diminished by the Lombard advance under King Liutprand. In these circumstances the papacy was for its own security forced to develop radically new ideas about its relationship with secular power.

The Christian world-view and its implications for the state

Theocratic monarchy and the papal claims were formulated within the context of a general Christian doctrine of the history and destiny of mankind. This view was elaborated most effectively by the Latin fathers of the church and was essentially theological in character, although it involved the most profound implications for ideas of government and the state. The story of man was seen to have been shaped by two crucial events: the Fall, involving the entry of sin into the world with the ensuing loss of God's friendship, and the incarnation of Christ who atoned for human sin by his death and founded the church as the vehicle of salvation. Augustine (354–430) produced the classic exposition of the doctrine of the Fall; his interpretation became completely dominant in the west.

According to the general patristic interpretation, man's true nature existed solely before the Fall, and survived thereafter only in a damaged form. In this view the nature proper to man was clearly a theoretical construct bearing only a distant relationship to the human condition in the world as we know it: mankind's present predicament lay in the realm of fallen nature. Sin, however, was not considered to have totally destroyed man's original nature, but rather to have obscured it: through his rational qualities there remained a scintilla of what he once had been. His ideal, primitive characteristics served as a standard against which the institutions of the fallen world could be judged. In their prelapsarian condition in paradise human beings enjoyed liberty, equality and the common use of all goods. Government, involving the subjection of man to man, like the institutions of slavery and property, was a divinely sanctioned remedy and punishment for sin and would not have been found in the original dispensation of nature: state authority, being perceived as essentially coercion, was inconsistent with man's original liberty. Humans, according to their unfallen nature, were indeed social beings but not political ones: although the structure of subordination within the family, specifically the wife's and children's to its male head, was natural, that within the state was not. This theory recognised no autonomous political dimension, and understood the content and purpose of government and the state according to a strictly theological perspective. Yet within this overall structure there were variations of view between individual Fathers: the role of rulership could be interpreted either in a relatively negative way in so far as its function as punishment was primarily stressed or in a more positive manner with the greater emphasis on its remedial purpose.[141]

It is particularly difficult to assess Augustine's contribution to the patristic theory of government and the state. He was a sophisticated, radical and profoundly spiritual theologian: his political ideas were incidental to his primarily religious purpose in writing and occupied a minute part of his vast output. In his mature thought, that is from about 405 onwards, and above all in *De civitate dei* (The City of God), his political ideas were subordinated to his developed theological thesis.[142] He divided mankind into the city of God and the earthly city – that is, the elect destined to be saved and those predestined to damnation. The cities were distinguished from each other by the objects of their love: 'Two loves have built the two cities: self-love in contempt of God the earthly city, love of God in contempt of self the heavenly.'[143] The city of God was composed of those loving the common good for reasons of

Christian charity, the earthly city of those consumed by a self-interested lust for power over others (*libido dominandi*). This was a deep insight into the way in which human beings make fundamental options in their lives, and thereby affect their relations with others and their ultimate fate in heaven or hell. The two cities were intermixed on earth and would only be distinguished eschatologically, that is at the last judgement. Thus the church in this world, although in a sense it represented the city of God, combined within itself members of both cities, with God alone at this stage knowing who belonged to which group. Given this orientation of his thought, Augustine was not much concerned with the political order as such. Indeed, he was highly sceptical about how much the state could achieve, attributing to it only the minimal role of preserving peace so that the good might not be disturbed. Political arrangements were entirely neutral as regards the human race's main business of salvation. Augustine reached the radical position that the state in itself was not a moral force at all. This became clear in *De civitate dei* where he discussed Cicero's definition of a people comprising a *res publica* as being 'a multitude united together by consent to law and the participation in a common good'.[144] It was fundamental to Cicero's political theory that the law (*ius*) of the state should be the embodiment of justice (*iustitia*). Augustine understood justice in the full Christian sense, which went far beyond Cicero's conception. Augustine's main discussion was in Book XIX, where in chapter 21 he maintained that without justice there was no true *respublica*, a view which appeared to echo his statement in Book IV, chapter 4: 'Remove justice, and what are kingdoms but bands of robbers on a large scale?'[145] But such was not his final opinion. Because he held that no state could in fact achieve Christian justice, he was in Book XIX, chapter 24, willing to leave justice out of his definition of the state entirely and to accept a minimalist and amoral description: 'A people is the association of a multitude of rational beings united by a common agreement on the objects of their love.'[146] Augustine had the Roman empire primarily in mind, and his words revealed how far he had departed in his later years from the tradition of Eusebius' equation of Roman and Christian, which he had himself espoused in his earlier works. Faced with the accelerating collapse of Roman power in the west, Augustine had lost confidence in any human state with the result that he freed the church from reliance on any particular political structure. Indeed, his pessimism about the whole political order is summed up in this statement: 'As for this mortal life, which ends after a few days' course, what does it matter under whose rule a man lives, being so soon to die, provided that the rulers do not force him to impious and wicked acts?'[147]

Augustine's mature thought was, however, quite irrelevant to the development of medieval political ideas. His removal of justice from the definition of the state was not perceived, let alone understood, and his doctrine of the two cities was only properly appreciated in the late Middle Ages, notably in the context of the disputes about the role of poverty in Christian life. Augustine kept church and state separate. Yet the later western patristic tradition, as represented by Gregory the Great and Isidore of Seville, travelled along a different road. Unlike Augustine, both were willing to move towards identifying society with the church understood in its wider sense as the community of Christians clerical and lay, and to view secular rulership as operating within this context. Gregory stressed the religious mission of Christian rulers, whether the Roman emperor or barbarian kings, whereas Isidore was not concerned with the empire but with a territorial Christian kingdom. The full development of this ecclesiastical conception of rulership was only reached in the Carolingian period and became a fundamental characteristic of clerical political theory in the Middle Ages. The monarch was perceived as an individual Christian and as such subject to the Christian normative structure as defined by the clergy. His prime duties to achieve justice and peace were understood to have a Christian content. Augustine's works were drawn upon in constructing this view, but only in a partial manner. In *De civitate dei*, II, 21, he stated: 'True justice is found only in that commonwealth whose founder and ruler is Christ ... There is true justice in that City of which the holy Scripture says, "Glorious things are said about you, City of God".'[148] Augustine was interpreted as meaning that true justice was only achievable in a Christian society understood as an existing body of baptised Christians; that only such a society, unlike the Roman state, could be a true *respublica*. This meant that the city of God became directly identified with the church in its wider sense, a less rigorist and more practical notion than Augustine's denial that it could ever be a perceptible community in this world. His subtle argument in Book XIX, 24, was ignored. The ideals of Christian justice and peace were to be the guiding lights of the Christian monarch, and their achievement his purpose for the good of those he ruled. From Augustine's standpoint this view would be naïve. Clearly, there is a distinction between Augustine's mature theory of rulership and the state and this early medieval doctrine. In order to mark the difference, while acknowledging the element of debt to Augustine, H.-X. Arquillière named this development '*augustinisme politique*', as he said, 'for want of a better word'.[149] Yet, although Augustine's mature theory was clear, he was sometimes inconsistent. He justified the forcible coercion of Donatist heretics by Christian rulers and public officials, and in *De civitate dei*, Book V he expressed the view that the establishment of the Roman empire and the good fortune of certain Christian emperors were the products of divine providence.[150] Although Augustine cast a long shadow over the western Middle Ages, it is possible to exaggerate his influence on political ideas. To categorise the emergent conception of Christian rulership as in any sense Augustinian may be a convenient shorthand, but is certainly a loose usage.

Patristic doctrines were to be selectively interpreted in the early medieval west in a manner which reinforced theocratic monarchy, although they were not in themselves its source. This process consolidated the great shift in Christian political ideas from the early recognition of any form of rule as being ultimately sanctioned by God in a religiously pluralist world, to the acceptance of theocratic monarchy as the sole form of rule in a totally Christian society.

2

THE GROWTH OF
SPECIFICALLY MEDIEVAL
POLITICAL IDEAS,
c. 750–*c.* 1050

The period from the mid-eighth to the mid-eleventh century was of crucial significance because it witnessed the consolidation of characteristically medieval ideas about both the nature of organised society and its structures of authority and power. Many of these concepts, although developed and modified later, were to remain basic for the remainder of the Middle Ages.

It was a time of fundamental change. In 751 Pippin III, with the support of Pope Zacharias, ousted the last Merovingian king, Childeric, and gained the Frankish kingship for himself. His dynasty, the Carolingian, was to last with varying degrees of authority and territorial control until 987. Under his son Charlemagne (768–814) the Frankish monarchy attained in western Europe a level of power unprecedented since the days of the Roman empire. In his reign Carolingian rule was extended over the whole of continental western Christendom, an area which extended from north-east Spain through what was to become France, to western and central Germany (including areas unconquered by the Romans), and down through most of Italy to the borders of the Byzantine lands in the south. A Frankish empire had been in fact established. In recognition of Charlemagne's imperial authority Pope Leo III crowned him Emperor of the Romans in St Peter's basilica on Christmas Day 800, an event the significance of which has been endlessly debated by historians. This marked the beginning of the medieval Roman emperorship in the west. The heyday of the Carolingian empire did not, however, outlast the troubled reign of Charlemagne's son, Louis the Pious (814–40). By the Treaty of Verdun in 843 the Carolingian inheritance was split three ways: Charles the Bald (840–77) was to hold West Francia, Louis the German (died 876) East Francia, and the

Emperor Lothar (died 855) a middle kingdom stretching from the Low Countries through Burgundy to north Italy. In 870, with the partition of Meersen, a more geographically simplified division was established between West Francia under Charles, East Francia under Louis and a kingdom in north Italy in the hands of the Emperor Louis II (855–75). Although towards the end of his life (in 875) Charles the Bald gained the emperorship, it was by this stage a title of no great practical importance. It was associated with the Italian kingdom and became defunct in 924.

In the political thought of this period from the mid-eighth to the late ninth century, monarchy, whether kingship or emperorship, certainly held centre stage. Ecclesiastics played a dominant role in the elaboration of ideas of theocratic monarchy. This trend reflected the markedly higher profile adopted by the papacy and the Frankish episcopacy in political matters, as shown above all by their active involvement in the making of rulers. The church was well and truly embarked upon its involvement in public life at the highest level, a function which it was to fulfil throughout the Middle Ages. Yet there was another side to Carolingian monarchy. Rulers relied also upon the co-operation of their secular magnates. The Carolingians were both theocratic monarchs and a noble family raised above the level of the others: the highest peaks in the range as it were. This meant that the element of the magnates' consent in the making of kings and assent to their rule survived. Furthermore, the bonds of society, quite apart from any considerations of Christian faith, were reinforced by the fidelity sworn to the king by those he ruled, both clerical and lay. Carolingian government was a form of combined operation between the monarch and his secular and ecclesiastical magnates. The Carolingian theory of rulership and society was an amalgam of theocracy, consent and fidelity.

The period from the end of the ninth century through to the middle of the eleventh contained many political legacies from the Carolingian era at its height. By the last decade or so before 900 royal authority had been eroded, partly under the cumulative impact of Viking invasions: real power came to lie in the hands of territorial magnates who had been consolidating their families' possessions for generations and were, for instance, strong enough to depose the West Frankish king, Charles the Simple, in 923. From 895 East Francia suffered the first wave of Hungarian attacks. Increasing fragmentation affected all Carolingian *regna*.

Yet the consolidation of territorial principalities at the expense of royal power should be interpreted not so much as a symptom of political decline but rather as a sign of change in political structure, especially in West Francia, whereby the nobility at all levels became more and more independent in their localities. Yet in tenth-century West Francia fragmentation often went further, so much so that real authority was in many cases restricted to the area which a castle could dominate: territorial magnates themselves faced constant war to claim their rights within their lordships. The last Carolingians found themselves competing with other magnates, notably the Robertian dukes, who eventually in 987 obtained the kingship through the election of Hugh Capet (died 996), the founder of the Capetian dynasty. The problem of the eleventh-century Capetians was survival, and their task the gradual pacification and extension of their demesne around Paris. The history of East Francia was very different. From the time of Henry I, 'The Fowler' (916–36), who was elected by the Frankish and Saxon magnates, a strong monarchy based upon the Saxon stem-duchy emerged and was consolidated by the Ottonians. Otto I's (936–73) victory over the Hungarians at the battle of the Lechfeld in 955 ended the period of the invasions of western Europe. His pre-eminence as the most powerful ruler in Europe was confirmed when in 962 Pope John XII crowned him Roman Emperor. This time the institution of emperorship was to prove extremely long-lasting: indeed the line of Roman emperors only came to an end when it was suppressed by Napoleon in 1806. This Saxon dynasty, which was succeeded by the Salian from the reign of Conrad II (1024–39) relied considerably upon the support of its bishops and abbots to provide resources and administration. The growing difference between conditions in West and East Francia only served to underline the increasingly permanent division into the kingdoms which were becoming France and Germany: the frontiers between them would vary from time to time, but this fundamental configuration of the map of western Europe was to be a legacy of the Carolingian and Ottonian eras. In 1050 the German kingdom was very much a reality, the French, however, still not much more than an idea, but one which was to prove triumphantly tenacious.

As regards political ideas this period from the early tenth to the mid-eleventh century in continental Europe saw the further development of theocratic ideas of kingship and emperorship, but in a way which clearly subjected the church to lay control. The popes crowned and anointed the Roman emperors; but in the years from 963 to 1049 the emperors managed to exert a considerable degree of domination over the papacy. Although the spotlight must be on the German monarchy there were important developments elsewhere. In England the tenth and eleventh centuries witnessed the unification of the most governmentally precocious early medieval kingdom, the Anglo-Saxon, which, although it drew on Carolingian and Ottonian ideas, had a unique contribution to make to medieval political thought.

CAROLINGIAN POLITICAL IDEAS

Theocratic monarchy

That Carolingian political ideas were overwhelmingly focused on theocratic rulership is both obvious and misleading because of the nature of the evidence. Theocratic notions were deliberately fostered by the monarchy as part of its programme for legitimising and consolidating the power of the dynasty. Royal and imperial official documents, such as capitularies[1] and letters, were a prime means to this end. The church supported this endeavour through the decrees of councils and the formulation of coronation orders (*ordines*). Individual ecclesiastics contributed through letters and tracts of various kinds, notably those which may be classed as early forms of the mirror-of-princes *genre*,[2] which sought to set forth the image of the ideal Christian ruler. Indeed, the royal programme itself was progressively taken over by the clergy in the course of the ninth century. Yet the prominence of theocratic conceptions should not obscure other ideas which, although fundamental, are not nearly so noticeable in the sources: the notions of fidelity and consent which, especially among the lay magnates, formed a bond of society and a basis for accepting the ruler's authority. These deep-rooted attitudes and assumptions remained predominantly at the level of word and action rather than written record. These problems in interpreting political ideas form part of the wider one of how to assess the Carolingian Renaissance as a whole. This overtly Christian movement was the programme of the ruling dynasty and the church: it left large parts of life untouched.[3]

The church stood at the cradle of the Carolingian dynasty through legitimising the transfer of the kingship from the powerless Childeric to Pippin. At the request of a Frankish embassy in 750 Pope Zacharias authorised this procedure. According to the Royal Frankish Annals written about forty years later, he replied to Pippin, 'That it would be better for him to be called king who had the power of one, than him who remained without royal power', and then 'commanded by apostolic authority that Pippin be made king lest order be disturbed'.[4] Whereupon Pippin was elected king of the Franks at Soissons, and in 751 the Frankish bishops participated in this king-making through anointing the new monarch, an innovation in Frankish terms: as a contemporary account tells us, 'Pippin the most high by the election of all the Franks to the throne of the kingdom, with the consecration by the bishops and the subjection of the lay magnates, together with his queen Bertrada, as the ancient order requires, was raised to the kingdom.'[5] In 754 Pope Stephen II himself anointed Pippin. The bare facts of papal authorisation and election by the Frankish magnates, followed by episcopal and then papal anointing, are clear; interpretation is more obscure. Because of the lapse of time after the event the Royal Frankish Annals cannot necessarily be taken as an accurate account of Zacharias's own words; they may be such, but may also represent a later justification in terms of the Isidorean notion that there must be congruence between the name (*nomen*) of king and royal actions, and the Augustinian view of the paramountcy of order in the microcosm and the macrocosm. Further, the church had by no means monopolised the king-making process. At this stage election by the Franks and clerical anointing are best seen as parallel and complementary forms of legitimation. Unction certainly indicated the ultimately divine source of royal authority, although, as we shall see, the developing significance of this liturgical act under the Carolingians became highly complex. Since the Merovingians themselves were theocratic kings, there was no innovation in stressing that Pippin's power came from God. The older historical interpretation that Christian monarchy by divine grace replaced the Germanic blood-right of the Merovingians is misleading.[6] What was new, however, was the prominent role adopted by the church, notably the papacy's involvement based on its long-established links with the Franks. In 751 the Exarchate of Ravenna had fallen to the Lombards who threatened the papacy. Zacharias and Stephen supported Pippin as potentially their strongest defender in the west; indeed, at his anointing Stephen also made Pippin 'patrician of the Romans' (*patricius Romanorum*) to perform this function. For Pippin the church gave additional confirmation that the change of dynasty was legitimate.

The clearest sign of the theocratic nature of Carolingian kingship was provided by the official adoption of the *rex dei gratia* formula as part of the royal title (*intitulatio*). Although there is a letter of Pippin, probably dating from 765, which uses the formula, it only became part of normal chancellery usage after his death from 769, and is to be found in the first official documents of both Charlemagne and Carloman. Between 769 and 774 the normal Carolingian *intitulatio* was 'N. by the grace of God king of the Franks illustrious man' (*N. gratia Dei rex Francorum vir inluster*).[7] The model for the *rex dei gratia* was the kings of the Old Testament, and the context the identification of the Franks as a chosen people with that of Israel. In these respects the Carolingians were developing Merovingian ideas. The king was the vicar of God (*vicarius dei*), as Cathwulf reminded Charlemagne in a letter of *c.* 775:

> Always remember, therefore, my king, with fear and love for God your king, that you are in his place to look after and rule over all his members and to give account on judgement day even for yourself. And a bishop is in second place: he is only in Christ's place. Ponder, therefore, within yourself how diligently to establish God's law over the people of God.[8]

Such kingship involved a religious role. At the Diet of Frankfurt of 794, for instance, Paulinus of Aquileia addressed Charlemagne as 'priest and king' (*rex et sacerdos*).[9] This usage did not imply any sacramental function, as indeed it had not for the Merovingians. Charlemagne both saw himself and was seen by those he ruled as having the prime responsibility before God for the Christian people divinely committed to his care – that is, for the church in the wider sense. He was a priest in that he promoted the worship of God and the spreading of his word. The church in the narrower and strictly ecclesiastical signification was included within the people which he governed; and his duty was to defend that church entrusted by God to his protection.[10] Indeed, as Alcuin, his teacher and adviser, explained, Charlemagne had been given two swords: one to keep the church internally clean from heresy, and the other to use against its pagan enemies – imagery derived from

Luke 22:38 and not yet used, as it was from the mid-eleventh century, to describe the relationship between spiritual and secular power.[11] The king's overridingly religious concerns were reflected in the large number of his capitularies devoted to spiritual and ecclesiastical matters. According to Alcuin, Charlemagne, like King David, combined the functions of royal leadership and priestly teaching (*praedicatio*) in order to guide his people, a community of belief, to salvation:[12] by means of correction (*correctio*) he aimed to spread and enforce the rule of uprightness (*norma rectitudinis*).[13] This usage of the Davidic theme became widespread in Carolingian literature from *c.* 794,[14] although it had been prefigured by Pope Stephen II's calling Pippin a 'new David' in 757.[15] The Old Testament idea of kingship as an office of service was thereby transposed into a Christian dimension.

In the course of the ninth century ideas of theocratic monarchy became more and more differentiated. The ecclesiastical perception, already partially articulated by Gregory I and Isidore, whereby society was identified with the church, became consolidated and predominant in Carolingian political thought. Secular rulership was understood to operate within the *ecclesia* conceived in the wider sense. Louis the Pious accepted this view and in so doing reflected the increasingly determinant role of the clergy in the formulation of political ideas. The church Council of Paris of 829 was a milestone in confirming this approach. Its decrees contained a number of chapters concerning the role and position of kings, and including an overt quotation from Gelasius:

> Principally therefore we know that the body of the whole holy church of God is divided into two distinguished persons, namely the priestly and the royal, as we accept has been passed on by the holy fathers. Concerning this matter Gelasius, the venerable bishop of the Roman see, writes thus to the emperor Anastasius, 'There are indeed', he says, 'two august empresses by which this world is principally ruled: the consecrated authority of bishops and the royal power. Of these that of the priesthood is a greater burden, in so far as they must also render account before God for the very kings of men.'[16]

A crucial shift was involved here. For Gelasius the *mundus* had been the Roman world, but for the council it had become the *ecclesia*. Jonas of Orleans, who played a leading role in the council, incorporated this interpretation of Gelasius in his tract, *De institutione regia* (c. 830).[17] Within this *ecclesia* secular authority existed in parallel with that of the priesthood, in accordance with the fundamental division understood to have been instituted by Christ. In the course of the ninth century the clergy gained considerably in self-confidence and were able increasingly to assert their rights and privileges. As part of this development there was produced the canonical collection known as the Pseudo-Isidorean Decretals. This was West Frankish in origin and was quite possibly compiled in the circle of Ebo, the deposed archbishop of Rheims (816–41). It consisted of forged and genuine papal decretals and authentic canons of councils. The main aim of the collection was to justify the freedom of the clergy from lay control. In the first instance it reflected the pretensions of the Frankish episcopate, but it did also stress the theme of papal primacy. It was to have an enormous influence later in the Middle Ages, being used as a treasury of quotations by the reform papacy in the second half of the eleventh century and by Gratian in his handbook of canon law in the twelfth.[18] But did this growth in clerical claims mean that the relationship between spiritual and secular authority was ceasing to be one of parallel roles? Within the context of the identification of society with the church Gelasius' notion of the superiority of the clergy in spiritual matters could lead to their erosion of the power of secular rulers, since the ultimate end of a community of this kind was understood to be spiritual. In the ninth century the beginnings of such ideas in ecclesiastical circles can barely be perceived. The Frankish clergy interpreted their inherently superior spiritual role to mean that they had the function of teaching the norms of Christian society and thereby determining the purpose and ideal conduct of the king. The clerical take-over of the process of king-making indicated not any loss of actual power on the monarch's part but an assertion that he exercised his authority within the context of the *ecclesia*, and in this had some similarity with a bishop. The episcopacy had no power to depose a ruler: thus in 833 it was the great men of the empire who had in effect deposed Louis the Pious by withdrawing their obedience, whereas the bishops confirmed their action by afterwards declaring formally the divine judgement that he had been shown to be unfit to govern, and by then degrading him from his rank as ruler and imposing a penance on him.

The papal interpretation of the relationship between spiritual and secular power within the *ecclesia* was also developed with increasing confidence in the ninth century. The clerical claims to superiority of role and thus independence of function were elaborated in a way which focused on the primatial position of the pope. Gregory IV, the pontiff at the time of the events of 833, argued that papal government was superior to that of the emperor in that it was concerned with souls, and that Christ had subjected emperors to the priestly authority of popes.[19] For Nicholas I (858–67) the Roman church was the head of all the churches and the pope was constituted *princeps* over the whole church. The priesthood was not therefore to be judged by the lay power, rather the reverse.[20]

Both the Frankish clergy and the papacy believed that the role of the secular ruler within Christian society was in its purpose one of Christian ministry. The Council of Paris (829) and Jonas of Orleans declared that 'The royal ministry is specifically to govern the people of God and to rule with equity and justice, and to strive that they may have peace and harmony.'[21] Indeed, Smaragdus of St Mihiel, writing before 814, had already classically defined the role of the king: 'Do [most gentle king] whatever you can for the part that you perform, for the royal ministry that you carry out, for the name of Christian that you have, for the place of Christ that you fill.'[22] In the Carolingian period, as Cathwulf showed, bishops were conventionally described as vicars of Christ. Through applying this nomenclature to kings Smaragdus was likening the royal role to the episcopal. Similarly, Louis the Pious, in his *Admonition to all the Orders of the Kingdom* (823–5), stated that divine providence had instituted him as ruler 'in order to care for His holy church and this realm (*regnum*)':[23] bishops and counts were to help him by sharing in the exercise of his function, which was thus a 'ministry divided into parts' (*ministerium per partes divisum*).[24] In the ninth century there was, admittedly, considerable fluidity in describing the ruler as vicar of God or of Christ; but with the growth in claims to liberty of the church, it was increasingly perceived that to attribute to the king the vicariate of Christ, the last possessor of both royal and sacerdotal power, would imply an increasingly unacceptable control over the clergy. Thus Hincmar of Rheims in the second half of the century was for this reason scrupulous to refer to the monarch only as vicar of God in an attempt to distinguish more clearly between the ministries of secular rulers and of bishops[25] – needless to say, Cathwulf's suggestion that the vicar of God was superior to that of Christ was not followed up. According to Hincmar, Christ had instituted not one ministry divided into two parts but two parallel ones within the church as a whole, although the episcopal enjoyed the greater dignity.[26]

The implications of understanding secular rulership as Christian ministry were profound, and in elaborating them the ninth-century writers were in essence developing the formulation of Gregory the Great. In a fundamental sense the king's ministry was that of any Christian, but of one who was also the king: of him, therefore, more was expected. And who but the clergy were to tell this exalted Christian what conduct was required of him? Hence there were written the clerical advice-books, or *Fürstenspiegel*, of which those of Smaragdus and Jonas of Orleans were prime examples. But this advice did not mean clerical control of the monarch. The fundamental thesis of medieval kingship was however established and in theory accepted. Kingship was an office of service within the Christian *corpus*, and as such its purpose was defined in terms of that of the Christian community as a whole, and its exercise limited by the normative structure of Christian morality.

The perception of kingship as an office of this kind was consolidated in the eighth and ninth centuries by the introduction of anointing into the inauguration rituals of kings. Unction became the liturgical expression of the making of the theocratic monarch. This was an Anglo-Saxon as well as a Carolingian development. There was, however, apparently no link between Visigothic royal anointing and Carolingian, although there may have been in the case of Anglo-Saxon.[27] As regards the anointing of Carolingian kings specifically, a distinction should be drawn between the eighth-century examples and those of the ninth. In 754 the pope also anointed Pippin's sons, Carloman and the future Charlemagne, and it is possible that they were reconsecrated by Frankish bishops in 768 and 771. Certainly, in 781 Pope Hadrian I crowned and anointed Charlemagne's sons Pippin and Louis (the Pious) as sub-kings, and on Christmas Day, 800, Pope Leo III crowned and anointed Charlemagne's son, Charles, as king. There appears, however, to have been no strongly entrenched Frankish tradition of royal anointing as such, because there were no non-papal unctions after at least 771, and also because it is most probable that no Frankish king was anointed during the first half of the ninth century. The examples of anointings in this period are the papal ones at the coronation of an emperor: in 816 that of Louis the Pious, and in 823 of Lothar. A significant shift occurred, however, when, in 848, Wenilo, the archbishop of Sens, crowned and anointed Charles the Bald as king of Aquitaine. From now on all West Frankish kings received episcopal coronation and unction, although the practice was only established in East Francia from 911.

Royal inauguration was thus incorporated in a church service, and was clothed in special liturgical forms, the coronation orders (*ordines*): the king at his very inception as monarch was dramatically shown to be such specifically within the church. These prayer-texts, although they must be understood primarily as liturgy, are sources for political ideas because they embody fundamental conceptions of rulership. This ceremonial creation of a king marked a significant stage in the institutionalisation of Christian ideas of kingship. There was a distinct process of development and crystallisation of ideas in the Carolingian *ordines*. The most important personal contribution was made by Hincmar of Rheims, who increasingly brought out the significance of anointing in his four *ordines*, and most notably in those for the coronation of Charles the Bald as king of Lotharingia in 869, and for that of Louis the Stammerer as king of West Francia in 877. His work formed the basis for the more elaborate West Frankish ('Erdmann') *Ordo* of the Sens tradition, and the 'Seven forms' *Ordo* of Rheims, both, probably, of the end of the ninth century. The last-named especially was particularly influential and was a prime source for the *Ordo* of 'Mainz' in the *Pontificale Romano-Germanicum* (*c.* 960), which was fundamental for the formation of coronation *ordines* for the rest of the Middle Ages.[28]

Such was the development in the mainstream in continental Europe. In Anglo-Saxon England royal anointing had certainly been introduced by the eighth century. The first English *ordo* was, however, composed later. Percy Schramm considered that there was no fixed rite until the 960s.[29] Janet Nelson has, however, argued that the 'Leofric' *Ordo* was English in origin, and that it was the oldest one, antedating Hincmar's first (for Judith, Charles the Bald's daughter, on the occasion of her marriage to Aethelwulf in 856). Nelson considers that the 'Leofric' *Ordo* was in use for most, if not all, of the ninth century, and that the English rite was imported into West Francia in the tenth century.[30]

The ultimate source for the idea of anointing kings seems obvious: the royal unctions in the Old Testament. Yet, as was most probably the case in Visigothic Spain, the direct liturgical source for the Carolingian coronation *ordines* appears to have been the episcopally performed ritual of post-baptismal unction, which treated the anointed priests, kings and prophets in the Old Testament as the models for all Christians.[31] Indeed, it is also most likely that Smaragdus' much-discussed reference to the anointing of a king refers to such a post-baptismal unction rather than to an inauguration as ruler.[32] The immediate context for Carolingian royal anointing was the designation of the Franks as the people of God (*populus dei*), and thus their identification with that of Israel. As the Old Testament showed, anointing was the form of royal inauguration instituted by God for his people: it was as though, ideologically, there were no gap between the Franks and ancient Israel.

The specific contribution which the anointing rituals made to the development of the idea of theocratic kingship appeared clearly in Hincmar's *ordines*. Anointing had become the constitutive element in the king-making process: it was the bishops who as mediators of divine grace made the king. There was thus a relative downgrading of other, traditional aspects of inauguration: the consent of the great men of the kingdom, enthronement and the feast. The episcopal anointing represented the third stage of the elaboration of the notion of kingship by the grace of God, the first being the Pauline view that all rulership was divinely sanctioned, and the second that the monarch derived his power directly from God. Anointing transformed kingship into another, higher dimension, because such unction was understood to be a sacrament. There was thereby involved a crucial change in the meaning attributed to the 'grace' by which the medieval king ruled. Whereas previously, *gratia* in this context meant 'favour', thus indicating the source of his power (the possibly sacramental nature of eighth-century unction remains obscure), now *gratia* also definitely signified 'supernatural grace' infused into the king through the mediation of the bishops in order to enable him to perform his specific ministry of rulership over clergy and laity within his kingdom understood as a church in the wider sense.

Hincmar made all this clear in the prayer he recited as he anointed Charles the Bald in 869:

> May the Lord, in his mercy and pity, crown you with the crown of glory, and may he anoint you to the rulership of your kingdom with the oil of the grace of his Holy Spirit, wherewith he anointed priests, kings, prophets and martyrs, who through faith defeated kingdoms, effected justice and gained his promises; and by the grace of God may you be made worthy of these same promises, so that you may merit enjoying their company in the heavenly kingdom. Amen ... And with peace given in your time, may he lead you with the palm of victory to the everlasting kingdom. Amen. And may he, who wished to set you up as king over his people, make you happy in this present world and his companion in eternal bliss. Amen. May he make you happily and long govern, by his dispensation and your administration, the clergy and people, whom he wished, with His help, to subject to your dominion, in order that, obeying divine commands, avoiding all adversity, abounding in all good things and obeying your ministry with faith and love, they may both enjoy the tranquillity of peace in this present world and merit winning with you the company of the citizens of heaven.[33]

A liturgical affinity with post-baptismal anointing would have suggested that royal unction was a sacrament. In addition another possible source was the opinion enunciated both by Gregory the Great and Isidore of Seville that the Old Testament anointings of kings were themselves sacraments.[34] In any case the notion that royal coronation unction was a sacrament proved peculiarly long-lasting: it can be found in the twelfth and thirteenth centuries even when the bulk of theologians no longer held this view, and such anointing was reduced generally to the level of a sacramental – that is, a sign instituted not by Christ, but by the church, in order, through its intercession, to aid the receipt of grace.

In one sense the king was like any other Christian, since all were 'anointed ones' through baptism, and to this extent he stood on an equal footing with his subjects, sharing their common religious and moral responsibilities. Through the additional, royal unction, however, the king was given the grace to perform a specific ministry within the church: as God's servant (*famulus dei*) to lead his people, ultimately, to salvation, a role in which

Christian responsibilities were focused and intensified. As a result, in his function as king he had been made, through anointing, more than simply a layman: his status as an ecclesiastical person (*persona ecclesiastica*) was enhanced. He was seen as the image or type of Christ (*typus Christi*); indeed, his co-regent in heaven.[35] The position of the king, therefore, combined aspects of both hierarchical superiority and equality, in relation to his fellow Christians whom he had been set above by God to rule as subjects of his dominion.

This dual character was reinforced by the complete liturgy surrounding king-making. The anointing and coronation preceded a Mass and therefore took place within the context of the creation of sacred community. The royal inauguration itself symbolically made real the unity of the kingdom through the participation of the king, the clergy and the nobility (whose acceptance of the proceedings came to be institutionalised later in a formal recognition (*recognitio*)). The Mass celebrated and confirmed the king's ministry within the community of the faithful: indeed, the Mass involved the first symbolic exercise of his vocation of service. The coronation Mass was a living symbol of a community of people equal as Christian souls, but ruled by a hierarchical structure of government.

In the developed Hincmarian rite of royal inauguration, coronation (as in 869 and 877) was not constitutive, but being secondary followed anointing, and was itself succeeded by the episcopal grant of the sceptre. Byzantine practice, introduced to Francia by the papacy, was the most likely source of such coronation. Initially the Franks did not consider it to be an episcopal monopoly: in 813 Charlemagne crowned Louis as co-emperor in an entirely secular ceremony, and in 838 Louis in turn crowned his son Charles (the Bald) as a sub-king. All this changed with Charles's inauguration by Archbishop Wenilo in 848. Indeed, Hincmar's *ordo* of 869 used coronation as a metaphor for anointing. In England royal coronation by bishops appeared by the early tenth century.

The episcopal domination of royal inauguration in West Francia appeared even more comprehensively in the 'Seven forms' *Ordo* which also included the archbishop's giving the king his sword (apparently an innovation shared with the West Frankish ('Erdmann') *Ordo*). Likewise, enthronement, probably the core of earlier secular king-makings, was placed in the hands of the bishops, and accompanied by the prayer *Sta et retine* enunciated by the archbishop, and which reminded the king, 'How the mediator between God and man [i.e. Christ] confirms you on this throne of the kingdom as mediator between clergy and people, and makes you reign with him in the eternal kingdom.'[36] Enthronement effectively symbolised the superior status of the theocratic king created on Christ's behalf by his representatives, the bishops – a process which had been developing, again, since 848.

The bishops had, therefore, come to control the ceremony of king-making and the formulation of the ideas associated with it: to this extent the ecclesiastical dominance of political ideas was institutionalised. The episcopacy represented itself as the mediator of power from God to the king. At the time of inauguration the ruler, on the face of it, accepted ecclesiastical notions of the nature, purpose and limitations of his kingship in so far as he agreed to undergo the whole procedure. How much he acquiesced during the exercise of his rulership was another matter. Certainly, the expression of ideas concerning the role of the king in a Christian society lay predominantly, but by no means entirely, in the hands of the clergy. There remained, however, the perennial problem of the Middle Ages: the ruler was limited in power in theory, but could he be controlled in practice?

In order to attempt to cope with this difficulty, Hincmar introduced a royal commitment into the process of king-making. The monarch-to-be bound himself by a solemn promise given to the bishops in word and writing before his consecration, which was therefore conditional on his undertakings being satisfactory. The first such promise preceded Charles the Bald's consecration in 869. Charles's *responsio* to the address of Bishop Adventius of Metz had the force of a commitment to uphold the honour and dignity of the church and the lay magnates, and 'to preserve the law and justice for each within his own order according to the laws both ecclesiastical and mundane relating to him'.[37] The procedure was more formalised in the case of Louis the Stammerer in 877. A week before his inauguration Louis made a *professio* to the lay magnates and the bishops that he would follow the 'rules' (*regulae*) of the church and continued, 'I also promise that I shall observe the laws and statutes for the people which by the mercy of God is committed to me to rule.'[38] At the inauguration itself, in response to a request by the bishops (*petitio episcoporum*), Louis made a formal promise (*promissio*) to uphold canonical privileges and laws.

The model for the royal profession was that made by bishops-elect prior to their consecrations, to demonstrate their orthodoxy and obedience. As Janet Nelson has shown, Hincmar's achievement was to perceive the relevance of the bishops' case to that of the king, the common link being that both were episcopally consecrated.[39] (Episcopal ordination anointing was, however, in no sense a model for the royal: it was only introduced into West Francia in the ninth century and in Rome in the tenth.) By undergoing consecration the king, like a bishop, became answerable to his consecrators and subject to canonical rules. The royal commitment was not a coronation oath as such, but rather the promise of an office-holder to obey the laws. The king was like a bishop in that he was consecrated to wield authority within the *ecclesia*: indeed, as the 'Seven forms' *Ordo* was to say, he participated in the bishops' ministry in exterior matters.[40]

But the fundamental question remained. Could the king, because of his promises and acceptance of consecration, be controlled ultimately by the bishops? Could they, if they thought it necessary, depose him, as they could a fellow-bishop for breaking his *professio*? There is some evidence that Charles the Bald thought that they were the only ones who could, because they had performed his anointing, 'from which consecration ... I should have been expelled by no one, at least without hearing and judgement by the bishops, by whose ministry I was consecrated king'.[41] Hincmar, however, never went so far as to claim the right to depose a king: any deposition would be in God's eyes alone. Yet whatever the practical restrictions on the bishops' powers, the ninth-century development of ecclesiastically controlled rituals of royal inauguration reinforced the general understanding that there was no such thing as an autonomous secular world. Through the extension of episcopal claims to jurisdiction over the king, the distinction between the spheres of operation of the spiritual and lay orders within the church was beginning to be eroded. This jurisdiction remained, however, at the level of spiritual and moral persuasion and instruction, rather than of the political power to dispose of a king deemed by the clergy to be unsuitable for Christian purposes and thus useless.

Consent and fidelity

The theocratic character of Carolingian kingship can be over-stressed at the expense of its other side, that of fidelity (*fidelitas*) and consent. The personal bond of sworn faith (*fides*) between ruler and ruled held kingdoms together and contributed to consolidating them. In 786, 792 and 802 Charlemagne had demanded such an oath from all free men in his dominions; but, above all, the fidelity of the magnates, both ecclesiastical and lay, was vital for the monarchy, which depended on their co-operation for its survival. The consent of these aristocratic faithful men (*consensus fidelium*) was exploited as a principle of government by the Carolingians.[42]

This idea of fidelity had its roots in the society of the noble followers of the king. The signorial interpretation of Frankish history, stressing an 'aristocracy with monarchical peaks' (*Aristokratie mit monarchischen Spitzen*), has been strongly in vogue amongst German scholars especially since the Second World War, and has replaced the myth of a Germanic free people electing its kings. Thus a historical link would be discerned between the Germanic band of the king's war-companions (*comitatus*), mentioned in Tacitus' *Germania*, and the Carolingian *fideles*. Yet precisely the same impediment of the lack of secure evidence, which helped to undermine the older model of the free people, has caused doubt to be cast on the very idea of 'original Germanic fidelity' (*urgermanische Treue*) as being itself mythic.[43] Certainly there are grave problems involved in trying to connect the *comitatus* with Carolingian *fideles*, not least because of ecclesiastical influence on the development of the idea of *fidelitas* in the intervening period. Because of the paucity of reliable evidence it is difficult to see how these matters can be satisfactorily resolved: care should be taken not to construct hard-and-fast models on shaky foundations. Whatever the truth of the matter, the question of the ultimate source of *fidelitas* is irrelevant to Carolingian conditions. The most that can be said is that the long-established duty of the magnates as *fideles* to give counsel (*consilium*) to their king provided the context within which the idea of the *consensus fidelium* developed, and that the consent given by Merovingian bishops to royal legislation, and required of them at ecclesiastical synods, served partly as a model for laymen.

Whether we may discern a feudal form of fidelity emerging at this time raises one of the thorniest controversies among historians. Rigorists would maintain that the term 'feudal' may only be applied when studying a period in which the word *feudum* (fief) was current to denote a service benefice, in land (or later in money), held by a vassal from his lord through a contract of personal dependence: that is from the late eleventh century. This view seems to go too far: in that landed benefices were systematically provided by the Carolingians for their vassals in order to enable these men to perform mainly military services for them as their lords in return for protection, it appears reasonable to understand these as feudal relationships. This is an example of a fundamental problem of historical interpretation: whether an idea or phenomenon of one period may be described by a term which accurately corresponds with its content, but which only becomes current later on. A properly historical approach would take account both of continuity in this respect and nuances of difference. The term 'feudal' has certainly been amongst the adjectives most abused by historians to describe the past, with its use ranging from solely the legal rights and duties relating to fiefs to highly generalised aspects of medieval society, including the position of the subject peasantry. Indeed, the more abstract term 'feudalism' has become no less than a pariah word amongst very many medievalists both because of its vagueness, and because it suggests a system where none existed, there being such local variations in forms of tenure.[44] Yet some scholars would hold that such a general model has a justifiable role in historical explanation.[45] Certainly, a systematic approach to feudal law only appeared later in the Middle Ages, notably in the juristic glosses, and, subsequently, commentaries, on the Lombard *Libri feudorum*, beginning with the gloss of Pilius in, or shortly before, 1207.

Feudal ideas were significant for political thought because of the contract of mutual consent between lord and vassal, and the resulting normative limitations on ruler and ruled, including the vassal's right of resistance if his feudal rights were infringed. This is, however, to anticipate, because the Carolingian period witnessed only the beginnings of feudal relationships. The concept of fidelity as such was what was important at this time. The monarchy extended vassalage to tie men to it and thereby raised the status of this condition. Yet whereas all magnates were *fideles* of the king, Carolingian sources appear to contain little reference to magnates as royal vassals.[46] Fidelity involved a large general obligation; vassalage added a specific extra one.[47]

Focus on fidelity reveals the dual relationship between the king and his magnates, spiritual and lay: the signorial aspect of his rule linked him to them as his faithful men, whereas the theocratic stressed the distance he stood above them. Yet the essence of Carolingian rulership in practice was that it was a partnership between the king and his magnates who shared in his ministry as agents exercising royal office. This partnership was reflected in the themes of fidelity and consent which emerged more and more strongly in the Carolingian period, initially as a means of consolidating the authority of the *parvenu* dynasty, and by the mid-ninth century arguably providing a partially contractual basis for royal power in West Francia under the pressure of the conflicts between the sons of Louis the Pious. Oaths of fidelity were crucial because no monarch relied solely on his theocratic claims for his legitimacy; and if such bonds were broken his position was gravely threatened. But *consensus* is a protean word. And what did it mean for the Carolingian *fideles*? If compulsorily demanded by a theocratic ruler it could amount to obedience. It could also mean formal assent; collective or universal consent without the possibility of individual dissent; or truly voluntary consent. Any answer can only be approached by considering the key areas of king-making, contractual monarchy and law-creation.

As regards the origin of royal power, in ninth-century West Francia lay magnates exercised an important role in choosing and deposing kings (as in 833) – a sign of the governmental partnership between the Carolingian ruler and his great men. Yet in the actual process of making the chosen candidate king, this lay participation was only reflected in an attenuated form beside the increasingly stressed theocratic interpretation: in these ceremonies the lay magnates expressed no constitutive consent but merely signified through assent by acclamation that they accepted the bishops' actions. Indeed, in the meetings leading up to Louis the Stammerer's coronation in 877 the magnates' swearing of fidelity took the place of any formal election on their part. Thus Louis' intitulation in his *Professio*, 'I Louis by the mercy of the Lord our God and the election of the people constituted king',[48] should be understood in this context. There was no contradiction involved in referring to God and the people (in the form of the magnates) as the sources of royal authority. In this respect divine grace and 'popular' consent existed in parallel, in that the magnates accepted the king whose power came from God. Equally well, God could be seen to be acting through them.[49] The

Carolingian acclamations were the origin of the later formal Recognition by the nobility at coronation services.

Although there was a clear distinction between the roles of the lay and ecclesiastical members of the magnate class in the ceremony of creating a king, they had in common the swearing of oaths of fidelity to him. The bishops were therefore themselves in a dual position. Because of their spiritual authority they were able formally to create the monarch, yet once he was instituted they were subordinate in temporal matters and were counted amongst his *fideles*. Indeed, it could well be that the theocratic elements, dominant at the time of the inauguration itself, might have less importance than the bond of fidelity as a basis for the exercise of royal power during the reign as a whole.

Such an interpretation is supported by the emergence of contractual aspects of kingship in West Francia in the 840s. Through the pact (*pactum*) of Coulaines in 843 Charles the Bald swore to uphold the honour of both his clerical and lay *fideles*, and the respective laws under which they lived, whereas they swore to sustain the honour of the king.[50] Thereby, reciprocity, co-operation and partnership within a form of community of the realm were established as aspects of what amounted to a fundamental law for the kingdom. Indeed, royal authority appeared conditional in so far as there was an implicit suggestion that king or magnates were released from the pact if either side broke its undertaking. Furthermore, in his oath taken at Quierzy in 858 Charles promised 'like a faithful king' (*sicut fidelis rex*) to honour and protect the persons and legal position of his *fideles*.[51] This contractual element was reflected at his coronation of 869, when his promise in his *responsio* repeated his words at Coulaines almost verbatim.[52] Fidelity, which in its pre-Carolingian origins seems to have imposed a unilateral obligation on the Frankish *fidelis*, had become a bilateral bond involving rights and duties for both ruler and ruled.

This contractual development was reflected in the process of law-making. Under Charles the Bald, capitularies, issued with the authority of the royal *bannum*, were promulgated with the freely given consent of his *fideles* – hence the statement in the Edict of Pîtres (864): 'law is made by the consent of the people and the constitution of the king'.[53] F.L. Ganshof held that a fundamental change in procedure was involved, in that the consent *formulae* contained in capitularies under Charlemagne and Louis the Pious reflected assent which could not be refused by the *fideles*, and which was thus in reality an unavoidable declaration of obedience.[54] Ganshof's views have been contested, in that some later scholars have attributed a more genuine role to magnate consent in the capitularies of Charlemagne and Louis the Pious.[55] This opinion would therefore see the reign of Charles the Bald more as consolidating a previous trend. Yet, even so, the consent given, being that of a group of *fideles*, would tend to be not individual but universal, partly in imitation of the procedure in ecclesiastical synods.

What, then, was the overall significance of the role played by the *consensus fidelium*? Certainly, the character of Carolingian monarchy was thereby considerably complicated, in that the signorial aspect of kingship came into clearer relief beside the theocratic. Because the central idea of theocratic monarchy was the divine origin of royal power, the king's relationship with those he ruled was based on *fides* in the sense of religious faith. As signorial monarch, however, the self-same king had with his *fideles* a relationship of *fides* in the sense of mutual fidelity, a bond useful to both parties. Such fidelity was not the source of his royal title, but it might consolidate his actual power. The theocratic–signorial model of kingship, clearly apparent in ninth-century West Francia, was to become the distinctive form of monarchical secular government in western and central Europe in the Middle Ages.

The transpersonal dimension

These theocratic and signorial aspects of kingship raise the further question of the extent to which Carolingian rulership and society exhibited impersonal and public characteristics, in addition to purely personal and private ones. Modern German scholars in particular have devoted considerable attention to this problem. They have used the term 'transpersonal' (*transpersonal*) to denote a range of meanings beyond the merely personal and individual, and stretching to the extreme of abstract state concepts. Notions according the kingdom an existence distinct from that of its king, organological ideas of society organised into a corporate body, and views of rulership as public office, would all be considered transpersonal. This word is now standard in German studies of the whole period of medieval political ideas, but has only been employed sporadically in English treatments. It is a useful term, however, since 'impersonal' only covers part of the meanings it denotes. For the moment the main focus will be on transpersonal ideas of kingship; those relating to Carolingian emperorship will be treated as part of the next section dealing with notions of empire.

The ninth-century elaboration of the idea of kingship as Christian ministry emphasised the distinction between the person of the individual king and his impersonal office. The normative standards, applying to such rulership, appeared objective, and, in theory at least, meant that the king should not govern in a subjective and thus arbitrary manner. The concept of a royal office, whose purpose was to serve the common good, involved the notion that the *regnum* or *populus* had a separate existence from that of its monarch. The Carolingian emphasis on the king's tutorial role of caring for those committed by divinity to his rule, only served to emphasise that the people of the realm had God-given rights which were to be protected.[56] This people was composed of free men who were Christians, a view which combined the Roman idea that members of the *respublica* were free and not slaves, and the Christian doctrine of the liberty of the sons of God. In addition to specifically Christian obligations, royal coronation promises respected the existing legal rights of those the king ruled. The signorial aspect of kingship was also not purely personal because of the way in which royal *fideles* held offices of the king and thus shared in his God-given ministry.

There is considerable further evidence supporting the view that in the Carolingian period there existed transpersonal ideas of the *regnum*. Charlemagne, for instance, from the beginning of his rule used the *intitulatio*, 'Charles by the grace of God king and ruler of the kingdom of the Franks, and defender and helper of the church'.[57] In that he did not designate himself simply 'ruler of the Franks', there was some idea of the kingdom as an entity in its own right. Similarly, to take a later example, the aim of the meeting at Coulaines was to consider 'the stability and good of the king and the kingdom ... and what would be to his [i.e. the king's] and the whole people's common profit'.[58] Of greatest significance, however, are the implications of the use of *respublica* in the ninth century after Charlemagne's imperial coronation, and notably from the reign of Louis the Pious onwards. The concept of the *respublica* was one of the most distinctive bequests of Rome to medieval political ideas. In antiquity it signified the state as such; was an eternal entity distinct from the ruler or government; and existed within an essentially public dimension. In itself the term *respublica* connoted no specific form of government: following the historical changes in the Roman world it signified the state under the Republic and the Empire. It was central to the idea of the *respublica* that it existed within a structure of law. Nithard, Paschasius Radbert, Sedulius Scottus and Hincmar of Rheims in particular used *respublica* in transpersonal senses owing a great deal to this Roman inheritance. They thereby distinguished between the king and the kingdom, the emperor and the empire. For them, *regnum* and *imperium* existed as entities which were public in nature and founded in law.[59]

It must, however, be said that some historians deny that such transpersonal ideas existed in the Carolingian period and stress the personal nature of authority and the bonds of society.[60] It is true that *fideles* who held office were in part performing a personal service to the monarch, but only in part. One meaning of *respublica* was the more down-to-earth one of fiscal possessions, yet even so there was a transpersonal element involved. More seriously, the principle of the personality of law persisted as the pact of Coulaines revealed. Against this should be weighed legislation of general effect, and the growing notion of territorial *regna*. As we shall see, the vicissitudes of the idea of empire in the ninth century reflected the interplay of patrimonial and transpersonal conceptions. In a sense, too, the royal household always was the basis for the Carolingian structure of government. Genuine problems of historical interpretation are at issue. Clearly, transpersonal ideas were at a very early stage of development, yet present they were.

The most serious difficulty, however, concerns organological conceptions. According to Carolingian theocratic ideas, the church in the wider sense was the *corpus* within which secular and spiritual rulership operated. There was no such thing as a state in the analogous sense of a politically organised body or community with an autonomous existence. In consequence it is possible to see ideas concerning society and its government as focusing on the person of the ruler, and thus lacking a transpersonal dimension.[61] Yet this interpretation goes too far, because within the over-arching context of the church in the wider sense, both the *regnum* or *imperium*, and the church in its narrower and purely ecclesiastical signification, exhibited transpersonal aspects, which is why the *Vita Walae* (Life of Abbot Wala of Corbie), written, perhaps, by Paschasius Radbert, characterised both of them as *respublicae* within the *ecclesia* as a whole.[62]

Ideas of empire

The re-establishment of a form of Roman emperorship in the west was a decisive moment in the development of medieval political ideas, and marked the entrance of a large theme which attracted varied interpretations over time. Indeed, within the Carolingian period itself notions of empire were very diverse. The whole complex of ideas of emperor and empire fluctuated widely in importance, with different writers, and in different times and places in the Middle Ages, yet remained one of the determining characteristics of specifically medieval political thought. These western imperial ideas were of marked longevity: they exerted an influence even into modern history, and thus far outlasted those of Byzantium from which they derived so much but from which they were so different.

Charlemagne was created Emperor of the Romans (*imperator Romanorum*) by two actions. As he was rising from prayer at the Christmas Mass Pope Leo III placed a crown upon his head, whereupon the assembled Roman people acclaimed Charles as emperor. The pope then most likely prostrated himself before the new emperor in a formal 'adoration' (*adoratio*). The significance of this sequence of events can only be understood against the background of the Byzantine process of making an emperor, which was its model. At Constantinople the formal popular acclamation was the more important component, and was followed by coronation by the patriarch. Clearly, the ceremony of 800 contained certain crucial innovations. The involvement of the pope was novel, as was the placing of the coronation first, thus emphasising the prominence of his role. The geographical Romans were also substituted for the Byzantines. The excuse for these actions was that, because a woman, the Empress Irene, ruled at Constantinople, the imperial throne was in effect vacant.

This event was open to more than one interpretation at the time.[63] According to the papal view, as expressed in the account of the ceremony in the *Liber pontificalis* (The Book of the Pontiffs), the whole process constituted Charlemagne Emperor of the Romans. The pope, in crowning Charlemagne, was given a pre-eminent role and presented as acting for God: indeed the Roman people's reported acclamation was 'to Charles, most pious Augustus crowned by God, great and pacific emperor, life and victory'. Yet this source did not treat the pope's action as being constitutive, but rather the popular acclamation: 'and he was constituted emperor of the Romans by all'. Nor was there any mention of papal anointing.[64] The Byzantine model explains much of this: the declaratory nature of patriarchal coronation, the lack of unction, and the function of popular acclamation to institute the emperor by declaring and effecting God's choice. Yet at Constantinople the role of the acclamation was by this stage very theoretical indeed. What is striking about the account in the *Liber pontificalis* is its stress on the constitutive nature of the ceremony. The reason why the pope wished Charlemagne to be made emperor was to consolidate his existing role as defender of the Roman church and the papacy, as was also made clear in the *Annales regni francorum* (Annals of the Kingdom of the Franks), written *c*. 801: 'and with the name of patrician removed he was called emperor and augustus'.[65] The patriciate of the Romans was supplanted by the emperorship which inherited its function. The overall context of the papal action was the developing process whereby in the eighth century the papacy increasingly exerted its independence and emancipation from Byzantium.

Charlemagne himself did not accept the papal interpretation. Indeed, he tried to downgrade the significance of the ceremony – as did the *Annales* which presented it as a normal Christmas crown-wearing, during which the pope intervened to replace the crown on Charles's head and the people inserted the title of emperor in the conventional Frankish praises (*laudes*).[66] Charlemagne never called himself *imperator Romanorum*: from 29 May 801 he employed as his official title, 'Charles most serene augustus, crowned by God, great, pacific emperor governing the Roman empire, and who [is] also by God's mercy king of the Franks and the Lombards'.[67] This apparently cumbersome wording reflected his real intentions.

His biographer, Einhard, writing about thirty years after the event, said that Charles would often maintain that he would never have entered St Peter's basilica if he had known what was about to happen.[68] This statement could be somewhat misleading, because Charles definitely knew that he was going to be made emperor: on 23 November he had been received outside Rome with imperial honours, and at a meeting in St Peter's on 23 December it had been publicly decided to make him emperor.

Charlemagne apparently expected to be acclaimed simply as 'emperor'; he objected to the words 'emperor of the Romans', and to the way in which the pope claimed a pre-eminent role through crowning him before the acclamation. He wanted in effect to be *a* Roman emperor rather than *the* Roman emperor; that is, to be emperor in the west without supplanting the Byzantine emperor in the east – hence the wording on his seal after the coronation: *Renovatio romani imperii* (Renewal of the Roman Empire). He desired recognition of the position which he in fact held: that he ruled so much of what had once been the western Roman empire together with additional lands in Germany. Indeed, he had already begun to adopt the external trappings of emperorship based on the Byzantine model available to him, and to treat his capital, Aachen, as a form of New Rome.

Charlemagne's idea of empire had a Frankish centre: the Franks were the imperial people. In including the geographical Romans within his dominion he did not wish to supplant the Franks, or indeed the Lombards, in any way. Adoption of the title, 'emperor of the Romans', would have been interpreted as favouring the Romans over them. He therefore employed the formula, 'governing the Roman empire', which had long been current in Italy, and was indeed to be found in three sixth-century Ravenna papyri containing oaths for the health of the emperor; he also stressed his royal titles.[69] Indeed, the fact that he ruled so many kingdoms gave him a further, hegemonial claim to emperorship. Carl Erdmann held that in Roman emperorship itself there had been such a hegemonial element which, in the early Middle Ages, had been transposed into barbarian kingdoms and become 'Rome-free'.[70] This interpretation has been criticised by Werner Suerbaum on the grounds that it is incorrect to maintain that in late antiquity the term *imperium* was only properly applied to the Roman empire as being composed of several *regna*, whereas it was also in fact applied to monarchies and indeed some cities.[71] Indeed, as we have seen, the empire itself was also called a *regnum*.[72] As far as the Franks were concerned, however, it seems dubious to insist on a clear-cut 'Rome-free' component in their idea of empire, because of the aping of Roman imperial characteristics so evident at Charlemagne's court: the hegemonial and Roman aspects of Carolingian emperorship were complementary.

The Christian character of Charlemagne's empire was also paramount: Alcuin, for instance, had already consistently referred to his rule over a 'Christian empire' (*imperium christ-ianum*).[73] That empire was in communion with the Roman church. Indeed, in the *Libri carolini* (written in 791–2) Charlemagne, in rejecting what he understood to be the theological errors of the Greek Council of Nicaea of 787, had denied the universalist claims of the Byzantine emperor and stressed the close links between the Franks and the Church of Rome, the guarantor of orthodoxy.[74] In this religious sense, therefore, his empire was Roman. Yet, although after his coronation he was happy to be called a 'new Constantine' (*novus Constantinus*), he had no wish to compete with the Byzantine emperor in the east: he desired no more than equality or parity with him. In contrast, the papally inspired title *imperator romanorum* definitely *was* a denial of the validity of Byzantine emperorship. The title itself was a neologism, at least as regards official documents: the correct Latin phrase would have been *imperator romanus* (the genitive plural was properly reserved for the names of peoples other than the Romans constituting the *respublica*). At Constantinople the emperor was simply referred to as the *Basileus*: indeed, since Heraclius I (610–41) he had not been called *Basileus ton Rhomaion* (emperor of the Romans).[75] Charlemagne and the Byzantines came to pursue a policy of compromise over the imperial title. In 812 the Byzantine emperor Michael Rhangabe sent to Charlemagne an embassy which saluted him at Aachen as *Basileus* and *imperator*, thus recognising his hegemonial claims to emperorship. From this time on, however, the Byzantine emperors began to style themselves *Basileus ton Rhomaion*, in order to make clear that they were the only true Roman emperors. In 813 Charlemagne replied to Michael in a friendly way stressing the independence and equality of the two empires, oriental and occidental: he began, 'Charles by divine grace emperor and augustus, and at the same time king of the Franks and Lombards, to his beloved and honourable brother Michael glorious emperor and augustus'.[76]

At heart Charlemagne believed that he had won his empire for himself with divine approval, and felt in no way dependent on the Roman people or the pope for the source of his power. He, therefore, considered that he could dispose of his empire as he saw fit. In 806 he had drawn up a formal division of the empire according to which his son Charles would succeed to an undivided Francia, and his younger sons Pippin and Louis to the acquired kingdoms of Italy and Aquitaine. Although this scheme retained the unity of the Frankish core of the empire,[77] it was evidence of a patrimonial attitude which envisaged the dismemberment of the empire as a whole, even though Charles was probably intended to be the heir to the imperial title itself. In the event the empire only remained a unity because Louis was the sole son to survive. Finally, in 813 at Aachen Charlemagne, in imitation of the Byzantine practice, crowned Louis himself co-emperor.

The reign of Louis the Pious marked the high point in the development of Carolingian ideas of empire. Louis himself stressed the Frankish and Christian aspects at the expense of the Roman. He consistently used the title of, simply, *imperator augustus*, and his seal bore the inscription, '*Renovatio regni Francorum*' (Renewal of the kingdom of the Franks). In his *Ordinatio imperii* (Ordering of the empire) of 817 he made provisions which both had immediate effect and applied after his death, and which went beyond Charlemagne's patrimonial approach in 806. He decreed that his eldest son, Lothar, was immediately to receive the imperial title together with the inheritance of Francia and the kingdom of Italy (in the event of Louis' death), whereas his son Pippin was to receive right away the kingdom of Aquitaine as was his remaining son Louis the German that of Bavaria. The younger sons were to be subordinate to their elder brother. He then proceeded to crown Lothar co-emperor. This arrangement combined both a unitary and a hegemonial approach. The overall unity of the empire was preserved by the subordination of the lesser kings to Lothar, who was also to rule a united Francia. In that the empire was identified with the church it shared the characteristic of being a transpersonal entity rising above subdivision: 'The unity of the empire which God has entrusted to us should not be rent by any human division ... lest haply this should give rise to a scandalous state of affairs in holy church.'[78] This sense of unity was not, however, to survive the reign of Louis the Pious, as the Treaty of Verdun and the partition of Meersen showed.

The papacy, for its part, pertinaciously developed its claim to create the emperor. When, in 816, Pope Stephen IV journeyed to Rheims, he crowned and anointed Louis the Pious emperor in a thoroughly ecclesiastical ceremony; the role of the Roman people to constitute by acclamation was thereby ignored. Louis may well have been in part manipulating the pope on this occasion, and certainly did not consider papal coronation to be necessary, as his subsequent coronation of Lothar revealed. Yet the papacy persisted: in 823 Pope Pachal I invited Lothar to be crowned and anointed in St Peter's. A shift, however, occurred by 850, when Lothar, who had not previously made his son Louis II emperor, petitioned the pope to do so. Already in 844 Pope Sergius II had crowned and anointed Louis as king of the Lombards. Pope Leo IV duly crowned and anointed the young king *imperator augustus* at Easter, 850, in St Peter's. The emperorship became steadily more Roman in complexion, as, after Lothar's death in 855, it was associated directly with Louis' rule in Italy and (in theory) his defence of the papacy. In his letter of 871 to the Byzantine Emperor Basil, Louis called himself 'Emperor and Augustus of the Romans', deriving his right to this title specifically from his consecration by the pope. 'Through our orthodox and sound thinking we [Franks] have received the government of the Roman Empire, and the Greeks, through their unorthodoxy and unsoundness, have ceased to be Emperors of the Romans.'[79]

Yet the true watershed was reached with Pope John VIII's coronation and unction of Charles the Bald in 875. For the first time the pope took the initiative as the sole, constitutive creator of the emperor: in the case of Charlemagne the Roman people, in papal eyes, had exercised a constitutive role, and all subsequent papally created emperors had been co-emperors. John made it clear that he had elected Charles as an officer called by God to act 'for the honour and exaltation of the holy Roman church and the security of the Christian people';[80] and the new emperor took an oath to defend that church. The emperorship was, even so, more important for the papacy than for Charles. Although he pursued his claim to Louis II's inheritance in Italy, the real centre of his interests remained in Francia. Indeed his idea of empire retained hegemonial aspects: when in 869 he won control of part of Lotharingia he styled himself *imperator et augustus* on the grounds that he ruled two kingdoms;[81] and his seal after his imperial coronation bore the inscription '*Renovatio imperii Romanorum et Francorum*' (Renewal of the empire of the Romans and the Franks). The papacy, on the other hand, had the most direct interest in who ruled south of the Alps, and made sure that the Roman emperorship remained linked to the protection of Italy and the church of Rome. Arab attacks in south Italy made the need for effective imperial aid all the more pressing. The medieval papacy was to stay obsessed with the empire mainly because of the security demands entailed by possession of the papal lands.

The status of the papal patrimony was a central concern of what is for modern historians one of the most important, and certainly the most enigmatic, documents, concerning the rights of the papacy as regards the empire, to be produced in the Carolingian period: the Donation of Constantine. This was a forgery which purported to be a constitution of Constantine (*Constitutum Constantini*) in favour of Pope Silvester I and his successors. It has attracted a vast amount of scholarly attention; but there is no agreement as to when, where or by whom it was produced. The suggested time-scale for its production has ranged from c. 750 to c. 850; and the places put forward have varied from Rome (notably the Lateran church and the papal chancery), France (Rheims and the abbey of St Denis), the library of the margrave of Friulì and the workshop of Pseudo-Isidore.[82] It is most likely, however, that it was produced, possibly in stages, before 806, the date of the St Denis manuscript, which is now accepted as the oldest. The Donation was based on the *Legenda sancti Silvestri* (Legend of St Silvester), composed between 480 and 490. According to the Donation, Constantine, in return for baptism and cure from leprosy by Pope Silvester, gave the Lateran palace and his imperial crown to him and his successors, together with the right to wear the other imperial insignia and garments. Constantine also expressly handed over the government of Rome, all of Italy and the regions of the west, as well as divers islands, as papal property. The Donation stated that Silvester refused the crown itself, and that Constantine had decided to transfer the seat of his imperial authority to the east, with its capital to be a city constructed at Byzantium, 'because, where the government of priests and the head of the Christian religion have been set up by the heavenly emperor, it is not right that there the earthly emperor should have power'.[83] Despite their vagueness, the terms of the Donation both confirmed papal claims to the patrimony and accorded the papacy imperial power in the west. The primacy of the pope was also affirmed: he was 'higher than and first of all the priests in the whole world'.[84]

There is, however, no hard evidence that the papacy directly used the words of the Donation in the eighth and ninth centuries. It has been argued that the phraseology of letters of Popes Stephen II, Paul I (757–67) and Hadrian I (772–95) presupposed the existence of the Donation, but this is no more, indeed, than supposition; and, although there appear reflections of the document in letters of John VIII, no verbatim use was involved.[85] The reality for the papacy was that the Carolingian rulers confirmed its claims to lands in Italy: witness Pippin's 'restoration' of papal territories in 754, and Charlemagne's 'donation' of the same and extra ones in 774. In 817 Louis the Pious in the *Pactum Ludovicianum* defined the papal lands and promised to defend them. In 824 Lothar, on Louis' behalf, issued the *Constitutio romana* which, in return for guaranteeing free and canonical papal elections, required that the pope should notify the fact of his election to the emperor who would then send legates to his consecration as bishop. An oath of loyalty to the emperors was also imposed on the pontiff. The Donation of Constantine was, however, to derive its historical significance primarily from its inclusion in Pseudo-Isidore, through which it entered the mainstream of the development of canon law. Explicit papal exploitation of the document came after the Carolingian period. The most likely explanation is that it was originally composed to support papal pretensions to the patrimony against Byzantine counter-claims.

POLITICAL IDEAS, *c.* 900–*c.* 1050

Rome-based emperorship

Although the original development of medieval ideas of Roman emperorship took place in the Carolingian period, and the rule of Charlemagne in particular was frequently referred back to in later centuries, the Carolingian era, because of political fragmentation at its end, was in effect a false dawn. The reigns of the Saxon and early Salian rulers of Germany formed the real starting-point for the continuous development of notions of Roman empire. The ideas produced then, relating to both ancient and Christian Rome, laid the basis for opening up a central and defining problem for the rest of medieval political thought: the relationship between temporal and spiritual power, and in particular that between the papacy and the empire. It was the prominence of this question which above all was to single out the political thought of the Middle Ages as being different from that of subsequent periods.

The lasting legacy of the Carolingian era was the acceptance of the principle that it was the pope who created the emperor. Otto I, desiring the title of emperor in recognition of his status and conquests, including that of the kingdom of Italy, initially petitioned Pope Agapetus II for the imperial crown in 951, only to be refused. His eventual coronation in 962 made him the protector of the Roman church and thereby singled him out from other rulers. There was, however, a difference between the pope's understanding of what was meant by such protection and the emperor's. John XII envisaged that Otto would act as the strong arm of the papacy to defend it in accordance with the fundamental papal conception of the function of the Roman emperorship, and of the patriciate of the Romans before it. Otto understood such protection as implying that the pope was thereby subordinated to the emperor's authority. Shortly after his imperial coronation in February 962 Otto confirmed in a pact with John XII the Carolingian donations to the papacy, the original *Ottonianum* which has not survived. After a papally inspired revolt Otto returned to Italy and called and presided at a Roman synod which deposed John in December of 963. At this time the emperor had the extant *Ottonianum*, purporting to be the pact with John XII, drawn up. This document indeed contained the genuine pact, but was a forgery in so far as it also featured the insertion of the requirement that every newly elected pope must take an oath before the imperial legates or the emperor's son before he was consecrated. This stipulation marked a severe infringement of papal liberty and was to form a justification for subsequent imperial depositions and appointments of popes by the Saxon and early Salian emperors.[86]

It is not clear what Otto understood the nature of his emperorship to be. Hegemonial aspects and also military were certainly included: Widukind of Corvey recorded that Otto had been acclaimed *imperator* by his victorious troops on the Lechfeld as had Henry I after another battle against the Hungarians in 933, a clear echo of the ancient Roman practice of honouring a successful general.[87] It is unclear what significance to attribute to the fact that Otto did not himself use the title of Roman emperor but rather that of *imperator augustus*, following Carolingian usage from the time of Louis the Pious. Nevertheless Widukind referred to Otto as '*imperator Romanorum, rex gentium*' (emperor of the Romans, king of peoples), and an imperial notary used the title *imperator Romanorum ac Francorum* in several imperial documents of 966.[88] The Rome-centred nature of emperorship became more apparent under Otto II whose chancery from 982 onwards adopted the title *Romanorum imperator augustus*.

Under his successor Otto III there emerged an unambiguously Rome-based concept of Christian emperorship. His programme was set out on his seal which was produced in 998 and was based on that of Charlemagne, being surrounded by the words, '*Renovatio imperii Romanorum*' (Renewal of the empire of the Romans). But he went beyond Carolingian conceptions of empire in his concentration on Rome as the supreme city in the world. He understood his imperial role as being to possess the summit of power in both temporal and spiritual matters. In this notion he was influenced by Byzantine ideas and ritual: indeed, as part of this tendency, he mimicked the eastern idea of a family of kings under the emperor by sending a crown to King Stephen of Hungary and making the Polish duke Boleslaw 'brother and co-operator of the empire' (*frater et cooperator imperii*).[89] But he also undermined the papal position by usurping its supreme role of Christian ministry: he was firstly 'servant of Jesus Christ' (*servus Iesu Christi*) and finally, in his famous diploma of 1001, 'Otto servant of the apostles and according to the will of God our saviour august emperor of the Romans' (*Otto servus apostolorum et secundum voluntatem Dei salvatoris Romanorum imperator augustus*). In this document Otto, as emperor ruling 'Rome the head of the world' (*Roma caput mundi*), claimed complete control over the Roman church, 'the mother of all churches' (*mater omnium ecclesiarum*). Otto went on to denounce the Donation of Constantine as a papal forgery (without proof), and then proceeded through his own munificence to donate the eight counties of the Pentapolis to the pope whom, he claimed, 'we have ordained and created' (*ordinavimus et creavimus*).[90] The pontiff in question was Silvester II, his former teacher Gerbert of Aurillac, who had indeed been appointed by Otto in 999. Just as the first Silvester was the supposed recipient of Constantine's Donation, it was probably no accident that it was a second Silvester who received Otto's.

It was Otto III's achievement to have permanently established the Roman character of the emperorship, although his successors varied in the importance they attributed to this aspect of their office. Henry II on his imperial coronation in 1014 adopted the title, 'Henry servant of the servants of Christ and august emperor of the Romans according to the will of God and of our saviour and liberator' (*Heinricus servus servorum Christi et Romanorum imperator augustus secundum voluntatem Dei et salvatoris nostrique liberatoris*),[91] a direct appropriation of part of the papal title. Conrad II was the first German monarch to call himself 'king of the Romans' (*Rex Romanorum*), implying a claim to the emperorship before imperial coronation; his son Henry III adopted the same style on his accession. Conrad's seal also bore the inscription, 'Rome the head of the world holds the reins of the earth's round orb' (*Roma caput mundi tenet orbis frena rotundi*).[92]

Whatever the claims of these rulers, from the papacy's point of view the Roman emperor remained a papal creation with a function within the church. The identification of the ruler as *vicarius Christi*, which became more prevalent during the Ottonian period and which passed from the Mainz coronation *Ordo* of 960 into the Roman imperial coronation orders, in theory placed defining limitations on the emperor's role by making him a participant in the episcopal ministry.[93] But, in reality, neither the fact that the pope crowned the emperor nor the latter's sacerdotal status were understood to entail his subjection in any way to control by the pontiff: quite the reverse. Indeed, Henry III acted decisively as *rex et sacerdos* and protector of a subordinated Roman church: although the details remain obscure, his assertive involvement in the synod of Sutri in 1046 contributed to the resignation of one pope, Gregory VI, and the deposition of two other claimants, Silvester III and Benedict IX. The citizens of Rome gave Henry the title of *patricius* which confirmed his leading role in papal elections; he proceeded to nominate four German popes in succession: Clement II, Damasus II, Leo IX and Victor II.

Despite the importance of ideas of empire produced under the Saxon and early Salian rulers, it would nevertheless be misleading to exaggerate the degree of reflection on such matters in this period. There was a notable paucity of writing relevant to political ideas. Many of the most characteristic statements of the monarchy's claims are to be found in iconographic evidence: illuminated liturgical manuscripts such as the Gospel Books of Otto III in which the Christ-like nature of the monarch was stressed.[94] Church and palace architecture also reflected the magnificence of the king-emperors: witness, for instance, the court buildings at Goslar and the mighty cathedral of Speyer founded by Conrad II as a fitting memorial to his imperial claim to be by far the greatest priest-king in Europe. Their stones were the most eloquent testimony to the power which these emperors possessed in temporal and spiritual matters. Yet when compared to the situation in the Carolingian period, the Saxon and Salian German kingdom witnessed a relative decline in political sophistication: it possessed very few institutions and worked almost entirely through the spoken rather than the written word. Legislation had virtually ceased; only one Ottonian administrative document, the *Indiculus Loricatorum*, survives.[95] In such circumstances it might seem misguided to seek out transpersonal ideas. The indivisibility of the realm appears to have been more the result of historical accident than established principle,[96] although, as far as the empire was concerned, the imperial insignia represented the continuity of the emperor's office.[97] Transpersonal notions can, however, be discerned in the *Gesta Chuonradi imperatoris* (Deeds of the Emperor Conrad), written in the early 1040s by Wipo, a court chaplain. Wipo distinguished between the person of the king and the kingdom, of the emperor and the empire. On the death of Henry II the citizens of Pavia destroyed the royal palace there on the grounds that it no longer had an owner. Wipo reported Conrad as responding: 'If the king has died, the kingdom remains, just as the ship remains whose helmsman has fallen. The house was public not private property.'[98] Wipo's use of the helmsman image, as elsewhere of the king as doctor bringing his kingdom to health, indicated that the monarch exercised an office of rulership over an entity, indeed an organism, separate from himself. Likewise, Wipo described the kingdom during the *interregnum* between Henry II and Conrad II as being a *respublica* without a ruler, an apt usage of the Roman term most suited to indicate transpersonal continuity, a term which he also equated with the *Romanum imperium*.[99]

Imperial kingship

Although these developments occurred under the Saxons and Salians, emperorship was not seen as a monopoly of those holding the imperial title conferred by the pope. A deeply rooted and pervasive idea of imperial kingship persisted. This attitude was reinforced by the biblically based view which saw kingship as the fundamental model for rulership, with the emperor being a particular kind of king.[100]

In West Francia imperial attributes rather than the formal title of emperor were commonly accorded to the king. Amongst the last Carolingians, for instance, Lothar was referred to as *augustus* because he ruled the *regnum Francorum* within the context of the now divided *imperium Francorum*.[101] This nomenclature, together with his use of imperial insignia, also reflected his hegemonial claims, notably to parts of Lotharingia. The early Capetians deliberately sought to legitimise and bolster their authority by using imperial epithets and *formulae* in their official documents. Thus Hugh Capet in charters referred to '*imperium nostrum*' and to himself and his co-ruler son (the future Robert II) as masters of the *imperium Francorum*; from the reigns of the same Robert and his successor Henry I, a continuous chancery tradition developed of calling the king *augustus*. Indeed, in one charter Henry I was referred to as 'supported by the imperial dignity' (*imperiali fultus dignitate*).[102] In literary sources the same equivalence between king and emperor could be found. Gerbert of Aurillac, while serving the Capetians, referred to Lothar as *Caesar* and to Hugh Capet and Robert II as *augustus*.[103] Abbo of Fleury saw no qualitative difference between kings and emperors. In his *Collectio canonum*, written from 994–6, he mentioned 'rules strengthened by the authority of royal, that is imperial, command' (*praecepta regalis, id est imperialis, iussionis auctoritate roborata*),[104] and the election of 'a king or an emperor' (*regis vel imperatoris*); he also said, 'every [king] within the borders of his kingdom exercises in piety a Christian emperorship' (*unusquisque [rex] infra sui regni fines imperium Christianum pietate exsequitur*).[105] Helgurd of Fleury in his biography of Robert II, written by *c.* 1041, called him 'such a great emperor of the Franks' (*tantus Francorum imperator*).[106] All these writers, and the chancery products, were seeking to strengthen the Capetians by applying the Carolingian imperial inheritance to the new dynasty; indeed, Hugh Capet and Robert expressly referred to kings and emperors as their predecessors.[107] Increasingly, Charlemagne would be appropriated by the French monarchy as well as the German. Certainly the imperial claims for the West Frankish kings were made in self-defence against the pretensions of the Ottonians.

From the reign of Athelstan (924–40) onwards the Anglo-Saxon monarchy had also adopted an imperial style, as was shown in royal charters, notably those of Edgar who was titled 'august emperor of all Albion' (*tocius Albionis imperator augustus*) and '*basileos* of the Angles and king and emperor' (*basileos Anglorum et rex atque imperator*); his kingdom was referred to as an 'empire' (*imperium*).[108] This imperial kingship was certainly hegemonial in character. It also rekindled the ancient memory of the Roman emperors once made in Britain and reflected the feeling that the island was 'another world' (*alter orbis*) which had never been part of the Carolingian empire. Byzantine models were clearly influential, as was the example of the Ottonians. There was, in addition, an extensive older literary basis: Adamnan of Hy, for instance, had in *c.* 690 called the victorious King Oswald, 'of the whole of Britain emperor ordained by God' (*totius Britanniae imperator a Deo ordinatus*);[109] and Bede referred to the royal *imperium* or *de facto* overlordship over the Saxon kingdoms.[110] Asser considered that Alfred ruled a *regale imperium*.[111]

In tenth-century Spain, the title of emperor was applied to the kings of Leon but was not personally used by them (although they did call themselves *basileus*). The earliest such reference was contained in three charters issued by Ordoño II in 916/17, in which he described his father Alfonso III as *imperator*. Subsequent usages of the title featured in chronicles and various charters rather than in official chancery documents. It is impossible to know what exactly the term meant. It was certainly honorific and appears to have embodied a claim to hegemony in the Iberian peninsula, a claim which drew on the tradition of the unity of Spain under the Visigoths and which involved the responsibility of winning back the land to Christian rule. Indeed, the epithet *Flavius* was applied to Ramiro III (967–84), as it had been to the Visigothic kings. The imperial style was also a response to the establishment of a caliphate in Cordoba in 929 and, in addition, may very well have been influenced by the example of the Carolingians – there is probably a core of truth in the document recording Ordoño's request for a crown from the Carolingian treasure held by the chapter of St Martin of Tours. The emperorship itself was firmly associated with the kingship of Leon, so much so that, when in 1034 Sancho III of Navarre captured that kingdom, which he called 'the summit of empire' (*imperiale culmen*), he minted coins featuring himself as *imperator*. His son Ferdinand I (1037–65), who united Leon with Castile, also bore this title, as did his successors.[112]

The existence of non-Rome-based imperial ideas put Roman emperorship into perspective. The Roman empire was important, but how important and to whom? It was only of direct significance for the papacy, Italy, Germany and Burgundy. There was no question at this stage of the Saxons and Salians seriously claiming any form of universal authority in Latin Christendom, despite the rhetorical flights of fancy of their court writers. Other rulers in the west, notably the French, recognised the higher dignity of the Roman emperor in so far as he fulfilled his prime and defining duty of defence of the Roman church: they did not accept that he had any jurisdiction outside the borders of his empire.[113] Cnut, for instance, through his presence at Conrad's coronation in 1027, was according him a precedence of honour. The *Imperator Romanorum* existed beside several royal emperors.

3

POLITICAL IDEAS IN THE HIGH MIDDLE AGES, *c.* 1050–*c.* 1290

Such fundamental and transforming developments took place in political ideas between the mid-eleventh and the late thirteenth century that this period can rightly be seen as being radically different from the early Middle Ages. The background was massive social, economic and political change. This was the time that medieval Europe took off as a civilisation. With the defeat of the last invaders, the Hungarians, western Christendom was no longer a threatened world but was able to expand geographically. The Germans continued the push to the east into Slav lands begun in the mid-tenth century; in the Iberian peninsula the *reconquista* made dramatic advances in the second half of the eleventh, culminating in the recapture of the old Visigothic capital of Toledo in 1085; Sardinia was conquered from Islam by the fleets of Pisa and Genoa in 1015/16, as was Sicily by the Normans between 1061 and 1091; the Byzantines lost their last toe-hold on the Italian mainland with the fall of Bari in 1071; the First Crusade and its aftermath established the crusading states at Edessa, and in Syria and Palestine at the turn of the eleventh and twelfth centuries; and, in Scandinavia, Denmark and Norway had been Christianised, officially at least, by the mid-eleventh century, and Sweden in the course of the twelfth. Within western Christendom, the economy, with regional variations, but aided by generally favourable climatic conditions, expanded rapidly through internal colonisation together with an accelerating growth in urbanisation and both long- and short-distance trade. Early medieval society in the west had been overwhelmingly agricultural, and indeed throughout the Middle Ages most people continued to live and work on the land, although by the thirteenth century this was no longer the case in Flanders and

Lombardy. The escalating development of city civilisation provided an environment specifically favourable for intellectual life and in particular for the emergence of universities: the Salerno medical school was the first from the mid-eleventh century; Paris and Bologna provided archetypes in the twelfth. Political ideas became more sophisticated in this urban ambience within a European world which was opening up.

At the political level, this growth in complexity resulted in the gradual emergence of territorial states, in England and the Norman kingdom of Sicily from the mid-twelfth century, and in France by the thirteenth, a position in marked contrast to that obtaining earlier in the Middle Ages, and one which was radically to influence the content of political thought. This is not to suggest that anything like modern forms of state came into being. But if one thinks of a state in fairly elementary terms as a politically organised community with a defined territory within which there exists a ruler or government with internal and external sovereignty, then such bodies began to exist from this time. They were characteristically medieval in kind with the question of sovereignty being complicated by competing ecclesiastical and feudal jurisdictions and, indeed, hierarchies of sovereign powers. Such states were made possible by nascent bureaucracies staffed increasingly by the burgeoning army of lawyers produced, on the Continent at least, by the new universities. By the late thirteenth century a variety of kinds of territorial state existed in different parts of Europe, ranging from the western monarchies, including by then the Spanish, to the city-states of Italy. A problem in terms of political and legal thought was posed by the coexistence of such territorial entities with the universalist jurisdictional claims put forward for the Roman emperor from the middle of the twelfth century.

Most marked was the development of the church as a legal and governmental institution. It adopted many attributes of a state and, indeed, in the papal patrimony acted as one, certainly from the time of Innocent III (1198–1216). With the increasing exercise of power by the church and the consolidation of ecclesiastical jurisdiction as existing parallel to that of secular rulers, there were more acute causes of dissension between temporal and spiritual authorities. Between the mid-eleventh and the mid-thirteenth centuries three major conflicts occurred between empire and papacy: the Investiture Contest and those featuring the emperors

Frederick I and II. Yet it was the papacy, through the medium of the canon law, which established itself as the only truly universal authority in western Christendom. The church, and the papacy in particular, had become a far more assertive and influential body than it had been in relation to secular rulers in the early Middle Ages.

Before the mid-eleventh century the raw materials for political ideas in the west were relatively restricted. The opening up of medieval society and civilisation in the high Middle Ages was fuelled at the intellectual level by a vast infusion of recovered knowledge of the literature, law and philosophy of the ancient world, so much so that the new sources transformed political thought. Through the so-called Twelfth-Century Renaissance the dissemination of the political ideas contained in Roman literature was widened, with pride of place being given to the works of Cicero. From the late eleventh century, the establishment of the scientific study of Roman law and its growth as a university discipline, in conjunction with the development of canon law and its scholarship, gradually produced in the *ius commune*, or common law, a comprehensive legal language, which provided an increasingly sophisticated mode of discourse for the elaboration of ideas relevant to political matters. Furthermore, the full recovery of Aristotle's political and ethical works by about 1260 presented an articulated naturalistic system for understanding politics. The result was that by the late thirteenth century classical-literary, civilian and canonist, and Aristotelian languages existed for the elaboration of political ideas, side by side with much-developed biblical forms of discourse. The extent to which such political thought operated at a purely theoretical level within each intellectual language, and the degree to which it was a response to the changes in society and its government, are questions which are central to our understanding of these writers.

SPIRITUAL AND SECULAR POWER, *c.* 1050–*c.* 1150

It was indeed ironic that Henry III, who had acted out the traditional role of *rex et sacerdos* at Sutri and through the subsequent appointment of German popes, had, by favouring the election of his relative Pope Leo IX (1049–54), given further impetus to the beginnings of the papal reform which was ultimately to destroy that early medieval relationship between temporal and spiritual power pre-eminently embodied in his exercise of the imperial office. This reform, belonging to a far wider movement partly inspired by monastic renewal, sought in the first instance to separate the church, in the sense of the clergy, from the concerns and influence of the lay world, an essentially spiritual aim. Common cause was made against simony, the purchase of ecclesiastical offices, which was understood to extend beyond the payment of money to include secular service and flattery. In treating this crime as a heresy the reformers struck at a central aspect of lay influence in church appointments. Equally important was the forbidding of clerical marriage and con-cubinage: family life was perceived as enmeshing the cleric in the concerns of this world and leading to the inheritance of clerical offices. The reform also stressed canonical election of bishops, that is by clergy and people, as Leo I had laid down.[1] Overall, there was an insistence on the primacy of the pope as the main agent of reform: Rome was the epitome of all churches and the guarantor of orthodoxy – on the basis of the Donation of Constantine, *principatus* over all churches in the world was claimed for the apostolic see. Indeed a new term, *papatus* (papacy), was first used by Pope Clement II in 1047 to reflect this increased status as a rank above that of a bishopric (*episcopatus*).

The differences of emphasis among these early reformers were summed up by the cases of Peter Damian and Humbert who were made cardinals in the 1050s. Although both heartily condemned simony, Peter Damian in his *Liber gratissimus* of 1052 followed the traditional line whereby he still recognised the episcopal and sacerdotal orders of simoniacs, whereas Humbert denied the validity of such orders in his *Libri tres adversus simoniacos* (Three Books against the Simoniacs), written about 1058 as a reply to Peter Damian's tract. On the question of canonical election matters were much more complicated, in particular because the custom had developed of lay investiture of ecclesiastical officers. Initially the episcopal or abbatial staff had been conferred by the ruler as symbolic of the bishop's or abbot's office; the first case of the giving of the episcopal ring as well was that of the investiture of Bishop Gebhard of Eichstätt by Henry III in 1042.[2] These actions were accompanied by the ruler's words, 'Receive the church' (*Accipe ecclesiam*). At the same time the new bishop or abbot gave homage and swore fidelity to the ruler for the feudal lands and jurisdictions of his bishopric or abbey. Peter Damian was not opposed to lay investiture as such so long as simony was not involved. The model for Peter Damian was co-operation between *regnum* and *sacerdotium*: in a letter he wrote to the young Henry IV in 1065 he referred to the 'mutual covenant' (*mutuum foedus*) between the royal and priestly powers.[3] Henry III was his ideal of an emperor who exalted the church,[4] and whose interventions at Sutri and in subsequent choices of pope he eulogised as God-given actions necessary for the achievement of church reform. For Peter Damian the king or emperor was indeed a layman, but still a sacral ruler whose coronation was a sacrament: this theologian adhered to the traditional view which saw no clear distinction between *regnum* and *sacerdotium*. In marked contrast, Humbert, in his *Against the Simoniacs*, clearly differentiated between the kingship and the priesthood. The king or emperor for him was as a layman no sacral ruler. Clergy were superior to laymen: 'Just as the soul excels the body and commands it, so too the priestly dignity excels the royal or, we may say, the heavenly dignity the earthly.'[5] Humbert totally rejected lay investiture on the grounds that the king as a mere layman could not confer a spiritual office on a cleric. Indeed, power was given to kings by priests for the good of the church. Striking though Humbert's opinions were, this tract had little immediate impact in subsequent decades, only being used by the publicist Placidus of Nonantula in 1111. In contrast, the views of Peter Damian had very great influence in the rest of the eleventh century.

It was also the case that Peter Damian's ideas rather than those of Humbert were more in tune with the attitudes of the popes themselves. Modern scholars used to believe that Pope Nicholas II (1059–61) had issued the first papal condemnation of lay investiture at the Lateran Synod of 1059, and that Pope Alexander II (1061–73) had reiterated this prohibition. As a result of the researches of Rudolf Schieffer, it now appears that no such papal prohibitions were issued before the pontificate of Gregory VII.[6] Where Nicholas II did make a decisive contribution as regards canonical election was in the case of the pope himself. At the same synod of 1059 a decree was issued which placed the election of the pope solely in the hands of the cardinals, primarily the cardinal-bishops. The role of the Roman clergy and people was reduced to one of mere assent to the choice. The historical participation of the emperor was by-passed with the formula 'saving the honour and reverence due to our beloved son Henry who is for the present regarded as king and who, it is hoped, is going to be emperor with God's grace, inasmuch as we have now conceded this to him and to his successors who shall personally obtain this right from the apostolic see'.[7] The Roman church thereby claimed its independence from both the Roman nobility and the emperors. This was a crucial step in the process whereby the papacy was to develop as an autonomous European-wide institution.

The full impact of the papal reform movement came with the pontificate of Gregory VII (1073–85). As subdeacon (later archdeacon) Hildebrand, he had been a leader of the reform at Rome since he had been brought back from exile by Leo IX. We have ample evidence for reconstructing his thought because his official Register (the oldest extant original) and some unregistered letters survive. Only fragmentary Registers are extant from before his reign: such as those of Gregory I, John VIII and Stephen V. The virtually complete run of papal Registers only commences from that of Innocent III. Gregory gave impetus to a process of differentiation between the church as an ecclesiastical entity and the sphere of secular power. This trend involved far-reaching claims for the autonomy of the church and challenged the earlier medieval view whereby temporal and spiritual power operated within the church understood in the wider sense. Significantly Gregory used the term *ecclesia* on all occasions except one to denote the strictly ecclesiastical body, and the word *Christianitas* with the wider connotation.

At the core of Gregory's thought lay the idea of the liberty of the church (*libertas ecclesiae*). This meant the freedom of the church as an ecclesiastical body from lay control and its subjection to that of the pope. Gregory worked with the traditional duality between clergy and laity but stressed with particular starkness the hierarchical superiority of the clerical order. The theme of hierarchy applied particularly within the *sacerdotium* itself: he developed markedly the idea of papal monarchy so important for the Rome-based reformers, as reflected in the addition of coronation to a pope's inauguration ritual from that of Nicholas II onwards. He used two biblical texts in particular to justify papal jurisdictional claims. Matthew 16:18–19 was interpreted as a form of divinely given privilege of liberty for the papacy: Christ had thereby committed to St Peter the power of the keys of binding and loosing as jurisdiction in both a governmental and a purely penitential sense. John 21:15–17 was also employed to reinforce the all-embracing scope of papal jurisdiction within Christendom: all were the pope's sheep; none was excluded.[8] Gregory identified himself with St Peter whose responsibility for the Christian world he saw himself as inheriting. His conception of papal monarchy was strongly legal in character and is best understood within the context of the development of canon law exemplified in Italian collections made before, during and immediately after his pontificate, such as the *Collection in Seventy-Four Titles* and those of Cardinal Atto, Anselm of Lucca and Cardinal Deusdedit.

The key to Gregory's conception of the relationship between temporal and spiritual power was his contention that the king or emperor was a layman: this involved a denial of the sacerdotal kingship underlying the claims of the Salians. He held that the clergy, as an order, were superior to the laity and that he, as the head of the church, had through the power of binding and loosing the capacity to judge rulers for their suitability (*idoneitas*). Early in his pontificate there was produced a document known as the Dictates of the Pope (*Dictatus papae*) which was inserted in the Register shortly after a brief account of the Roman Lenten Synod of February 1075. There has been no overall agreement among modern scholars about the nature of these twenty-seven propositions which Erich Caspar, who established the critical text of the Register, called 'papal guiding-principles' (*päpstliche Leitsätze*).[9] The suggestion that they were headings for a canon law collection to support papal claims cannot be decisively demonstrated. They can also be described in a more neutral way as a memorandum.[10] Whatever they were originally, they certainly set forth trenchantly the rights of papal authority. Most were concerned with strictly ecclesiastical questions; three, however, dealt with aspects of the pope's powers in temporal matters: 'That he may depose emperors' (Dictate XII), 'That he alone can use imperial insignia' (Dictate VIII) and 'That he can free the subjects of wicked men from their fealty' (Dictate XXVII).[11] It is noteworthy that at this point Gregory claimed only to be able to depose emperors, not kings. This might be because the pope personally crowned the emperor and not kings, and could therefore more plausibly assert a right of deposition. The contemporary Dictates of Avranches, however, were less restrained: 'Every power in the world should be subject to the pope ... He can change kingdoms.'[12] The appropriation of the emperor's insignia reflected the use of the Donation of Constantine in the papal reform and was part of the process whereby an imperial papacy emerged – that is, one with the attributes and trappings of secular power. Most far-reaching of all, however, was the claim to be able to release subjects from their oaths of fidelity. This was an innovation with revolutionary implications, because it would totally undermine the whole institution of kingship. It would, after all, be up to the pope alone to decide who were wicked rulers, since he was the judge of sin.

Gregory put these principles into action during his conflict with Henry IV of Germany, a conflict which marked the beginning of the most important medieval dispute between papacy and empire. Misleadingly known as the Investiture Contest, it was to last from 1075 to 1122. Lay investiture of ecclesiastical offices was only one of the complex of issues at stake: fundamental questions were addressed concerning sovereignty in the Christian community, the relationship between temporal and spiritual power, the nature of kingship, and the status of episcopal authority as regards that of the pope and secular rulers. Lay investiture itself only became the predominant issue after 1100. The immediate reason for the outbreak of the dispute was the ongoing affair of the appointment to the archbishopric of Milan. In 1072 Henry had invested Godfrey in the traditional manner to the fury of the popular party, the *Patarini*, who chose their own candidate, Atto. Pope Alexander II recognised Atto as canonically elected and excommunicated five of Henry's counsellors for their supposed role in ordering the Lombard bishops to consecrate Godfrey. At the beginning of his pontificate Gregory did not make an issue of lay investiture, since he hoped for a reconciliation with Henry: indeed, in the first explicit negative reference which a pope had made to lay investiture, Gregory had in September 1073 advised Anselm of Lucca to refrain from royal investiture *until* such time as Henry should make peace with the pope through ceasing to consort with his excommunicated counsellors.[13] The situation deteriorated in 1075, however, because the king, continuing to associate with his counsellors, appointed the bishops of Spoleto and Fermo and nominated a third achiepiscopal candidate for Milan – Thedald. Modern historians are divided as to whether Gregory had issued a formal decree against lay investiture at the Lenten Synod of 1075; there were measures against simony and clerical fornication. In any case, the pope, finding Henry's actions intolerable, on 8 December sent him a letter calling on him to cease associating with his excommunicated counsellors and complaining about his actions as regards the sees of Spoleto, Fermo and Milan.[14] This marked the beginnings of hostilities. In January of the crisis year of 1076 Henry, having gained the support of his bishops at a synod at Worms, wrote to Gregory addressing him as 'Hildebrand, now not Pope, but false monk' and calling upon him to descend from the throne of St Peter.[15] In response Gregory at the Roman Lenten Synod in February excommunicated and suspended Henry from his kingship,[16] whereupon at Easter Henry together with many of his bishops declared Hildebrand deposed. However, the king had overestimated the strength of his position, and his support gradually drifted away; so much so that a growing opposition amongst the princes culminated in the October meeting at Tribur-Oppenheim which forced Henry to swear obedience to Gregory and to revoke his sentence of deposition. The princes made their allegiance conditional on the king's seeking a meeting with the pope in order to be freed from excommunication, and also swore to meet early in 1077 at Augsburg in Gregory's presence. They had therefore invited the pope to arbitrate in the affair of the kingship of Germany. Henry regained the initiative in January 1077 by presenting himself as a penitent before Gregory who was wintering at the castle of Canossa in northern Italy before crossing the Alps. The pope, acting as a pastor, freed him from his excommunication without restoring him to the exercise of his kingship. From this point Henry began to recruit his strength again; but civil war broke out in Germany, because in March his opponents elected Rudolf of Rheinfelden, duke of Swabia, as king. Gregory never did reach Germany. He claimed that he was going to arbitrate in the matter, but delayed and appeared ambiguous as to whether he was treating Henry as a king. The result was prolongation of hostilities and loss of support for the papacy. The pope's attitude to lay investiture hardened: in March 1077 he definitely referred to it as an abuse and at the Lateran Synod of November 1078 unequivocally condemned it.[17] Finally at the Lenten Synod of March 1080 Gregory definitely deposed Henry, reimposed his excommunication, freed his subjects from their oaths of allegiance, declared that the kingship was conceded to Rudolf and issued another decree against investiture. In response Henry, with the agreement of most of his German bishops, declared Gregory deposed, and at the synod of Brixen in

June an anti-pope Wibert of Ravenna was elected. Henry's position improved markedly with the death of Rudolf in October after the battle on the Elster. It took Henry and Wibert till 1083 to fight their way to Rome: in March 1084 Wibert was crowned pope as Clement III and in turn crowned Henry emperor. Henry was thus only made emperor by his own anti-pope. Gregory was forced to flee Rome with his Norman allies and died, largely deserted, an exile at Salerno in May 1085. His pontificate was apparently a failure; but through his actions he had put into effect ideas, concerning the government of the Christian community, which were to cause enormous reverberations in the subsequent course of medieval political thought.

Gregory's Register contains elaborate justifications for his actions. These are to be found especially in the proceedings of the Lenten synods of 1076 (*Reg.* III, 10a) and 1080 (*Reg.* VII, 14a), and in two lengthy *apologiae* sent to his friend Bishop Hermann of Metz in August 1076 (*Reg.* IV, 2) and in March 1081 (*Reg.* VIII, 21). Gregory based his measures against Henry directly on the Petrine commission: the power of binding and loosing in Matthew 16:18–19 extended to temporal matters and gave him the authority to suspend and then depose Henry, and to excommunicate him and free his subjects from their allegiance. Likewise Henry, as a king, was not excepted from the sheep committed to the pope's care (John 21:15–17) – that is, jurisdiction. In the sentences of both 1076 and 1080 Gregory addressed himself in supplication directly to St Peter and acted as his vicar. Henry's sins were disobedience and pride. In the second letter to Hermann of Metz in particular Gregory elaborated the theme of the clergy's superiority entitling them to judge laymen. Indeed, to make his point he went so far as to say, 'Greater power is conceded to an exorcist [a sub-diaconal grade of cleric], when he is made a spiritual emperor for expelling demons, than could be given to any layman for secular domination'[18] – a deliberate attempt to shock and to challenge the presuppositions of lay rulers. In both letters Gregory sought to provide authorities and historical precedents for his actions against Henry. In so doing he was trying to show that he was doing nothing new, because it was fundamental to his understanding of papal authority that he enjoyed precisely the same powers as any pope from the time of St Peter. In fact he was interpreting these sources in ways which supported his conception of papal powers but which deviated from their original significance.

Thus he used the statement by Gregory I that a king who went against one of his decrees 'should lose his office of honour and power' and, if not repentant, suffer excommunication and final damnation. Whereas Gregory I had been referring to excommunication, Gregory VII understood the passage to justify the deposition of a king as well as his excommunication. The assumption behind Gregory VII's attitude was that excommunication, being spiritual in nature and thus a far worse punishment than deposition from secular office, implicitly contained within it the loss of merely temporal power.[19] Likewise, in *Reg*. VIII, 21 he quoted the famous *sententia* by Gelasius:

'There are indeed two things, emperor *augustus*, by which this world is principally ruled: the consecrated authority of bishops and the royal power. Of the two that of the priesthood is a greater burden, in so far as they must also render account before God for the very kings of men.' And after a further few words he said, 'You know therefore that in these matters you depend upon their judgement, not they who are willing to be subjected to your will.'

The 'few words' omitted were crucial and showed that Gelasius meant that the royal power was subjected to the priesthood only in religious matters.[20] Gelasius, as we have seen, considered that temporal and spiritual power existed in parallel within their own spheres; Gregory interpreted him to hold that temporal power was in general subject to spiritual. Of the historical precedents he quoted, the most relevant was Pope Zacharias's role in the deposition of Childeric and his replacement by Pippin as king of the Franks. Gregory represented his predecessor's legitimising involvement in a way most favourable for his own understanding of papal monarchy. In both letters he referred to Zacharias as deposing Childeric and freeing his subjects from their oaths of allegiance, thus disguising his own innovation in this latter respect. By the second excommunication and clear deposition Gregory's attitude had hardened considerably: he claimed that the power of binding and loosing included that 'to remove from and concede to anyone according to his merits earthly empires, kingdoms, principalities, dukedoms, marches, counties and the possessions of all men'.[21] His opinion of lay rulers had declined further:

Who would not know that kings and dukes took their origin from those who, ignorant of God, through pride, rapine, perfidy, murders and, finally, almost any kind of crime, at the instigation of the Devil, the prince of this world, sought with blind desire and unbearable presumption to dominate their equals, namely other men?[22]

In contrast, the sacerdotal order was so superior that, 'Who would doubt that the priests of Christ are considered the fathers and masters of kings, princes and of all the faithful?' – they were the 'eyes of God'.[23] Those whom the church has called to temporal rulership should obey the clergy in all humility.[24] But of course Gregory fully recognised that theoretical statements about the due relationship between temporal and spiritual power were not enough; he realised that in the political conditions of the late eleventh century personal bonds of sworn fidelity were the strongest sinews of society. He therefore favoured the development of feudal links between the papacy and secular rulers. After the death of Rudolf of Rheinfelden, for instance, he made it known in a letter to the abbot of Hirsau that the Roman church would require an oath of fealty to St Peter and his vicar in the flesh from whomever was elected king in Germany.[25] Although Gregory's feudal language was far from precise, and although there is not enough evidence of a wide-ranging curial feudal policy, there is documentation of his desire to increase the number of kings and lords who were St Peter's *fideles*, in addition to his southern Italian Norman vassals. Overall, Gregory's vision of the relationship between *regnum* and *sacerdotium* existed within his conception of the pope's mission of service, a view summed up in a letter written in 1083 towards the end of his life (*Reg.* IX, 35) and in which Gregory showed that he remained true to his sense of heavy responsibility for all Christendom as the heir and successor of St Peter whose privileges, expressed in Matthew 16:18–19 and John 21:15–17, he exercised.

Gregory VII's ideas concerning the relationship between temporal and spiritual power raise fundamental questions regarding the interpretation of medieval papal theory. He himself was, clearly, no great theoretician, which in itself illustrates the problem involved in trying to apply an articulated interpretative structure to the understanding of his thought. Yet it is precisely such structures which have been routinely employed by modern historians as ways of making sense of the governmental claims of and for the medieval popes. Two terms in particular have been defining ones in this debate: hierocratic and dualist. Both are modern constructs applied to the Middle Ages. The term 'hierocratic' is derived from the Greek words for priest (*hiereus*) and power (*kratos*) and describes a model of papal monarchy. The pope, as the successor of St Peter, is the divinely appointed head of the body of Christians which has been committed to his care by Christ. Within this body the clergy are superior to the laity and spiritual jurisdiction is superior to temporal. The pope being responsible before God for the Christian community has the right to judge, depose and concede power to secular rulers. Indeed, in its developed form this theory attributed to the pope the role of mediator of a ruler's power from God. There was absolutely no autonomy for secular authority and indeed no means of judging the pope. A difficulty involved in applying this model is that its fully articulated form only appeared with papal publicists of the early fourteenth century. The dualist theme we have already met:[26] it corresponds to the fundamental distinction between clergy and laity. As applied to the papacy it interprets sacerdotal and secular power as existing in parallel, with each being derived from God. The pope's authority is essentially spiritual in nature, with the result that there is no justification for the pope to be able to interfere with the power of a temporal ruler. The acknowledged greater dignity of the sacerdotal order does not mean that temporal power is subjected to it. A fundamental problem involved in adopting these terms, 'hierocratic' and 'dualist', is that they are not mutually exclusive. Any hierocratic interpretation includes an element of duality in that the distinction of function between clergy and laity is of necessity adhered to. There is no denial that the role of the secular ruler is to exercise temporal power and that the pope does not do so directly (except in the special case of the papal lands). Likewise, however thorough-going a dualist view might be, the headship of the pope in the Christian community is accepted. Medieval thinkers often did not fit easily into these broad modern categories and it has often been suggested that it is anachronistic to operate with the terms 'hierocratic' and 'dualist'.[27] It is perfectly true that it is possible to treat the political and governmental ideas of the medieval papacy without any recourse to them. Should they therefore be abandoned? That would seem to go too far because, so long as the limitations involved in their use are borne in mind, they serve as a useful shorthand, but nothing more.

However famous and dramatic his conflicts over temporal and spiritual power might be, Gregory probably contributed more to the growth of papal monarchy through developing the other aspect of liberty of the church – namely, the hierarchical subjection of the *sacerdotium* to the pope. Gregory sought to strengthen existing papal powers over bishops. His ideas in this respect illustrated a central problem of the medieval church. There could be tension between the increasing concentration of powers in the hands of the pope as the apex of the ecclesiastical hierarchy, and attempts by the episcopacy to retain something of the greater and divinely instituted autonomy which it had enjoyed earlier in the history of the church. When conditions were favourable bishops were able to stage rearguard actions in this respect. Fundamental questions concerning the source and extent of episcopal powers of jurisdiction were at stake. In the *Dictatus papae* (*Reg.* II, 55a) Gregory reiterated the papal claim to be the sole authority able to depose (or reconcile) bishops, but went further by his statement, 'That the pope can depose the absent',[28] a rejection of a rule of due process according to existing canon law and a striking extension of monarchical power. The idea of appeal to the Roman church as the ultimate authority was ancient, being found in Gelasius and repeated in Pseudo-Isidore, where it was treated as a procedure expressly meant to protect bishops.[29] Gregory reiterated this right stating, 'That no one may dare to condemn anyone appealing to the apostolic see'.[30] He took a large step, however, when he permitted inferiors at papal bidding to accuse their superiors.[31] This definitely infringed existing canon law and involved a revolution in the understanding of hierarchy. By allowing a cleric of a lower order to accuse his ecclesiastical superior and by-pass the intermediate hierarchical grades by appealing to the top, Gregory was undermining the principle of a graduated and layered hierarchy. In his eyes hierarchy was thereby strengthened, in those of bishops it could well appear damaged. Appeal to Rome, given new life by Gregory, was to be a prime means by which direct papal control over the church was extended and the power of bishops curtailed. In all, Gregory, through strengthening the position of the papacy as the ultimate court of appeal, had given a more articulate meaning to the ancient formulation of legal sovereignty included in Pseudo-Isidore and repeated in the *Dictatus papae*: that the pope may be judged by no one.[32]

Gregory also expanded papal claims to sovereignty with specific reference to the canon law as such. He stated of the pope, 'That no chapter and no book may be considered canonical without his authority' (a considerable expansion of a Gelasian tradition) and that, 'No synod may be called a general one without his command.'[33] The prime source for this conciliar view was Pseudo-Isidore, and it had also been put forward by Leo IX. Gregory's formulation was particularly important because general councils posed a serious potential threat to papal sovereignty; it was therefore essential for the pope to have control over whether one was summoned or not. A general council might, if uncontrolled, provide a forum for episcopal independence and could be an autonomous source of canon law. Gregory's two statements taken together meant that the existence of such councils and their decrees were subject to papal approval for their validity in canon law, a clear departure from the position obtaining in the ecumenical councils of antiquity and a sure sign of the burgeoning pretensions of the papal monarchy. Gregory went even further, saying of the pope, 'That he alone may create new laws as time makes necessary'.[34] The argument from necessity was one particularly suited to the extension of monarchical power. Here was, indeed, an assertion that the pope could through his will produce innovatory legislation, in itself a significant development of papal claims but one made with a conservative intention to counteract harmful innovations which, for this pontiff, sullied the purity of the church. The earlier medieval view was that the pope was bound to conserve the traditions of his predecessors; Gregory expanded the papal role by also reserving the right to legislate afresh for changing times, but in a way which would conform to the traditions of the gospels, the fathers of the church and previous popes.

The impact of Gregory VII's pontificate was enormous: for the church nothing was to be the same again. From his active lifetime can be traced the settling of the church in its long-term direction as a body of power and coercion; the character of the papacy as a jurisdictional and governmental institution, evident in a primitive form from the fourth and fifth centuries, became far more sharply focused from the time of the reform papacy. This orientation could be perceived as creating tension with the papacy's spiritual mission which Gregory himself always held to be its more important role: his was a 'power better than that of the world'.[35] For Gregory the pope's jurisdictional powers facilitated the exercise of his pastoral function. Nevertheless there arises the intrusive thought, out of bounds for a historian: this was the moment of the great wrong direction taken by the papacy, one which was to outlast the Middle Ages and survive into our own day. From the time of Gregory can be dated the deliberate clericalisation of the church based on the notion that the clergy, being morally purer, were superior to the laity and constituted a church which was catholic, chaste and free. There was a deep connection between power and a celibacy which helped distinguish the clergy as a separate and superior caste, distanced in the most profound psychological sense from the family concerns of the laity beneath them. At the time of the reform papacy the church became stamped with certain characteristics which have remained those of the Roman Catholic church: it became papally centred, legalistic, coercive and clerical. The Roman church was, in Gregory's words, the 'mother and mistress' (*mater et magistra*) of all churches.[36] Gregory VII was an archetypal conservative revolutionary: his opponents maintained that he was overturning the existing world-order; he claimed that he was true to the early church and was rooting out customs which had no warrant in canon law.

Gregory's pontificate stimulated a debate about the relationship between temporal and spiritual power, a debate which was conducted by means of tracts throughout the remainder of the Investiture Contest. This was the first such publicistic exchange in the Middle Ages, with protracted discussion leading to a sharpening of political and ecclesiological ideas. The impact of individual tracts varied widely and their oral audience is unknowable; but the overall effect was that the issues involved in the dispute were exhaustively dissected in political and ecclesiastical circles for half a century. The intellectual ferocity of the argument resulted from the challenge which the church reformers posed to traditional kingship, and from the Henrician rejection of the extension of papal claims in secular matters. Both sides argued within a shared intellectual tradition based on the Bible, the Fathers, canon law, statements of previous popes and ecclesiastical writers, church history and the practice of previous rulers. In this sense the debate belonged to the thought-world of the early Middle Ages; but this interpretation is misleading to the degree that in this period of fundamental transition writers were grappling with an increasingly more clearly defined differentiation between temporal and spiritual power.

Both sides claimed to be seeking to preserve unity within the Christian community; both accepted that such unity was procured by the co-operation of the two parts into which the body of the faithful was divided – the clergy and the laity. There was agreement concerning the sacramental and teaching roles reserved to the priesthood, but disagreement over the function and boundaries of secular and ecclesiastical jurisdiction – this was the heart of the dispute. The underlying reason was that, although the traditional division into clergy and laity was taken as something given, there was dispute about who was a cleric, who a layman in jurisdictional matters. Indeed, the differences were irreconcilable. Did the king possess ecclesiastical jurisdiction or the priesthood secular? What was the proper function of each?

The pro-papal tracts can be briefly characterised because they developed the reformers' arguments. They espoused a clear distinction between clergy and laity and treated the king as a layman. They supported the papal interpretation of the Petrine commission in Matthew 16:18–19 and defended the power of the pope, as head of the church, to judge and depose a king whom he considered to be useless. Three writers deserve special mention. Bonizo of Sutri in his *Liber ad amicum* (Letter to a Friend) of 1085/6 gave a lengthy justification for Gregory VII's actions and in his protracted discussion of Christian kingship sought to show that royal power was subject to that of the pope.[37] Manegold of Lautenbach in his *Liber ad Gebehardum* (Book for Gebhard), also written in 1085, undertook a comprehensive defence of Gregory VII, treating kingship as an office from which an unsuitable incumbent could be deposed.[38] The *Summa gloria* of Honorius Augustodunensis (written in the early twelfth century), through a lengthy interpretation of human history, presented a unified view of Christendom as a corporate body (*universitas*) in which, the clergy being superior to the laity, the priesthood was superior to kings who were no more than laymen: 'The king is to be constituted by the priests of Christ, who are the true princes of the church; consent is merely required of the laymen. Because, therefore, the priesthood by right constitutes the kingship, the kingship will by right be subject to the priesthood.'[39]

The pro-royal writers denied the basic presuppositions of the Gregorian case. They continued to maintain that the king as Christ's vicar was not merely a layman but rather *rex et sacerdos*, in effect a special kind of bishop. For them the king or emperor was in terms of jurisdiction the head of the church with the power to appoint bishops, to have a decisive role in papal elections and, if necessary, to bring about the deposition of a pope. This approach involved, of course, a rejection of the Gregorian interpretation of Matthew 16:18–19 and John 21:15–17.

The letters of Henry IV himself passed through the hands of a number of *dictatores* of whom the most important for the theoretical elaboration of the royalist position was Gottschalk of Aachen, an imperial chaplain. Gottschalk's claim to fame is that in Letter 13 (written in 1076) he initiated the use of the two-sword analogy to describe the relationship between *regnum* and *sacerdotium*, a brilliant allegorical interpretation of Luke 22:38, once heard, never forgotten, and destined to become a mainstay of subsequent political thought. Gregory, he claimed,

> without God's knowledge usurped the *regnum* and *sacer-dotium* for himself. In so doing he despised God's pious arrangement which He wished principally to consist not in one, but in two: two, that is the *regnum* and *sacerdotium*, as the Saviour in his passion had intimated should be understood by the figurative sufficiency of the two swords. When it was said to Him, 'Lord, behold here are two swords,' he replied, 'It is enough,' signifying by this sufficient duality that there were to be borne in the church a spiritual and a carnal sword, by which every harmful thing would be cut off: the sacerdotal sword would be used to encourage obedience to the king on God's behalf, whereas the royal would be employed for expelling the enemies of Christ without, and for enforcing obedience to the *sacerdotium* within.[40]

Alcuin had not used the two-sword imagery in such a sense.[41] It used to be thought that Peter Damian in Sermon 69 had first used the allegory of the sacerdotal and royal swords, but that work is now accepted as twelfth-century, and perhaps by Nicholas of Clairvaux, St Bernard's secretary.[42] Gottschalk was using the two-sword analogy to support a pro-royal understanding of Gelasius' doctrine of the two powers, but the image could equally well be used by the papalist side, as John of Mantua shortly showed by indicating that both the secular and the spiritual sword were in the hands of the pope.[43] There has, however, been acrimonious debate amongst modern scholars about the meaning of the two-sword analogy in ecclesiastical sources. The kernel of the dispute has been whether the two swords were intended to signify spiritual and secular power as such, or powers of spiritual and material coercion, the sense in which ninth-century popes had applied the image to their own authority. These allegorical interpretations of Luke 22:38, strange to modern eyes, adhered to the medieval exegetical method which sought to discern deeper mystical meanings transcending the lowest level, the literal signification of the words of the text. That the apostles had brought swords to the garden of Gethsemane was recorded in the New Testament: one of them had cut off Malchus's ear (Luke 22:50) and then been enjoined by Christ to put up his sword (Matthew 26:51–2). Pope Nicholas I, for instance, following John 18:11 identified the apostle as Peter who, he said, had thereby used the corporeal sword.[44]

For Gottschalk, Gregory's crime indeed lay in arrogating kingship and priesthood to himself: he accused him of intending to subvert the divine dispensation of two swords by making them one.[45] In Letter 13 Gottschalk maintained that Christ's will was that the two swords should work together in harmony within a unity (the church). Henry's power came directly from God, not Hildebrand, who had not constituted him as king and was nevertheless trying to deprive him of his kingship. The two powers were not completely distinct, however, but shaded into each other: 'In charity the province of one extends into the other, as long as neither the kingship is deprived of honour by the priesthood nor the priesthood is deprived of honour by the kingship.'[46] His approach was essentially unitive, reflecting that of the Salian monarchy. In his eyes, it was Hildebrand who was undermining the peace and harmonious order of the Christian community. He wrote Letter 12 (also of 1076) to defend that order. In it he upbraided Hildebrand for inciting laymen to disobey and, indeed, remove their bishops. Furthermore, Henry could be judged only by God from whom alone he derived his power, and in whose hand kingship and empire lay, not Hildebrand's. The king, in any case, could be deposed only for deviation from the faith. Gregory, in contrast had not been properly appointed, but had obtained the pontifical throne by cunning, simony and force. The letter ended with the ringing demand: 'I, Henry, King by the grace of God, together with all our bishops, say to you, "Descend! Descend!" '.[47]

The theme of the co-operation of the two divinely instituted powers to achieve peace and concord within the overall unity of the Christian community was fundamental for other pro-royal writers, although some were more willing to stress the distinctiveness between the two than were others. This duality, designed to protect the power of the king or emperor from papal encroachments, produced inequality in that the secular ruler was perceived as having ultimate jurisdictional control within the church: he could bring about the deposition of the pope, but the pope could not remove him. In terms of this world, the two powers were not strictly parallel and certainly unequal. It was Henry's duty to preserve the peace which Gregory had shattered. Peter Crassus in his *Defensio Heinrici IV. Regis* (Defence of King Henry IV), written in 1080 or 1084, emphasised the specific role of the Roman emperor in this respect. Peter was notable for his use of Roman law to justify the legitimacy of the secular ruler's role as guarantor of religious orthodoxy, referring to C.1.1.1 (*Cunctos populos*) and C.1.11.1 (*Placuit*), and quoting the historical examples of the emperors' calling the early general councils of the church.[48] He held that God had instituted two laws for mankind: canon law and the laws of emperors and kings.[49] Through his twenty extracts from the *Code*, five from the *Institutes* and one from the *Epitome Iuliani* he made the most extensive use of Roman law yet made by supporters of the Salians. Although the profundity of Peter's usage of that law should by no means be exaggerated, his work illustrated the increased study of Roman law in Italy in the second half of the eleventh century before the development of the school of Bologna, and was significant for its application of such legal texts to a work of political discourse in support of a lay ruler. The Roman law was increasingly to provide material for articulating the theme of secular rulership and set forth a model whereby the *princeps* exercised jurisdiction in ecclesiastical matters. Peter Crassus' text also formed part of the more general theme of Romanism developed among Italian supporters of the Salian monarchy, as witnessed by Benzo of Alba's *Liber ad Heinricum IV.* (*c.* 1085), a partly metrical attack on Gregory VII, with its emphasis on the central role of the emperor as ruler of the world (with Rome its head), 'vicar of the Creator' (*vicarius conditoris*) and maker of popes.[50] Wido of Osnabrück in his *De controversia inter Hildebrandum et Heinricum* (Concerning the Controversy between Hildebrand and Henry) (1084/5) also reiterated the fundamental theme of dualism within a unified church under the jurisdictional headship of the emperor. 'If these two heads of the church [i.e. the *regnum* and the *sacerdotium*] are in discord, everything which benefits either the soul or the body is disturbed and sinks to destruction.'[51] The emperor was, however, the senior partner: when by ancient ecclesiastical custom, previously accepted by the church, the clergy and people chose a pope according to canonical rules, imperial consent was required.[52] This meant that the two powers were not completely distinct: there were, indeed, strictly ecclesiastical rights which were protected by canon law, and over which no layman had any authority, but, as Wido went on to say, 'Although a king is rightly separated from the number of the laity in this way, having been anointed with the oil of consecration he is recognised as a sharer in the sacerdotal ministry.'[53]

The most comprehensive treatment of the Henrician position in the early Investiture Contest was contained in the *Liber de unitate ecclesiae conservanda* (Book Concerning the Preservation of the Unity of the Church) written by an anonymous monk from the abbey of Hersfeld between 1091 and 1093. This stressed the need for unity in the church and accused Gregory VII of trying to destroy that concord,[54] especially through his deposition and excommunication of Henry IV: 'Whether he be Gregory or Hildebrand or someone else, who is the head of a party, not the church, he was not able to condemn King Henry, who certainly strove after, chose and worked very hard for this: that there should be one body of the church, so that likewise there could also be one body of the *respublica*.'[55] The Anonymous sought to attack the Gregorians on their own ground by using many of the same proof-texts as they did, thus setting out to refute their arguments by presenting what he considered to be the true interpretations. He threw back at his opponents the charge that they had misrepresented their authorities and history. He made a number of references to Gelasius in support of a relatively strict division between the spheres of secular and spiritual power. If this arrangement were properly observed then unity and concord would be maintained in the Christian community. Gelasius' words, he considered, reflected the divine dispensation which

102

was infringed by Hildebrand and his bishops whose crime was to usurp the office of both powers, and 'who, when for the sake of their pontifical dignity they should not involve themselves in secular affairs, usurped the ordering of the royal dignity against God's decree'.[56] The king's power, being from God, should be immune from attack by the church. The Anonymous also made use of the teaching of Gregory I that divinely ordained rulers, good or evil, should be obeyed. This doctrine of obedience was crucial for the pro-Henrician writers because the Gregorian case for resistance to and deposition of a useless ruler rested on the church's capacity to judge a king and find him wanting. The Anonymous also expressly rejected the way in which Gregory VII in *Reg.* VIII, 21 had interpreted Gregory I's *Reg.*, XIII, 12 as justifying the deposition of Henry: he undermined Gregory VII's understanding of the passage by comparing it with Gregory I's general teaching on the obedience due to secular power, and denied that the text, as reported, was meant to apply to a truly Christian king like Henry anyway.[57] Gregory VII's use of history was also criticised by the Anonymous, notably the pope's interpretation of Pope Zacharias's role in the deposition of Childeric as a precedent for his own treatment of Henry IV: for the Anonymous there was no comparability – Childeric had no royal power or dignity only the name of king, whereas Henry thoroughly deserved his crown.[58]

The preservation of unity and harmony in the Christian community remained a persistent theme in pro-royal tracts in the early twelfth century. Sigebert of Gembloux in his *Epistola Leodicensium adversus Paschalem papam* (Letter of the People of Liège against Pope Paschal) (*c.* 1103) blamed Gregory VII for undermining the order of the world by inciting laymen against the clergy. 'Who', he said, 'can separate the cause of the *regnum* from the cause of the *sacerdotium*?'[59] The *Orthodoxa defensio imperialis* (Orthodox Defence of the Empire) of 1111 treated the *regnum* and *sacerdotium* as united in office after the example of Christ: they must, therefore, co-operate. But the secular ruler was the head of this unity: the king was *caput ecclesiae*. As a result the consent of clergy and people, generally required for canonical election of bishops, included that of the prince as the head of the people (*caput plebis*). The emperor, in particular, had a legitimate function in the appointment of popes, indeed one enshrined in canon law: 'The pope is therefore ordained with the agreement of the emperor, so that by his obedience the church may be supported in temporal matters.'[60]

Since both the royal and the papal sides perceived temporal and spiritual power as being combined within a unity, it says very little to characterise the Henrician tracts as dualist. The protagonists differed over the relationship between the two powers which were not distinct, but shaded into each other: the Henricians accorded the king or emperor the supreme position as regards secular and ecclesiastical jurisdiction, whereas the Gregorians attributed to the pope ultimate sovereignty in both. King and pope claimed to be able to depose each other. Within the overall context of the unity of the Christian community, the Henrician approach remained traditional, whereas the Gregorian was innovative in that it provided the catalyst for an increasing differentiation between the two powers and, indeed, contributed in the long term to the secularisation of kingship by stripping the king of his sacerdotal attributes.

Consideration of the issues which the Investiture Contest raised concerning the relationship between temporal and spiritual power was not confined to Germany and Italy, but was evident in France from the 1090s and in England from the turn of the century. Indeed, the most radical treatment was contained in a tract produced in the Anglo-Norman lands. The writer, who was originally known to modern scholars as the Anonymous of York, but, following the research of George H. Williams, is now commonly called the Norman Anonymous, produced his work on the Continent, perhaps at Rouen in c. 1100.[61] He expressed the traditional view that royal and sacerdotal powers were combined in Christ, and hence in the king, the vicar of Christ; but the author's independence of mind was revealed in his development of his argument. He held that Christ was king by virtue of his divine nature and priest by that of his human, with the result that kingship was superior to priesthood within both Christ and his vicar, the king. Whereas, however, Christ was divine by nature, the king was God and Christ through grace, that is through unction: the king, therefore, had a dual personality – 'in one by nature an individual man, in the other by grace a *christus*, that is a God-man'.[62] The anointed king as the 'figure and image of Christ and God' (*figura et imago Christi et Dei*) reigned together with Christ.[63] As a result, 'It is clear that kings have the sacred power of ecclesiastical rule even over the priests of God themselves and dominion over them, so that they too may themselves rule holy church in piety and faith.'[64] The priesthood was subject to the king, as to Christ. The king could in consequence appoint and invest bishops. Behind the Anonymous's statements lay the view that jurisdiction was superior to sacramental power, a notion common both to Gregorians and their royalist opponents. But he reversed the papalist position by denying governmental powers to the priesthood and reserving them solely to the king. He did not consider, incidentally, that the fact that bishops consecrated kings made them in any sense superior, because there were many examples of lesser powers elevating superior ones to office.

Of all the issues treated in the publicistic literature of the Investiture Contest the crux was clearly whether the pope in fact had the authority to free subjects from their oaths of allegiance and depose kings. The papacy was here on its most insecure ground and its claims most shocking, indeed no less than a sign of contradiction to the presuppositions of lay society. Fundamental questions concerning obedience to authority and the justifiability of rebellion were at issue. Both sides accepted that kingship was an office in the tradition of the ideas of Gregory I and thus limited by its function; but whereas the Henricians followed that pope in leaving an errant king solely to God's judgement, the followers of Gregory VII interpreted the notion of royal office as justifying human action to remove a ruler who was perceived to have failed in his duties; they thereby contributed further to the desacralisation of kingship. Their main focus was on the pope's role in this respect. Manegold of Lautenbach, however, went further by saying that a king (a name not of nature, but of office), who was unjust or tyrannical had broken the pact (*pactum*) with his people by which he had been constituted, and that as a result of his severing the bond of faith his people was already freed from its oath of allegiance.[65] This was by no means, as some scholars once thought, an expression of popular sovereignty, but one of aristocratic resistance along the lines of the arguments used by the Saxon rebels in 1073: the *populus* was identified with the great men of the kingdom.[66]

There were also problems with the papal position at the most fundamental level: the interpretation of its basic proof-text, Matthew 16:18–19. The Gregorian view identifying Peter with the rock on which the church was founded was, as we have seen, only one possible reading.[67] The main alternative understanding which equated the rock with Christ had a venerable ancestry in Christian exegesis, including Augustine, and was common in the preceding medieval centuries, being supported also by 1 Corinthians 10:4.[68] Furthermore, Matthew 16:18–19 could be understood to apply to all the apostles, who received thereby the same powers as Peter, as indeed the Norman Anonymous believed. This interpretation was also followed by the Anonymous of Hersfeld who supported his case by referring to chapter 4 of the early church father Cyprian's text *De ecclesiae catholicae unitate* (On the Unity of the Catholic Church). The little-known version, which he used, accurately reflected Cyprian's own view, unlike the alternative one, favouring papal primacy, which was widely known and used by the Gregorians.[69] The papal interpretation of Matthew 16:18–19 only convinced its own supporters and was never to achieve universal acceptance: the view that Christ's commission was made to the episcopacy as a whole retained its strength throughout the remainder of the Middle Ages.[70]

The intellectual debate stimulated by the Investiture Contest brought no solutions to the fundamental questions raised: the presuppositions of the two sides were too opposed for this. The dispute was ended by a series of practical compromises based upon the distinction between the spiritual and temporal aspects of bishoprics. Guido of Ferrara in the 1080s had already distinguished between the bishop's *spiritualia*, pertaining to his episcopal office, and his *saecularia*, signifying the possessions of his see.[71] In the Anglo-Norman lands a solution was reached by 1107 whereby Henry I renounced investiture, but election of bishops and abbots still took place in the royal presence and those elected had to do homage for the temporal possessions of their churches. In France a decisive contribution had been made by the canonist Ivo of Chartres in a letter written in 1097 to Archbishop Hugh of Lyon: in this he maintained that royal investiture did not concern a bishop's *spiritualia* but solely the estates and worldly goods given the see by the king (known generally as *regalia*).[72] By the solution in France, very likely influenced by Ivo's ideas, the king renounced investiture and homage but held on to the right to confer the temporalities of sees and to demand fealty. In both England and France the royal grant of *regalia* followed consecration thus saving the outward forms of canonical election. As regards the papacy and the empire, Pope Paschal II, influenced by the tract *De episcoporum investitura* (Concerning the Investiture of Bishops) in 1111 attempted, briefly and unsuccessfully, to surrender church *regalia* in return for the renunciation of investiture by Henry V. This initiative was not, as was once thought, the product of a desire to achieve apostolic poverty, but an attempt to remove the root reason for royal investiture in order to free the church from lay control: Paschal intended that the church should retain all its possessions (*ecclesiastica*) which were not *regalia*, together with the patrimony of St Peter.[73] The final solution to the Investiture Contest was reached through the Concordat of Worms of 1122 between Pope Calixtus II and Henry V. The pope conceded election of bishops in the royal presence and that the king should grant *regalia*; Henry in turn surrendered investiture and accepted canonical election and free consecration, but the granting of *regalia* and the accompanying giving of homage were to take place before consecration, thereby undermining in practice the principle of the liberty of the church. Calixtus was clearly influenced by the English solution and the ideas of Ivo of Chartres.

The differentiation between the spiritual and temporal aspects of a bishopric was the net intellectual result of the Investiture Contest. The only solution reached was that to the narrow question of investiture itself. This differentiation went against the initial views of reformers like Humbert who saw a bishopric as a unity, but it adequately explained the desire for royal involvement and, above all, permitted both sides to compromise in order to achieve peace at the end of a long-drawn-out and increasingly dreary conflict.

In the decades succeeding the Investiture Contest, however, there took place development in the formulation of ideas concerning the relationship between temporal and spiritual power. This was mainly in terms of canon law and is best discussed as part of the elaboration of legal language as a vehicle for political ideas. In terms of a theological approach, two writers in particular made contributions of a particularly lasting nature: Hugh of St Victor and Bernard of Clairvaux. Their statements on this question provide further proof of how misleading it is to try and force the ideas of a medieval author into a hierocratic or dualist straitjacket. Not only that: there was a marked discrepancy between whatever might have been their original intention and how their thought came to be interpreted subsequently.

Hugh (c. 1098–1142) was a luminary of the Parisian school of St Victor. In his *De sacramentis christianae fidei* (Concerning the Sacraments of the Christian Faith) he argued that the *regnum* and *sacerdotium* formed an organic unity as two sides of the body of Christ, but that the priesthood was of greater worth than kingship because it was prior in time. Furthermore,

> Just as the spiritual life is worthier than the earthly, and the spirit than the body, so the spiritual power is superior to the earthly or secular power in honour and dignity. For the spiritual power has to institute the earthly power, *in order that it may be*, and to judge it, if it has not been good.[74]

This might well appear to mark a clear development in hierocratic thought in that the secular power appears to depend for its very existence on the spiritual – and indeed this passage was often to be interpreted in precisely this way by pro-papal writers in later centuries – but it is highly dubious whether this was the meaning which Hugh intended, because he attributed power only over *spiritualia* directly to the clergy. It was perfectly possible that he was simply referring to the clergy's role in consecrating a king, without suggesting thereby that they were the original source of royal power.[75]

Bernard (1090–1153) was abbot of the Cistercian abbey of Clairvaux and became the most influential ecclesiastic of his age in the west. His message about the relationship between temporal and spiritual power was striking but confusing and only formed a tiny part of his vast literary output, being mostly to be found in his tract *De consideratione* (On Consideration) written c. 1150 and addressed to a former pupil who had become pope as Eugenius III in 1145. True to his vocation as a monk of the ascetic new religious order he criticised the papacy for having taken a wrong direction through becoming excessively involved in the affairs of this world, notably in its exercise of jurisdiction: 'And indeed every day the laws resound in your palace; but they are the laws of Justinian, not of the Lord. Is this right?'[76] Yet, although he stressed the pope's spiritual and pastoral role above all, he did this in a way which emphasised papal primacy, maintaining that Christ in John 21:17 had committed the whole flock to the care of one shepherd, Peter, in the presence of the other apostles, as a sign of unity. He also produced a classic definition of the pope's monarchical power in terms of the formula, plenitude of power (*plenitudo potestatis*), which was to play an increasing role in the development of papal governmental claims:

> Others have been called to a part of the care, you to plen-itude of power. The power of others is curtailed by certain limits: yours extends also over those who have accepted power over others.[77]

There was thus ambiguity in Bernard's approach, an ambiguity which remained in his most famous statement which applied the two-swords imagery to explain the relationship between the pope's power and that of secular rulers. Referring to Christ's injunction to Peter to put up his sword into its scabbard, he said:

> This sword is yours to be drawn, perhaps at your command, if not by your hand. Otherwise, if it no way belonged to you, when the apostles said, 'Behold, there are two swords here,' the Lord would not have replied to them, 'It is enough', but, 'It is too much.' Both belong to the church, that is the spiritual sword and the material, but the one is to be drawn for the church, and the other also by the church: the one by the priest's hand, the other by the soldier's, but, to be sure, at the priest's command and the emperor's order.[78]

The meaning of this passage has been hotly disputed by modern scholars, on the whole according to the ways in which they interpret the jurisdictional claims of the medieval papacy. Interpretations have ranged over a very wide compass. Alfons Stickler maintained that the material sword referred to the coercive power of the church, not to temporal power as such: in consequence Bernard was not claiming that the papacy was the source of secular power. The exercise of the material sword was delegated to the laity, because clerics were forbidden to shed blood. A case in point would be the papal summoning of a crusade. Indeed, an earlier letter by Bernard to Eugenius, calling for such an expedition, used the two-sword imagery in the same way, and can be seen as being consistent with this form of interpretation.[79] At the other extreme, some scholars have under-stood the passage from *De consideratione* as having a thoroughly hierocratic meaning, whereby the pope distributed temporal power to secular rulers, who exercised it at his command in a derivative and subordinate way. It is certainly true that later, definitely hierocratic writers, notably in the fourteenth century, were to interpret this passage in such a manner, but there is no certainty that this was Bernard's own meaning, which remained to some degree unclear.[80]

THE LANGUAGES FOR POLITICAL THOUGHT: THE REVIVED LEGACY OF ANTIQUITY

Classical-literary: John of Salisbury

The differentiation between the temporal and spiritual spheres, increasingly evident during the Investiture Contest, provided the basis for the developing consolidation of ideas of a secular, political dimension in the remainder of the twelfth century. A prime source for such notions was to be found in literary culture, heavily reliant on classical models.

Fundamental to this way of looking at the world was a changed conception of nature: certainly in this century there was a move from interpreting nature in purely religious and moral categories to seeking a physical explanation of it in terms of cause and effect. Modern scholars dispute about the significance of the treatment of nature in twelfth-century literary, theological and jurisprudential sources, but beneath all the differences of emphasis in different medieval authors, there can be perceived a growing tendency to accord to nature a certain autonomy.[81] Although God was understood ultimately to stand behind nature, the latter could to a degree be discussed in its own this-worldly terms. The common equation of God with nature was expressed in more sophisticated theological language as signifying the relationship between the divinity as *natura naturans* with His creation as *natura naturata*.[82] The main problem for the modern interpreter is that nature is such a slippery concept that it is difficult to be at all precise over the meaning attached to it by a medieval writer. As regards classical-literary sources, Seneca and, notably, Cicero provided treatments of nature which were seminal for twelfth-century political thought. Cicero's influential ideas were contained above all in his tract *De officiis* (On Duties). For him there was an intrinsic link between nature and reason (*ratio*): natural law as a rational order underlay the life of the universe and of man.[83]

From the point of view of political thought the most important representative of twelfth-century literary culture was John of Salisbury (1115/20–80), an English-born, Paris-educated ecclesiastical bureaucrat and man-of-affairs, who initially served Archbishop

Theobald of Canterbury, was a close friend of Thomas Becket, Henry II of England's Chancellor, and after the vicissitudes of exile ended his career as bishop of Chartres. Of his voluminous writings his tract *Policraticus sive de nugis curialium et vestigiis philosophorum* (Policraticus or Concerning the Trifles of Courtiers and the Footsteps of Philosophers) had the greatest direct relevance to political ideas. This work of some 250,000 words was completed in 1159 and was dedicated to Thomas Becket. Although it has often been treated as the first political thought treatise of the Middle Ages, this approach is misleading because it could only in part conform to such a description: it was certainly to some extent a mirror for a prince, but it was also a more general work of philosophy, a tract on the political *mores* of his time, and a work of personal consolation. It reflected the way in which literary *genres* were still relatively unfixed in this period.

Nature was of fundamental importance in John's view of the world: on several occasions he referred to the Stoic–Ciceronian formulation that 'nature is the best guide to life', and specifically to man's civil life in the *respublica*, a view which he reinforced by quoting at length the passage from Vergil, *Georgics* 4, in which the bees are praised as a model for a civil existence.[84] But he went further than the purely mundane level by incorporating Neoplatonic ideas which saw nature as the will of God, and man, on a cosmological scale, as the microcosm, or 'little world' (*mundus minor*) which reflected the macrocosm.[85] This view bore witness to the long-term impact of Chalcidius' commentary on Plato's *Timaeus* and was, most probably, influenced by William of Conches' commentary on that work.[86]

Within this natural context John elaborated the most thorough-going organic treatment of the 'body of the *respublica*' (*corpus rei publicae*) yet produced in the Middle Ages. The clergy are the soul of that body;

> But the *princeps* occupies the place of the head in the *res publica*; he is subject to the one God and to those who are His vicars on earth, because in the human body as well the head is animated and ruled by the soul. The senate occupies the place of the heart, from which proceed the beginnings of good and bad works. Judges and governors of provinces claim for themselves the functions of the eyes, the ears and the tongue. Officials and soldiers coincide with the hands.

Those who always accompany the *princeps* are similar to the sides. Treasurers and record-keepers ... relate to the likeness of the stomach and intestines which, if they accumulate with huge greed and tenaciously guard their hoards, create countless incurable diseases, so that by their vice the whole body's ruin is threatened. But with the feet, which adhere perpetually to the ground, coincide farmers, for whom the head's foresight is the more necessary, in that they encounter many obstacles, while they obey the body in walking on the ground; the help of coverings is more justly owed to them who hold up, sustain and propel the mass of the whole body. Remove the help of feet from the strongest body and it will not proceed by its own strength, but will either basely, uselessly and laboriously crawl with its hands, or will be moved by the aid of brute beasts.[87]

Although the ultimate origins of medieval organological concepts were to be found in the works of St Paul, Augustine and Chalcidius, John's more immediate sources seem to have been William of Conches' commentaries not only on the *Timaeus* but also on Macrobius' commentary on the *Somnium Scipionis* (Dream of Scipio), Bernard Silvestris' commentary on Vergil's *Aeneid* and glosses on the Roman law.[88] John presented these ideas (and indeed the whole of Books V and VI) as being based on a supposed work of Plutarch, the *Institutio Traiani* (The Instruction of Trajan). Modern scholarship has discussed whether this was a genuine work of Plutarch, or a pseudo-Plutarchian piece produced in late antiquity, or an invention on John's part. The consensus appears to be that it was a literary device: that no such work existed. There has been found no reference to it other than those in the *Policraticus*. John probably produced this fiction in order to give his ideas greater weight by providing them with a purported ancient authority; there was, after all, no full-scale ancient treatment of political thought available to him. Plato's *Republic* and Aristotle's *Politics* had not yet been rediscovered; of Cicero's *De republica* only the part known as the *Somnium Scipionis* was extant.

Embedded in John's organic metaphor was the idea of the common good: the interdependent members of the *corpus rei publicae* aimed at the achievement of this goal. John produced an emphatic intensification of this fundamental concept and in doing so was heavily influenced by the Ciceronian notion of the *utilitas publica*. The ruler was limited in the exercise of his power by this norm which was used by John to elaborate the Christian ministerial idea of rulership: 'The *princeps* is therefore the minister of the common good and the servant of equity.'[89] Indeed, the *princeps* was characterised by ruling according to law which 'is the gift of God, the form of equity, the norm of justice, the image of the divine will', whereas the tyrant dominated his people with violence.[90] John devoted Book VIII, chapters 17–21, to a lengthy treatment of the problem of tyranny, confronting in it the basic question: could anything be done about a tyrant? That quintessential crux of medieval political ideas was at issue: all rulers were understood to be limited by theoretical norms, but could they be controlled in practice? John's response has caused much debate among modern historians. Although he repeated the Augustinian view that tyrants were sent by God as a punishment for the people's sins, he also made statements that appeared to advocate tyrannicide: for example, 'the tyrant, the picture of depravity, is for the most part even to be killed'.[91] Yet he hedged this position around with so many provisos that it is difficult to see that he was envisaging it as an option for action: poison could not be used and, above all, no one bound by a feudal oath to a ruler could kill him, even if he were a tyrant, which would prevent anyone from eliminating their own monarch. It seems most likely that John was putting before rulers the terrible image of the fate of tyrants in order to dissuade them from evil-doing, with the sure promise that God would punish them.[92]

John's organic theory of the common good could be seen as contributing to the development of a transpersonal natural state concept. It is perfectly true that his sophisticated use of Roman political terms, notably derived from Cicero and the Roman law, served to raise the level of discourse for describing the political dimension in which the *respublica* existed. Indeed, the law, he said, was that 'according to which all should live who dwell in a political corporate body'.[93] Yet he can only be understood as going part of the way down this road. He made no clear distinction between church and state. The clergy, after all, were the soul of the body politic. Furthermore, he produced a thoroughly hierocratic application of two-sword imagery:

> The *princeps*, therefore, receives this sword from the hand of the church, since it in no way has the sword of blood. Yet it

does have it as well, but uses it through the hand of the *princeps*, on whom it has conferred the power of coercing bodies, while reserving authority over spiritual matters to itself in the form of its priests. The *princeps* is therefore a minister of the priesthood and exercises that part of the sacred duties which seem unworthy for priestly hands. For every duty of the sacred laws is religious and pious, but that one is inferior which is exercised in the punishment of crimes and seems to represent the image of an executioner.[94]

For John the *respublica* was a Christian community in which the theocratic and the political dimensions coexisted. In one passage, for instance, in a naturalistic context, he suggested a purely human source for the ruler's power:

Rightly the power of all subjects is conferred on him [the *princeps*] so that he might be sufficient by himself to seek out and create the good of one and all, and the condition of the human *res publica* be best served, while all are members one of another.[95]

But he never suggested that the people itself possessed the exercise of power: this for him was concentrated in the person of the ruler. It was in this sense that the *princeps* represented his subjects: he acted in the place of the *corpus rei publicae* and bore the *persona* of the corporation of his subjects.[96] Yet ultimately power came from God and the laws of all rulers were subject to the law of God and those of his church: 'The censure of all laws is in vain, if it does not bear the image of the divine law, and the constitution of a *princeps* is useless, if it does not conform to ecclesiastical discipline.'[97] Indeed, the *princeps* was 'an image of the divine majesty on earth'.[98]

In so far as the *Policraticus* was a work of political thought, it had obvious faults of organisation: it can appear as a strange farrago of political and moral observations interspersed with more sustained passages containing something like a systematic treatment of issues. Yet it was to remain one of the most influential political works for the remainder of the Middle Ages.

The language of Roman and canon law

A long-term, indeed permanent, development in the language of political thought occurred through the emergence and growth of legal science, a phenomenon which had the greatest effect on European cultural history. This new, jurisprudential method was anchored in the scholarship of Roman and canon law which, from its late eleventh-century origins, blossomed in the course of the twelfth century. Although these two branches of law were initially distinct, they developed in tandem, so much so that at least in the course of the thirteenth century they became combined in a *ius commune*, or common law, approach. Civilians and canonists built up a rational, differentiated jurisprudence which constituted a characteristic way of looking at the world, or in their own terms a 'true philosophy' whose priests they were.[99] Their works may be categorised as being a subdivision of scholasticism in that the dialectical methodology employed involved the application of Aristotelian logic to an authoritative body of texts. Although most of Roman law was concerned with private rather than public law, and the vast bulk of canon law related to matters unconnected with politics and government, these jurists did make substantial contributions which may be considered relevant to political thought, and in so doing they provided a systematic approach which had not existed before in the Middle Ages.

The scientific study of Roman law began with the school of jurists known as the Glossators. They originated with the work of Irnerius from the turn of the eleventh and twelfth centuries at the archetypal university of Bologna and were centred on that *studium*. The availability of the full text of the *Corpus iuris civilis* was crucial for the development of their work. Whereas the *Institutes* and the *Novels* had been current in Italy throughout the Middle Ages, and the first nine books of the *Code* had been to hand since the ninth century, the text of the *Digest* had only surfaced in the south of the peninsula in *c.* 1070, whence it found its way northwards (the last three books of the *Code*, known as the *Tres libri* were to come into use by the mid-twelfth century). The school of the Glossators reached its maturity in the late twelfth and early thirteenth centuries with the work of the Bolognese jurist, Azo, whose *Summa codicis* (1208–10) and *Summa institutionum* exercised enormous influence. The culmination of the labours of the Glossators came with Accursius' *Glossa ordinaria* on the whole of the *Corpus iuris civilis* (completed in the 1230s): this was to serve as the standard gloss for the remainder of the Middle Ages and into the early seventeenth century, as is witnessed by the very large number of surviving manuscripts and early printed editions of it. The Glossators initially sought to establish the meaning of the Justinianean texts, but, with the growing sophistication of their method, increasingly produced interpretations reflecting the requirements of the society of their own times.

The turning-point in the development of canon law scholarship came in 1139/40 when Gratian produced at Bologna his *Concordia discordantium canonum* (Concordance of Discordant Canons) which became known as the *Decretum*. By applying the dialectical method pioneered by the theologian Abelard (1079–c. 1142), Gratian sought to produce some coherence out of the contradictions in the existing undifferentiated mass of canon law. His work, which had no official status, became the standard handbook for the study of the subject: a whole school of jurists, known as the Decretists, devoted their energies to elucidating the *Decretum*. Amongst them Huguccio (d. 1210) was pre-eminent. Yet in the second half of the twelfth century the body of canon law had been steadily growing through the marked increase in the issuing of papal decretals, especially during the pontificate of Alexander III (1159–81). The result was that official compilation on the part of the papacy was required. Pope Innocent III authenticated the first such collection, the *Compilatio tertia* of 1209/10. This contained a selection of the decretals issued in the first twelve years of his pontificate and was supplemented by the second official collection, the *Compilatio quinta* promulgated by Honorius III in 1226. This initial stage of compilation culminated in Pope Gregory IX's codification, the *Liber extra* (1234). The canonists commenting on decretal collections were known as the Decretalists, amongst whom the most important in the mid-thirteenth century were Pope Innocent IV (d. 1254), Hostiensis (d. 1271) and Bernard of Parma (d. 1266), the writer of the *Glossa ordinaria* on the *Liber extra*. Because the canon law was a living and growing one reflecting the conditions of medieval life, the works of the canonists were closely connected with the needs of the societies in which they lived. Indeed, because virtually all the popes of the twelfth and thirteenth centuries had been trained as lawyers, the academic canonists influenced the development of the canon law itself. As far as political thought was concerned the canonists had a great impact over a wide spectrum, greater indeed than that of the Glossators: they exhibited more versatility than their civilian brothers who were to some extent tied to an authoritative text completed in the sixth century with only a very few high medieval additions.

Roman and canon law jurisprudence focused more and more sharply on the role of the ruler's will in law-making, but within the context of the limitations imposed by higher norms in the form of divine law, natural law and the *ius gentium*. This was a medieval interpretation of the classical Roman law notion of legislative authority, a notion which had accepted such norms but accorded them a minimal role in limiting the emperor's power to make law. The jurists' treatments of the content of these higher laws and their interrelations were varied indeed, reflecting for instance differing approaches to Ulpian's and Gaius' definitions of natural law and changing theological understanding.[100] Although the main emphasis of the approaches of the Glossators, Decretists and early Decretalists was to concentrate on the legislative aspect of monarchical rulership both temporal and spiritual, there was also some acknowledgement of the people's function in law creation. Civilians discussed whether the *lex regia*, the supposed source of imperial power, was irrevocable or revocable by the Roman people. Indeed, Gratian included all human law under the general heading of custom and stated, 'Laws are instituted when they are promulgated, and confirmed when they are approved by usage.'[101] The Glossators, reflecting the contradictions in the *Corpus iuris civilis* concerning custom, discussed whether custom could abrogate imperial laws and came to the general conclusion that it could, if it arose after the law in question.[102]

Yet it was precisely on matters associated with the will of the ruler that twelfth- and thirteenth-century jurists exhibited a remarkable fecundity of mind, thereby making important contributions to the development of the languages of law and politics. They recognised that the ruler, operating within a normative context, in no sense exercised untrammelled power. Yet the Roman law principle of 'what pleases the prince has the force of law' stood behind the counterpoint of two fundamental principles in law-making – reason and will. The universal twelfth-century juristic assumption was that law, to be valid, corresponded with reason. The beginnings of the process, however, whereby there was an increasing emphasis on the law-creating function of the ruler's will, became encapsulated in the formula 'his will is held to be reason' (*pro ratione voluntas*) which derived from Juvenal's *Satires* (6.223) and had come to be used by jurists from the end of the twelfth century. Kenneth Pennington has stressed the role of the canonist Laurentius Hispanus (writing between 1210 and 1215) in developing the idea, on the basis of this formula, that the pope could change canon law in such a way that what was previously just became unjust, with the implication that the papal legislative will was distinct from the rational content of law, a view which ran counter to that of Huguccio.[103] The use of this formula, in that it focused on the notion of law as legislation, could serve ultimately to reduce the objectively rational or moral aspect of law, and lead to a purely positivist approach. Indeed it was precisely in the twelfth century that French canonists had begun to employ the term 'positive law' (ius positivum), a usage with roots in Chalcidius' commentary on the Timaeus, and found also in Abelard, before it later appeared in the work of Laurentius Hispanus.[104] Yet there was no question of such a solely positivist conception of law in Laurentius nor in the thirteenth-century canonists and civilians: the law-maker for them still operated within a normative context expressed in terms of the common good. Nevertheless, the positivist seed had been sown.

It was a principle of Roman law that, although the princeps was freed from human laws (legibus solutus), he should none the less obey them, because his power was a legal one founded by the lex regia.[105] This view meant that he was in no way an absolute ruler, and twelfth- and thirteenth-century jurists, while accepting that such obedience, being voluntary, had a purely moral force, agreed that his power was subject to higher norms.[106] Yet the very term 'absolute power' (potestas absoluta) was a medieval juristic coinage made by Hostiensis, drawing on theological sources, to distinguish between the pope's extraordinary power to transcend the provisions of canon law, where he judged necessary, and his 'ordinary power' (potestas ordinata) which he exercised on a day-to-day basis according to the canons.[107] Again, potestas absoluta was at this stage understood within a normative context, but it was a formulation which would be very useful for extending the scope of the sovereignty of the ruler's will. Nevertheless the general understanding was that the pope could only 'with cause' (ex causa) deviate from the canons or derogate from higher norms.

The term potestas absoluta was related to the concept of the pope's plenitude of power (plenitudo potestatis) which had not been employed by Gregory VII, but emerged in the twelfth century as a way of expressing papal sovereignty, a usage which diverged from Leo I's original meaning, and was to be found frequently, and definitively, in Innocent III's decretals.[108] Hostiensis was to give the classic treatment of this idea. Plenitude of power expressed the jurisdictional primacy of the pope, but was in no sense arbitrary, since it existed within the normative framework of the papal office. The term was clearly ideal for the articulation of the idea of sovereignty, and as such was applied by and to secular rulers in the course of the thirteenth century.[109]

Although there was this evermore sophisticated treatment of the expression of the ruler's will, these jurists also gave considerable attention to refining ideas constituting the normative and limiting context of the exercise of his power. A recent direction of research taken by Brian Tierney has highlighted the twelfth- and thirteenth-century canonists' contribution to the development of notions of individual rights based on natural law: that human beings have subjective natural rights as distinct from the objective law of nature. Tierney has disputed the earlier consensus that such subjective rights only emerged later, for instance, in the theological and philosophical writings of William of Ockham or Gerson. Tierney's findings have been disputed, but his arguments carry a lot of weight and have certainly introduced a most fruitful line of enquiry into the political ideas of these canonists.[110] For the jurists the whole subject was fraught with the greatest difficulties. On the fundamental topic of rights to private property, Decretists wrestled with the apparent contradiction between Gratian's position that the common possession of all things was a precept of natural law, and his statements elsewhere which assumed the licitness of individual property. The view that the law of nature was included in the *ius gentium*, which sanctioned property, was followed by some Glossators including Accursius. It is also, of course, a fundamental right for a litigant to enjoy due process in any court of law. Although one could argue that trial by ordeal was more rational than it might seem, being a means of revealing the immanent judgement of God as an alternative to the feud, it was precisely in the twelfth and thirteenth centuries that the Romano-canonical legal tradition began to develop rational due process (*ordo iudiciarius*) which jurists from the thirteenth century argued was based on natural law.[111]

The most trenchant discussion of the limitations on the ruler's power was to be found in an area at the heart of the pope's authority. What was to be done about an heretical pope? This

119

topic became a set-piece of Decretist discourse. Gratian had included the statement in his *Decretum* that the pope was to be judged by no one 'unless he be found to deviate from the faith' (*nisi deprehendatur a fide devius*).[112] The problem was, who could judge the pope in order to protect the *status ecclesiae*, which amounted to the church's constitution, its divinely revealed hierarchical structure and repository of faith? No juridically convincing answer was reached; but it was significant that the question was asked. The most famous Decretist treatment was that of Huguccio who held that the pope could be condemned for heresy, a category which, he held, included a range of scandalous crimes: by way of illustration he indulged in flights of juristic fancy, such as the speculation that the pope might have intercourse with his concubine on the altar of a church, in which case he would be committing both fornication and heresy.[113] The problem remained: who was to say that the pope was heretical, if he denied it? Huguccio held that an heretical pope had already judged and deposed himself – not a practical solution.

The canonists also gave lengthy treatments to the question of the relationship between temporal and spiritual jurisdiction. The basic problem, which caused fundamental divergences among their views, was produced by the tension between the acceptance of Christ's division of the two powers and the recognition that the clergy were superior to the laity. Did this superiority entail that temporal power was derived from the spiritual, or did they exist in parallel, with the spiritual enjoying a higher dignity?

Where Gratian had tried to make sense of the canons, the Decretists tried to make sense of Gratian. His dialectical method of assembling contrary texts left his commentators with a confusing collection of material on this question with the result that no consensus emerged. Out of the mass of commentaries three stood out. Rufinus in his *Summa decretorum* (1157–9) argued that, whereas the pope possessed a 'right of authority' (*ius auctoritatis*) over secular matters, and indeed confirmed the emperor in his rulership, the latter had the 'right of administration' (*ius administrationis*) over them.[114] Huguccio (writing in the years 1189–91) took what may be described as a more dualist line. He held that the imperial and papal powers were directly instituted by God and that neither was derived from the other, with the result that the emperor obtained his office from election by the princes and people. There was, after all, an empire before there was a papacy. The emperor possessed full power before unction and confirmation by the pope, who only gave him the imperial title. The pope could, indeed, depose him, but only with the will and consent of the princes.[115] In contrast, Alanus Anglicus writing in *c.* 1202, expressly disagreed with Huguccio, maintaining that the emperor derived his sword from the pope who possessed both the material and the spiritual one.[116]

Innocent III, in a series of decretals, then injected what were to be the most important papal contributions to this debate. Anyone seeking to understand his pontificate is faced with a veritable quagmire of radically differing interpretations by modern historians. His reign was the crux of the medieval papacy. He was involved in the widest possible range of ecclesiastical and political affairs. He became embroiled in the question of the imperial succession in the civil wars after the death of Emperor Henry VI in 1197. Through his policy of recuperations he earned the title of the second founder of the papal states. The Fourth Crusade was preached by him. Through his conflict with King John of England over the appointment of Stephen Langton to the see of Canterbury he became a protagonist in one of the most prolonged and bitter disputes between the temporal and the spiritual power. His most positive achievement was his favouring of the beginnings of the friars. The pontificate culminated in the Fourth Lateran Council. But despite all this activity the traditional (and justified) question is, just how successful was he? Was it all a tremendous effort for little practical result? Where he certainly did make a long-term impact was within canon law through his vast decretal production and the *Compilatio tertia*. Almost six hundred of his decretals were to find a permanent place in the canon law. Yet even at this point there is uncertainty amongst modern scholars. It used to be almost an article of faith amongst church historians that Innocent was the most eminent of virtually two hundred years of a string of lawyer-popes in the twelfth and thirteenth centuries. Kenneth Pennington has now thrown so much doubt on the claim that Innocent was formally trained as a lawyer that it seems sensible to modify this interpretation. The latest trend is to stress Innocent's formation as a theologian at Paris. He may have sat for a while at the feet of Huguccio at Bologna, but, if so, for how long?[117] Historians have long debated whether Innocent was a hierocrat or a dualist; now he is increasingly seen as above all a pastoral pope.[118]

The problem as regards the interpretation of his ideas concerning the relationship between temporal and spiritual power is in part caused because he wrote no tract on this subject. His ideas were mostly contained in *ad hoc* decretals which tended to use arguments that came to hand to support the points he wished to make. His most important statements concerning the empire were contained in the decretal *Venerabilem* of 1202 in which Innocent justified his claim to be able to choose between the two claimants to the imperial crown, Otto of Brunswick and Rudolf of Swabia. The pope accepted the princely electors' rights to choose a candidate but maintained that these derived from the papacy through the translation of the empire (*translatio imperii*) from the Greeks to the Germans in the person of Charlemagne. Innocent stated that, since he as pope anointed, consecrated and crowned the emperor, he had the right to examine and, if necessary, reject a candidate chosen by the princes. He was explicitly applying the procedure for the confirmation of elections to bishoprics.[119] Elsewhere Innocent had maintained that the choice of emperor belonged to the pope 'principally and finally' (*principaliter et finaliter*) – that is, in its origin and purpose.[120] Innocent was insisting that the pope, because he instituted the emperor, was the source of the latter's authority.

It was clear enough that Innocent could argue in this way because of his direct role in the imperial coronation. But what were his powers as regards secular jurisdiction in general? In his decretal *Per venerabilem*, also of 1202, he maintained that the pope could 'exercise temporal jurisdiction incidentally after having examined certain cases', and (with specific reference to his plenitude of power) that the pope 'is accustomed to perform the office of secular power sometimes and in some things by himself, sometimes and in some things through others'. Furthermore, in a passage glossing Deuteronomy 17:8–12, and much discussed by modern historians, he could be interpreted as meaning that the pope could judge in both civil and ecclesiastical cases.[121] In the decretal *Novit* of 1204, which was concerned with the dispute between King Philip Augustus of France and King John of England, he eschewed judgement in feudal cases but reserved the right to intervene where sin was involved (*ratione peccati*).[122] In the decretal *Licet* of 1206 he argued, in the case of the Italian city of Vercelli, that if laymen felt they had not found justice in secular courts then they could appeal to the papacy, especially when the empire was vacant.[123]

But what did all this amount to? What did it mean? Innocent's words are very difficult to interpret because of the amount of allegorical language he employed, in part, probably, a result of his theological formation. There was a heavy emphasis on texts from the Old Testament to justify papal claims, such as 'I have set thee over nations and over kingdoms, to root up and to pull down, and to waste and to destroy, and to build and to plant' (Jeremiah 1:10).[124] The traditional New Testament proof-texts were, of course, also much in evidence. To illustrate the inferior and derivative relationship of royal power to that of the pope, he used the well-worn allegory of the moon, which shone by the reflected light of the sun.[125] He also argued that he acted as vicar of Christ in the order of the Old Testament figure Melchisedech who was both priest and king of Salem.[126] Modern historians have been unable to agree about what Innocent meant by this claim. According to the hierocratic interpretation, as represented pre-eminently by Walter Ullmann, the claim to the vicariate of Christ, the last person to combine within himself the powers of priest and king, was the source of the supreme spiritual and temporal power of the pope.[127] In Michele Maccarrone's opinion Innocent intended a purely spiritual meaning by using this title – a view which is consistent with a more dualist reading of his intentions.[128] Kenneth Pennington has seen this vicariate as being used by Innocent as justification for the pope's right to use divine authority on those occasions on which he sought to transcend the canon law, a usage which, he has argued, laid the foundations for Hostiensis' formulation of the pope's *potestas absoluta*.[129] All this further illustrates that it is misleading to attempt to force the ideas of any medieval pope, and especially those of Innocent III, into a hierocratic or dualist interpretative strait-jacket. Whatever the nuances of Innocent's thought, reconstructed out of *ad hoc* statements made for different purposes at different times, he certainly claimed the right to intervene in secular matters.

The long-term significance of the decretals mentioned was that they provided abundant fodder for subsequent jurists. The notion of papal intervention *ratione peccati* in particular gave much food for thought, because it could be understood as being tantamount to a blank cheque for papal interference in secular affairs, on the grounds that it would be up to the pope alone, as the supreme spiritual authority, to judge whether sin was involved; any temporal ruler could always be outmanoeuvred in this way. On the whole, the thirteenth-century Decretalists may loosely be described as tending towards a hierocratic interpretation of papal powers. It would be misleading to say that Innocent IV went much beyond Innocent III. The former certainly held that a king would receive short shrift, should he try to bring a feudal action before a papal court.[130] Innocent IV's perception was that there had been historical development in the regal powers of the pope: these had originally been potential and had only become actual over the course of centuries. His deposition of the Emperor Frederick II at the First Council of Lyon in 1245 was on the basis of the pope's vicariate of Christ and powers of binding and loosing.[131] Hostiensis, however, with his rhetorical elaboration of the divine foundations of papal authority, could appear more hierocratic in approach.[132] But it was in another area that these two jurists differed significantly: over the question of whether infidels possessed valid jurisdiction. Innocent IV, arguing that the pope possessed jurisdiction over non-Christians *de iure*, but not *de facto*, was in consequence willing to recognise the practical validity of rulership by pagans. Hostiensis, in contrast, would not accept that infidels could exercise any valid jurisdiction. The disagreement between them was, in the sixteenth century, to provide material for the debate over the treatment of the Indians in the New World.[133]

Although the relationship between temporal and spiritual power remained a preoccupation for jurists, the emergence of territorial states in the twelfth and thirteenth centuries, and specifically kingdoms, posed a growing problem: how to reconcile this new phenomenon with the universalist pretensions of empire and papacy. The question was acute in terms of Roman law with its claim that the emperor was 'lord of the world'; there was much more flexibility as regards canon law. In order to express the territorial sovereignty of kings, jurists developed two formulae which were in origin distinct but became combined. The first equated the king with the emperor and became consolidated as 'the king in his kingdom is the emperor of his kingdom' (*rex in regno suo est imperator regni sui*). The origins of this equation were to be found in canonist writings at Bologna in the years shortly before and after 1200, notably those of Alanus Anglicus.[134] The civilian Azo also produced the idea in a *quaestio* composed soon after 1200.[135] Although the original meaning of this equation has been debated by modern historians there is scholarly consensus that, in the course of the thirteenth century, jurists, notably

English, French, Spanish and Neapolitan ones, elaborated this formula as a claim to the sovereign independence of kings in the sense that the king within the territory of his kingdom exercised the same authority as the emperor did in the empire as a whole. The second formula related to the king who did not recognise a superior (*rex qui superiorem non recognoscit*). This derived from a phrase in Innocent III's decretal *Per venerabilem*: 'since the king himself [i.e. of the French] does not recognise a superior in temporal matters' (*quum rex ipse [Francorum] superiorem in temporalibus minime recognoscat*). Innocent here seems to have been repeating phraseology contained in a petition sent to him on 2 November 1201 by Philip Augustus.[136] Canonists commenting on *Per venerabilem* differed as to whether this text indicated the *de iure* or the *de facto* independence of the French monarch from the emperor. Civilian jurists in the thirteenth century, with the possible exception of the Frenchman Johannes de Blanosco, retained the view that *de iure* sovereignty remained solely with the emperor: Johannes argued that the king of France was emperor in his kingdom because he recognised no superior in temporal affairs.[137] The Neapolitan jurist Marinus da Caramanico (d. 1288) produced a different way of justifying the independence of his king in terms of Roman law. He argued that the Roman empire had been based on force not law, and that the emperor only had authority where he could actually exercise power; elsewhere monarchs ruled by virtue of the *ius gentium*.[138] There existed in effect a plurality of territorially sovereign powers of which the emperor was but one.

Aristotelian language

In the course of the thirteenth century there also occurred the rediscovery of Aristotle's political ideas through the recovery of his *Nichomachean Ethics* and *Politics*. Both texts were translated into Latin from Greek manuscripts, although the *Politics* was already known by repute from Arab scholars' references to its existence, and the *Ethics* had been commented on in Arabic. Fragmentary versions of the *Ethics* were produced in the twelfth and early thirteenth centuries; but Robert Grosseteste translated the work in its entirety by about 1246/7, to be followed rapidly by an anonymous revision of his translation which became widely known. The *Politics* was translated, in a literal manner,

by William of Moerbeke who became the most prolific and influential translator of Aristotle. His first attempt, in c. 1260, was an
incomplete one terminating at 2.11; his second, a version of the
whole text, can be dated to the first half of 1265 and showed a
much better understanding of the philosopher.[139] The recovery of
the *Ethics* and *Politics* formed part of the rediscovery of the whole
corpus of Aristotle's philosophy in the west between the 1120s
and the 1270s. Earlier in the Middle Ages only two of Aristotle's
logical works were known, in Latin translations by Boethius: the
Categories and *On Interpretation* (comprising, together with
Porphyry's *Isagoge*, the 'old logic'). The medieval Latin translations of Aristotle, made overwhelmingly from Greek texts
rather than Arabic versions, spanned the period from somewhat
before 1150 to 1295, when Durandus of Alvernia finished his
revision of the anonymous translation of the *Economics*. Only
partial renderings of the *Eudemian Ethics*, however, survive; the
Poetics was, indeed, translated by William of Moerbeke in 1278,
but remained unknown; and only two anonymous translations of
the *Rhetorica ad Alexandrum* are extant, possibly produced in the
fourteenth century.[140] The process of assimilation of the new
Aristotle at the universities of Paris and Oxford was very slow.
There is evidence that lectures on the 'new logic' and some of the
works on natural philosophy were being given in both universities in the first decade of the thirteenth century. It was, however,
only in the 1240s and 1250s that Aristotelian studies really
flowered at Paris and Oxford. Although Latin scholastics used
(almost without exception) translations based on Greek texts for
their commentaries, they were also influenced by Arabic versions
of Aristotelian ideas derived from twelfth-century Latin translations of, for example, Alfarabi and Avicenna. The most important
Moslem interpreter of Aristotle, however, from the point of
view of the Latin west, was Averroes (Ibn Rushd) of Cordoba
(1126–98), who did not have access to the *Politics* but whose
middle commentary on the *Nichomachean Ethics* was translated
into Latin in 1240; indeed, most of his commentaries on Aristotle
were available in Latin versions by about 1250. The case of
Averroes illustrated the importance of Moslem Spain as a source
for the revived western knowledge of Aristotle.

The enthusiastic reception accorded to Aristotelian ideas was
matched by fierce opposition. The main problem concerned
the relationship between those ideas and Christian revelation.

Indeed, as early as 1210 lecturing on Aristotle's works on natural philosophy was proscribed at Paris. Scholars in the mid-thirteenth century expressed a wide variety of views ranging from the synthesis of Thomas Aquinas (c. 1225–74) to the 'Averroist' distinction between the truths of theology and those of philosophy. The reaction against the study of Aristotelian and Arabic philosophy culminated in the condemnations of 1277 at Paris and Oxford, whereby 'Averroist' and some Thomist propositions were proscribed.

The works of Aristotle provided a systematic treatment of the natural order on a metaphysical basis. The acceptance of this approach was already prepared by the pre-existing naturalistic, this-wordly direction shown in twelfth- and thirteenth-century theology, literature and jurisprudence. The recovered *Ethics* and *Politics* presented a systematic study of an avowedly political dimension and, specifically, made possible the establishment of political science (*scientia politica*) as an autonomous scholastic discipline: the subject gained thereby its own books of authority. The Aristotelian categorisation of politics as a separate branch of the practical sciences, which, together with ethics and economics, comprised moral philosophy, had, indeed, been known throughout the Middle Ages from, for instance, the works of Boethius, Cassiodorus and Isidore of Seville, and was used by Hugh of St Victor, in his *Didascalion*, and by Gundissalinus in his *De divisione philosophiae* (Concerning the Division of Philosophy) of c. 1150. Yet thirteenth-century introductions to philosophy, written before the reintroduction of the *Politics*, could only point to the Roman and canon law (*leges et canones*) as the textual subject-matter of political science.[141] Evidence survives of other occasional usages of the word 'political' and its cognates before the Aristotelian revival, but it was that movement which established it as a central and defining term in political thought.[142]

Aristotle taught that 'man is by nature a political animal',[143] meaning thereby that the fulfilment of human nature, as the realisation of its potentialities, could be achieved only within the perfect community, the Greek *polis* (city-state). The political aspect of man's life was the defining one and included all others within it. The origins of the political community, therefore, lay within man's nature. This view, understanding human nature to be as it is in the here and now, was radically different from the patristic approach which held that man's true nature existed only before the Fall, after which rulership and property became necessary as remedies for sin: that man's original nature was, in short, social but not political. The adoption of Aristotelian ideas could facilitate further development of ideas of state concepts within a natural, and secular, political dimension.

Because Aristotle held that the existence of the political community was demanded by man's nature, he considered the purpose of that community to be supremely important: it served to attain the life of virtue, the achievement of human potentiality. He viewed the city-state as being a self-sufficient community which had grown from smaller ones lacking this attribute. Likewise, because purpose was so pre-eminent, the form that rulership took was unimportant: he classified constitutions according to whether the state was ruled by the one, the few or the many – right constitutions aimed at the common good, deviant ones at the private good of those ruling. He was, in short, a relativist, considering that no one form had a monopoly in securing the ends of the state. The influx of Aristotelian political ideas meant that it became possible for thinkers to deepen arguments concerning the common good, and to accommodate more easily the variety of medieval forms of government, ranging from monarchies to Italian city-republics, although it was necessary in the process to widen the applicability of Aristotle's ideas from the city-state to include larger political units.

The first generation of scholastics to use Aristotle's *Politics* did so in a variety of *genres*, and in ways which can, on the whole, be described as theoretical in character rather than thought-out responses to contemporary political reality. Amongst literal commentaries on the text it is debatable whether the first was that of Albert the Great (*c.* 1200–80) or of his pupil, Thomas Aquinas, who wrote his between 1269 and 1272. Aquinas's commentary broke off at 3.8, and it has generally been accepted that Peter of Auvergne continued the remainder of the commentary. It is, however, not clear whether Peter wrote solely to complete the Dominican's work or whether he produced a complete commentary separately, the latter part of which was later used as a continuation of Aquinas's text. Another kind of commentary, in *quaestio* form, was also produced at Paris: by treating specific questions this permitted the author greater freedom of interpretation. Peter of Auvergne wrote his *Quaestiones super libros Politicorum* between 1272 and 1295/6, and most probably in the

1270s; the so-called Milan Anonymous produced his *quaestio-*commentary between 1295 and the beginning of the fourteenth century. The *Politics* were also used in mirror-of-princes tracts. Aquinas wrote his *De regno ad regem Cypri* (On Kingship for the King of Cyprus) between 1271 and 1273 for King Hugh III. The first section up to 2.4 was by Aquinas: the remainder of the work was written by Ptolemy of Lucca (*c.* 1236–1327). Similarly Giles of Rome (Aegidius Romanus, *c.* 1243–1316) produced his tract *De regimine principum* (On the Government of Princes) in *c.* 1280 for the future King Philip IV of France. The *Politics* was also used by Aquinas in his *Summa theologiae*, during the writing of which he began from 1267/8 to cite verbatim William of Moerbeke's complete translation.[144]

Aquinas's treatment of politics was fragmentary and must be seen within the wider context of his theology. In the main, he exemplified a metaphysical and theoretical approach to political questions. His attempted synthesis of Aristotle and Christianity rested on the distinction between the natural and the super-natural orders: 'Grace', as he said, 'does not destroy nature, but perfects it'.[145] There was thus a hierarchy of ends for human existence: both orders were created by God, but the spiritual was superior, since it encompassed man's final destiny in heaven. The natural order was to be discussed, at least partly, in Aristotelian terms, the supernatural in those of Christian revelation. Human nature had, indeed, been damaged by the Fall but the principles of nature enshrined in the rational precepts of natural law could still be understood: sin only affected man's capacity to fulfil the requirements of natural law. Since man was political by nature, politically ordered society existed before the Fall, although in the state of innocence dominion would have been directive rather than coercive in kind: it would have directed free men to the common good.[146] Aquinas's concept of the state, like Aristotle's, was organic: a unity of order for the common good, composed of its members rather than being distinct from them, but a congregation distinguished by its purpose from a mere aggregation of individuals. This was a notion of the common good which combined a this-worldly Aristotelian approach with a Christian transcendental one:

> Because man living according to virtue is ordained to a higher end, which consists in the enjoyment of God ... there

should be the same end for a multitude of men as for one man. The final end of a congregated multitude, therefore, is not to live according to virtue, but through a virtuous life to arrive at the enjoyment of God.[147]

A fundamental problem, however, in interpreting Aquinas's thought was that, for him, the common good of the political community was in some senses identified with and in others different from that of its individual members. Certainly, the common good was the determining criterion for the legitimacy of the political community: again, purpose rather than origin was the predominant consideration.[148]

For Aquinas, the normative context of political life was articulated in an interlocking structure of law linked by reason. At the highest level was the eternal law of God which expressed the divine rational guidance of created things. Because men, being made in the image of God, shared in the divine reason, they could participate in the eternal law, which rational participation was called natural law. Human law in turn was a rational application of natural law either in general terms (*ius gentium*) or particular ones (*ius civile*). There was also divine law which directed man to his final end of eternal blessedness.[149] The sources of this structure clearly lay in Christian and Stoic ideas. In understanding human law as 'an ordinance of reason for the common good promulgated by him who has care of the community',[150] Aquinas held that for such law to be valid it must be rational and thus derived from natural law: the mere will of the law-maker did not constitute valid law.[151] Natural law, according to Aquinas, was an objective rule rather than a source of individual natural rights. Furthermore, although it was immutable, it could be added to by human reason, as in the case of the institution of private property and slavery which supplanted the common liberty and possession of all things in the state of innocence.[152]

Because of his emphasis on the primacy of purpose, Aquinas was willing to accept the validity of a variety of forms of government ranging from monarchies to popular regimes in city-states. There is much in his writings in favour of monarchy, especially in the *De regno*. He used the metaphysical argument that monarchy, in that it expressed the principle of unity, was best suited to bringing about peace and thus procuring the common good. Likewise, he interpreted the organic approach as favouring monarchy:

'Every natural government is by one; for in the multitude of the body's members there is one which moves all, namely the heart.' Furthermore, 'There is one king amongst the bees, and in the whole universe one God, maker and lord of all.'[153] He also used the hierarchical argument of the relationship between the macrocosm and the microcosm to justify monarchy: 'A king should understand that he has undertaken the duty to be in his kingdom like the soul in the body and God in the universe.'[154] There were, however, limits on monarchical power: the ruler's will was to be governed by reason, which was the context in which Aquinas understood the Roman law tag, 'What pleases the prince has the force of law', although any such limitation had only directive rather than coercive force.[155] A king ruling according to the laws exercised 'political rule' (*regimen politicum*) rather than 'regal rule' (*regimen regale*) – that is, full and unlimited power (*plenaria potestas*).[156] On the whole, Aquinas favoured a limited monarchy in the form of a mixed constitution containing monarchical, aristocratic and popular elements as being most likely in practice to secure the common good through ensuring the participation of all.[157] He also accepted government by the people as a valid form for cities. This provision underlay his general theory of legislation: 'Making law belongs either to the whole multitude or to the public person who has care of the whole multitude', as also did the power of legal coercion.[158] Indeed,

> If it is a free multitude, which could make law for itself, the multitude's consent, manifested by custom, has more weight in observing something than the authority of the prince, who only has the power to make law, in so far as he bears the person of the multitude.[159]

Furthermore, as republican Rome in its heyday showed, general political participation could engender a greater commitment to the common good than existed under a monarchy, because each would make the common good his own, with the result that 'It seems by experience that one city administered by annual rulers can achieve more sometimes than a king, if he were to have three or four cities.'[160]

Where, however, experience really informed Aquinas's political ideas was in his contention that popular forms of government were prone to fall into disunity and dissension and thus fail to secure peace. The result was that government by the many was more likely to result in tyranny than rule by one man, as, he maintained, was shown by the fall of the Roman republic and observation of events in his own day: for this reason 'the simple conclusion is that it is more expedient to live under one king, than under the rule of many'.[161] Although he condemned the tyranny of the majority as shown in oppressive rule by the many over the rich (following Aristotle in classifying it as democracy, a perverse form of government), he had to admit that rule by one man was potentially both the best and the worst form of government: that as far as unjust governments went, democracy was better than the rule of a tyrant.[162]

Aquinas gave sparse treatment to the relationship between temporal and spiritual power. In his early commentary on Peter Lombard's *Four Books of Sentences* (the standard textbook of medieval theology written from 1155–8) Thomas followed a traditional line. The powers were distinct: both derived from God, but in such a way that the temporal was not derived from the spiritual, with the result that temporal power was subject to spiritual in matters affecting salvation, but was to be obeyed before the spiritual in civil ones. This division applied,

Unless perchance the secular power is also joined to the spiritual as in the case of the pope, who occupies the summit of both powers, spiritual and secular, through the dispensation of Him who is priest and king, priest for ever according to the order of Melchisedech, King of kings, and Lord of lords.[163]

It was, however, far from obvious what precisely Aquinas meant by this, as was also the case elsewhere in this commentary when he incorporated Bernard of Clairvaux's argument that the church possessed the temporal sword which was exercised at its command.[164] In the *De regno*, however, his own voice became far clearer. Because of the hierarchy of ends of human life he was unable to accord total autonomy to secular government. Spiritual guidance to man's higher end of eternal blessedness was entrusted to priests, not kings. In order to maintain the distinction between the powers, the ministry of Christ's kingdom was entrusted to priests,

And in particular to the High Priest, the successor of St Peter, the Vicar of Christ, the Roman Pontiff to whom all kings of the Christian people should be subject, just as to the

Lord Jesus Christ himself. For thus those who care for antecedent ends, should be subject to him who cares for the ultimate end, and be directed by his command.[165]

Aquinas, however, went into no further details concerning the relationship between the two powers and did not treat the problem of possible conflicts between them. He had, furthermore, nothing to say about disputes between papacy and empire; indeed, being concerned with kingdoms and city-states, he had no contribution to make about the Roman empire of his own day.

Aquinas was writing in the context of a Christian society: there was no question for him of accepting the full autonomy of a secular, political order within Christendom. He did, however, recognise that infidel governments, being based on the *ius gentium*, were valid, but did so only in a provisional way. He reserved to the church the right to abrogate existing infidel rule over Christians and maintained that the church could never permit the new establishment of such rule over the faithful. His harshest condemnations were reserved for those who had rejected the faith: heretics deserved death, and the subjects of any ruler excommunicated for apostasy were *ipso facto* freed from his rule and their oaths of allegiance to him.[166]

Despite his stature as a thinker, Aquinas was not the main transmitter of Aristotelian political ideas to the Middle Ages. This role was played by Giles of Rome (Aegidius Romanus) through his *De regimine principum* (On the Government of Princes), the most influential medieval example of the mirror-of-princes *genre*. The book enjoyed a vast influence and was translated into the main vernacular languages of western Europe, beginning with the French version of *c.* 1286. The reason behind the success of this work becomes clear as one reads it: the text is very readable – it flows on and on inexorably. By the standards of the Middle Ages it is systematic. It is, however, intellectually undistinguished: a classic example of the great impact of a work of, essentially, popularisation, albeit for a highly restricted governmental audience.

Giles's approach was different from that of Aquinas in that it was far more secular: it treated the state as something earthly and made no mention of relations between temporal and spiritual jurisdiction. Although Giles accepted the variety of political regimes, including republican ones in Italian cities, he strongly favoured monarchy, and, indeed, hereditary and unlimited monarchy at that.[167] Monarchy he considered to be in harmony with the natural order and a reflection of the divine hierarchy. The king for him was the 'living law' (*lex animata*), 'like a demigod' (*quasi semideus*), and 'intellect without concupiscence' (*intellectus sine concupiscentia*).[168] He used the metaphysical argument for unity and the Aristotelian view of a leading principle in any body or organism. The true monarch brought peace and, being the guardian of justice, ruled for the good of his people. Although the monarch was not subject to limits in the exercise of his power, Giles understood him as ruling within a normative framework: 'It should be known that the king and any ruler is the mediator between natural and positive law, for no one rules rightly unless he acts as right reason dictates; for reason should be the rule of human acts.'[169]

The assimilation of Aristotelian ideas by the 1280s completed the process whereby medieval political thought was transformed through the introduction of literary, juristic and philosophical languages derived from the ancient world. Nothing less than an intellectual revolution had progressively occurred in the twelfth and thirteenth centuries.

4

POLITICAL IDEAS IN THE LATE MIDDLE AGES, *c.* 1290–*c.* 1450

A fundamental shift in the nature of political thought became increasingly apparent from the turn of the thirteenth and fourteenth centuries. At the methodological level discourse became more sophisticated, largely because writers could draw on a developed *ius commune* and a received Aristotelian language. There emerged a noticeable trend towards a confrontation with political reality, and in particular with questions of power, a confrontation facilitated by these juristic and Aristotelian approaches. Reality became more and more the touchstone of political thought: acceptance of it, accommodation with it, attempts to change it – to advocate what should be the case. The first three decades of the fourteenth century were also noteworthy for producing lengthy treatises, which may be classed as political thought texts, and which in depth of treatment went far beyond exemplars of the existing mirror-of-princes *genre.* Indeed, fourteenth-century political thought as a whole was to prove the most productive and profound of the Middle Ages.

These intellectual developments took place in a context of radical historical change and deep crisis. By about 1300 population growth had reached the limits of subsistence, given available technology, with the result that deterioration in the climate early in the fourteenth century contributed to recurrent famines. The levelling-off of the population preceded the demographic catastrophe of the Black Death of 1347–51 which initiated a three-centuries long plague-cycle. Although the impact of the Black Death is highly debatable, the cumulative effect of these events was to produce massive changes in medieval society, so much so that the period after the mid-fourteenth century seems in many ways a different world from that which went before. The other great scourge of fourteenth- and fifteenth-century Europe, war, had direct political effects in that military financial demands led to the development of state machinery, as was notably the case in France and Italian cities.

The political history of the territorial states of the fourteenth and fifteenth centuries became increasingly complicated. Despite all the vicissitudes occasioned by wars and internal disorder, a general trend towards the further consolidation of territorial states could be perceived. This movement was reflected in political thought. Nevertheless, the claims of the Roman emperor were by no means dead. Although there was a growing tendency for emperors to concentrate on trying to conserve and increase their own family's lands within Germany, Henry VII (1308–14) tried to impose his authority on the whole of Italy during his expedition there from 1310–13, as did Lewis IV of Bavaria (1314–47) from 1327–30. Charles IV (1347–78), on his visit to the peninsula in 1355 to gain the imperial crown, came not as an invader but as a purveyor of imperial privileges; he made one return from 1367–8. Because, in legal terms, the Roman emperor remained the ultimate *de iure* sovereign in north and north-central Italy, there was good reason for the survival of the imperial idea in Italy as well as Germany; there also existed French pretensions to the crown of the empire. As a result imperial notions were strongly represented in political thought. Indeed, the theme of the relationship between universal and territorial sovereignty remained fundamental.

The other universalist power, the papacy, experienced a succession of deep troubles, beginning with the conflicts between Pope Boniface VIII (1294–1303) and King Philip IV of France (1285–1314). These disputes were followed by the papal sojourn at Avignon from 1309, during which the external prestige of the institution suffered despite (or partly because of) the pope's increasing jurisdictional and financial control over the clergy. During this period the papacy became embroiled in its last conflict with the empire in the Middle Ages, a lengthy one with Lewis IV, whom it never recognised as emperor. The papacy's return to Rome was immediately followed in 1378 by the outbreak of the Great Schism, the worst crisis of the medieval church. From that year there were two men who claimed to be pope with rival courts at Rome and Avignon. Europe became split along political lines. The Schism stimulated the emergence of the conciliar movement as an attempt to solve the problem through the calling of a general council of the church. The first such council held at Pisa in 1409 only succeeded in creating a third papal claimant. The Schism was finally ended at the Council of Constance in 1417. Conciliarism, which stressed the supremacy of the general council over the pope, was a diverse phenomenon which infused the subsequent councils of Pavia–Siena (1423–4) and Basel (1431–49). Although the popes survived the conciliarist threat and concentrated on building up their power as Renaissance princes, the credibility of the papacy as an institution was weakened through the legacy of the Schism, the effects of heresy (notably the Hussite revolt), and the criticism levelled by poverty movements. Conciliarist ideas occupied a particularly important place in the political thought of this period; notions of the role of poverty also contributed to the understanding of the nature of power and powerlessness.

By concentrating on the theme of the confrontation with political reality it is possible to give some shape to the complex and variegated mass of political thought in this century and a half. The crisis of church and state in the period up to the Black Death produced a rich crop of political ideas. The contributions of the jurists, both civilians and canonists in a *ius commune* context, were particularly important throughout the whole time-span, precisely because of their accommodation of authoritative texts to the political, social and economic realities of their society. Conciliarist ideas, in their origins, expression during the Great Schism and radical elaboration at the Council of Basel, were responses to the perceived needs of the church, and, through their concentration on its constitutional and governmental structure, had profound political implications.

IDEAS OF CHURCH AND OF STATE,
c. 1290–*c.* 1350

The conflicts between Philip IV and Boniface VIII

The pontificate of Boniface VIII and its immediate aftermath marked the watershed between the high and late medieval papacies. He was involved in two disastrous conflicts with Philip IV of France. The first concerned taxation of the clergy. Philip had taxed his to help pay for his war with Edward I of England, who had done the same with the English church. These royal actions contravened the decree of the Fourth Lateran Council according to which the clergy could not pay taxes to lay rulers without papal consent, although monarchs had taxed their clergy with papal acquiescence throughout the thirteenth century. Boniface could easily have compromised but chose not to. In April 1296 he issued the bull *Clericis laicos* which, without mentioning either king by name, forbade secular rulers to tax the clergy and the clergy to pay such taxes without licence from the apostolic see: the bull expressly stated that lay rulers had no jurisdiction over clerics or their property. Faced, however, with a royal embargo including the export of money from France, Boniface had to back down and, humiliatingly, in the bull *Etsi de statu* of July 1297 give Philip the privilege of exemption from the prohibition in *Clericis laicos*: the king could tax his clergy without papal permission in case of emergency. The second dispute was far more serious. In 1301 Philip had the Bishop of Pamiers, Bernard Saisset, arrested and tried in his presence at Senlis for blasphemy, heresy and treason. Saisset was then held there at the king's pleasure in nominally ecclesiastical custody. This was a breach of a fundamental principle of canon law whereby a bishop could only be judged by the pope. Boniface could have been accommodating with the French king; instead he opted for confrontation. In so doing he was following what may be broadly termed the hierocratic rather than the dualist tradition in canon law. He demanded Saisset's release, revoked the privileges granted in *Etsi de statu* and called all French bishops to a council in Rome to discuss the preservation of ecclesiastical liberty, the reform of the kingdom, the correction of the king's past excesses and the good government of the kingdom.[1] He thereby considered the temporal government of the French crown to be a matter of church concern. His onslaught culminated in the notorious bull *Ausculta fili* of December 1301 in which he reminded Philip, as his dearest son, that he had a superior and was subject to the head of the ecclesiastical hierarchy,[2] and also that no power over clerics was conceded to laymen. Because he did not qualify his claim to superiority, Boniface could well have appeared to be maintaining that the king was subject to him in both temporal and spiritual matters. The response of the French court was ferocious, including the whipping up of Parisian public opinion, condemnation of the pope at a form of Estates General, and pressure on northern French clergy not to attend Boniface's council. As in the first dispute, fundamental questions were at issue. From the royal point of view the sovereignty of the crown was at stake; the pope considered that he was defending the liberty of the church.

From the aspect of political thought the culmination of the second dispute was Boniface's bull *Unam sanctam* in which he deliberately chose to confront the question of the ultimate relationship between temporal and spiritual power. It was dated 18 November 1302, but may have been issued a few months later. This curious document was unique in that it was an official papal exposition of the general principles determining the subordination of secular to ecclesiastical power. There had been no decretal like it, not even Innocent III's *Venerabilem* or *Per venerabilem*, which had been focused on more specific issues. *Unam sanctam* contained no overt reference to the conflict with Philip IV. The bull contained nothing new: it was stitched together from statements and arguments culled from theological sources, although there was some juristic matter. Boniface set forth the model of a church within which all authority, spiritual and temporal, existed, and which was a mystical body (*corpus mysticum*) in a juristic, corporational sense, united under one head, Christ, and his earthly representative, the pope. Within this body, the relationship between spiritual and temporal power was strictly hierarchical. Boniface used a hierocratic interpretation of Bernard of Clairvaux's two-sword imagery in order to illustrate the way in which secular power was derived from, and exercised at the will of, the priesthood. Indeed, he said, 'The spiritual power has to institute the earthly power and judge it, if it has not been good', a paraphrase of the words of Hugh of St Victor, again to support his hierocratic argument.[3] The final sentence of the bull was the statement, 'We declare, state, define and pronounce that it is entirely necessary for salvation that every human creature be subject to the Roman pontiff'; but even this was based on Aquinas's words in his *Contra errores Graecorum* (Against the Errors of the Greeks).[4] All that was new about *Unam sanctam* was that the pope had chosen to make an official pronouncement of this kind.

In practical terms the bull achieved nothing at the time. It was a thoroughly damp squib. Boniface's pontificate ended in disaster: he died a few weeks after being imprisoned and manhandled by French forces at Anagni. Indeed, Pope Clement V, faced with intense pressure from the French crown, decreed in *Meruit* in 1306 that he did not wish there to arise from *Unam sanctam* anything prejudicial to the king or his kingdom, that the French king, kingdom and people should be no more subject to the pope than they had been before the bull, and that everything as regards the church and the king, kingdom and people should be in the same state as it was before.[5] In the years following Boniface's death there was very little canonist interest in the bull. Indeed, it only became part of the canon law in the sixteenth century, when it was included in the *Extravagantes communes*. Although *Unam sanctam* was referred to in the remainder of the Middle Ages, its real fame grew later, and notably in the works of modern historians.

Boniface had refused to accept the reality of the way in which the French state had grown; he denied, by implication, the validity of ideas which accorded any autonomy to the secular sphere. His whole approach must have somewhat bewildered the French monarchy which considered itself to be the guardian of the French church, a role which its clergy accepted. Indeed in 1290 Cardinal Benedict Gaetani, the future Boniface VIII, had as papal legate negotiated an agreement with Philip whereby a royal ordinance confirmed clerical privileges and the right of the Parlement of Paris to judge prelates and hear appeals from their temporal courts. The principle was reinforced that the king was the supreme judge in secular matters within his kingdom: in this respect there were no islands of clerical immunity, although ecclesiastical jurisdiction was protected. The French monarchy had always been seen by the papacy as its greatest support.

The conflicts between Philip and Boniface produced a flood of tracts devoted to the questions raised: as a crisis which stimulated political thought it bore comparison with the Investiture Contest. But the use which these works made of jurisprudence, scripture, Aristotle and historical examples revealed just how much development there had been in political thought since the late eleventh century. These writings fell into two broad groups: less extensive tracts, directly related to the disputes, and major theoretical works produced in the context of the conflicts. All shades of opinion, pro-papal, pro-royal and those seeking a middle way, agreed that Christ had divided the two powers; but this statement created more problems than it solved. In temporalities, was the king subject to the pope or was the church to the king? What did it mean to say that the powers were distinct?

Could either be involved in the sphere of the other in any way? Did the admittedly greater dignity of the spiritual power mean that the temporal was derived from it? Indeed, in sheer exasperation Boniface rejected the French suggestion that he was in any way usurping or minimising the power of the French king: 'It is forty years that we have been expert in the law and we know that there are two powers ordained by God' – a response which begged all the questions.[6]

Amongst the lesser tracts, the pro-royal *Disputatio inter clericum et militem* (Dispute between a Cleric and a Knight) was produced in *c.* 1297 in the context of the first dispute, and, as its title suggested, was couched in the dramatic form of an argument between a priest, putting forward a pro-papal position, and a knight refuting him in support of the king. The writer denied the pope any jurisdiction in temporal matters, asserting that the pope was the vicar of Christ in the humility of the latter's earthly life and not in the power and glory of his risen one; furthermore, the church had not used its temporal possessions and rights properly. The king's role was to protect the church; priests in return should pay taxes for the defence of the realm. Indeed, if the clergy were not co-operative, royal privileges to them could be revoked. In the conclusion, the knight reiterated the claim that the kingdom of France was independent of the empire and that the French king, as exercising imperial power in France, had supreme power over laws, customs, privileges and grants of liberties in his realm.[7] The tract *Rex pacificus* argued that the two powers were distinct on the Aristotelian analogy of the functions of the head and the heart, with the king being the heart and the pope filling the directing role of the head. In temporal matters the church was subject to the power of the king, who was Christ's vicar for such things. Although the spiritual power was higher in dignity than the temporal, this did not mean that the temporal was in any way derived from the spiritual. The sublime status of the Pope entailed neither that he was the temporal lord of all nor that he possessed temporal power over all.

The *Quaestio in utramque partem* (Both Sides of the Question), written in 1303, adopted a moderate approach. The writer began from the premise that 'temporal and spiritual things are in every way distinct and neither belong to the same genus nor share the same matter; temporal and spiritual powers are therefore distinct and do not depend on each other'[8] – a view diametrically opposed to a hierocratic one which could be seen as treating the two powers (in so far as they were possessed by the pope) as different aspects of one power. Human beings led a double life (*duplex vita*), a corporeal and a spiritual, and hence were citizens of two worlds (*duplex civilitas*). The author established the autonomy of secular government on the basis of naturalistic and ethical arguments from Aristotle and Cicero: the pope had, therefore, no predominance over the temporal order. Indeed, Christ had fled worldly power and ambition, advocating instead a life of poverty. He had possessed temporal power, but having chosen not to exercise it, had also forbidden its use to St Peter (and therefore his successors): he had only passed on his spiritual power. Hierocratic interpretations of papal power had made much use of Old Testament priesthood as a model: the author of the *Quaestio* denied the relevance of this approach on the grounds that they were not priests in a New Testament sense. The papal office was simply too sublime to exercise temporal jurisdiction. The tract, as it progressed, however, modified the strict distinction between the two powers by accepting that the pope could assume temporal jurisdiction in the cases recognised by canon law. The pope could even indirectly bring about the deposition of a king by absolving his subjects from their oath of allegiance (or rather declaring them so absolved) on the grounds of heresy or contumacy against the Roman church. In extraordinary cases the pope could assume both powers. The author was rejecting extreme papalist or royalist positions and stressed the interdependence of the two powers.

The three major theoretical tracts written in the context of the conflicts amounted to a new *genre* for the Middle Ages, in that they were not mirrors-of-princes but works of synthesis focused on specific themes, and in particular that of power. They were produced within a year or so of one another: all three were products of intellectual formation at the university of Paris. Giles of Rome's *De ecclesiastica potestate* (On Ecclesiastical Power), completed in 1302 and dedicated to Boniface VIII, was extremely hierocratic in content and would appear to have formed a basis for the construction of *Unam sanctam*. At Paris Giles had been the most prominent member of the Augustinian order, having been their first to hold a professorship in theology; in 1291 he had become Prior-General of the order and in 1294 had been made archbishop of Bourges by Boniface VIII, although he spent most of his time thereafter at the papal curia. The tract itself was devoted to the relationship between temporal and spiritual power, the topic omitted in Giles's earlier *De regimine principum* (On the Government of Princes) with its thoroughly secular and this-worldly tone. There was no contradiction involved because the two tracts argued on different levels and in different ways: they were connected, however, in that both were systematic treatments of monarchy according to hierarchical principles. *De ecclesiastica potestate* (On Ecclesiastical Power) was an extended essay on the implications to be drawn from the proposition of the spiritual sphere's supremacy over the temporal: the superiority of the priesthood over secular power was grounded on priority in time, dignity and scope. The tract's extreme papalism was reflected in its identification of the church with the pope who, 'a creature without halter and bridle', enjoyed absolute power in terms of positive law, which he should nevertheless normally observe.[9] The concept of lordship (*dominium*) was central to the tract: by it Giles denoted both power and property. The temporal power was subordinate to and derived from the spiritual which, following a hierocratic interpretation of Hugh of St Victor, instituted it. He also incorporated into his argument Bernard of Clairvaux's contention that temporal power was exercised at the command of the spiritual. The *dominium* of the church was universal, superior and primary; that of the faithful laity was particular and inferior. Although Giles accepted that the church would not normally intervene in secular matters, he dealt at great length with the cases which canon law accepted as justifying such intervention. His most extreme statements, however, concerned property. He argued, on the basis of the subordination of the body to the soul, that all property was subject to the church and the pope in particular. Estrangement from God deprived a person of any rights in this respect: a sinner in short could not rightly possess property. Since all people were sinners, and it was the church that reconciled sinners to God, property rights could only be derived from the church. As he said, 'The church is more lord of your possessions than you are yourself.'[10]

Giles's approach was eclectic in that he drew primarily on the Bible, canon law, Augustine, Aristotle and Pseudo-Dionysius; but the overall trend of his arguments was a form of *Augustinisme politique* in that he considered *dominium* infused by Christian justice to be the only true form. His text could appear thoroughly theoretical and removed from the needs of the contemporary church and society: an unreal response to a real crisis and, as such, an unhelpful encouragement to Boniface to part further from any real hope of influencing events. But Giles, like the pope, clearly thought he was being realistic. The clue lay in the idea of the hierarchy of realities: both men were seeking to express the higher reality lying behind and beyond the lower and purely surface reality of political life. Both Giles and Boniface thought that they were making statements of eternal truth. The irony was that truly hierocratic texts were produced in the early fourteenth century at precisely the time at which the papal monarchy as an institution was beginning its long, late-medieval decline. Giles was to be followed by other extreme hierocratic writers: Augustinus Triumphus, for instance, with his *Summa de potestate ecclesiastica* (Summa on Ecclesiastical Power) (1326) and Alvarus Pelagius with his *De planctu ecclesiae* (Lament of the Church) (1330–2).[11]

The second major theoretical text produced during the conflict between Philip IV and Boniface VIII was James of Viterbo's *De regimine christiano* (On Christian Rule) of 1302. James was also an Augustinian and his work, dedicated to the pope, used Giles's *De ecclesiastica potestate*. At the time of composition James was a master at the university of Paris; he was nominated archbishop of Benevento by Boniface in September of 1302 and became archbishop of Naples at the end of the same year. James's very clear and well-argued tract was justly called by Arquillière 'the oldest treatise on the church',[12] in that it was the first medieval attempt at ecclesiology. James began by defining the church as a *regnum*, because it was a community composed of many faithful. The first part of his work was concerned with the character of that *regnum*, and the second with the power (*potentia*) of Christ and his vicar, the pope. For James the church was hierarchically organised according to Gregory I's 'great order of difference' (*magnus ordo differentiae*), that is its gradated structure of orders and functions, an approach which differed from Giles of Rome's identification of the church with the pope.[13] In treating the relationship between temporal and spiritual power James developed Aquinas's concept of the connection between grace and nature in a particularly clear way:

> A middle way can be followed ... to say that the institution of temporal power materially and originally has its being from

144

the natural inclination of men, and through this from God in so far as the work of nature is the work of God; as regards its perfection and form it has its being from the spiritual power, which is derived from God in a special way. For grace does not destroy nature, but perfects and forms it ... Because the spiritual power looks to grace, and the temporal to nature, the spiritual does not exclude the temporal but forms and perfects it. All human power is imperfect and unformed unless it is formed and perfected by the spiritual. This forming is through approbation and ratification.[14]

Ultimately, therefore, temporal power served spiritual ends. James's argument was a hierocratic one. Temporal power pre-existed in the pope, whose temporal and spiritual powers of juris-diction were two aspects of the same royal power – 'a double power because it concerns diverse acts' relating to the two orders of beatitude, temporal and spiritual.[15] The pope had temporal power in a higher, directing and ordering way. James disposed of the objection that Christ did not exercise temporal power by saying that his choice not to do so did not mean that he could not pass it on to his vicar.

The third theoretical tract was that of John of Paris (Jean Quidort): his *De regia potestate et papali* (On Royal and Papal Power) was produced in 1302/3.[16] It was an abstract and scholarly work focused on questions of temporal and spiritual power and jurisdiction. It professed to argue in a way which would have general validity: it only contained a couple of references to the conflicts between Philip IV and the pope. Its purpose was, by defining the limits of the pope's power, to protect the monarchy against papal claims: John expressly sought to refute the hierocratic arguments of Giles of Rome and another pro-papal writer in the disputes, Henry of Cremona.[17] The tract could to this extent be classed as pro-royal, but was by no means excessively so with the result that some modern scholars have seen it as setting forth a middle way between polarised positions in the conflicts.[18] John's rejection of a hierocratic approach was shown by the way in which he pursued the theme of the separation of secular and spiritual power on the grounds that they were different in kind. Kingship he defined in naturalistic, Aristotelian terms:

It is clear that it is necessary and useful for man to live in a multitude and especially in one which can suffice for all the purposes of life, like a city or a region, and especially under the rule for the common good by one man who is called a king. And it is also clear that this government is derived from the natural law, because man is naturally a civil or political and social animal.[19]

Priesthood, in contrast, was purely spiritual: 'Priesthood is a spiritual power conferred by Christ on the ministers of the church to dispense sacraments to the faithful.'[20] According to John the natural origins of political communities entailed that different forms of state and government had arisen in different places in response to variations in climate, language and human conditions. This explained why any form of universal temporal rulership was unsuitable and, in fact, in terms of the realities of physical coercion, unworkable. John's political world was one of a plurality of territorial states, mostly kingdoms. In contrast he accepted the universality of the pope's spiritual government as being divinely ordained and practical, in that it operated verbally rather than by the material sword.[21]

As regards the relationship between secular and spiritual power, John considered that they existed in parallel, with the secular being greater in temporal things and the spiritual in spiritual ones. Both powers derived directly and ultimately from God. John struck at the central argument of a hierocratic position by differentiating the notion of hierarchy: he accepted the absolute superiority of the spiritual order over the temporal in terms of dignity, but by distinguishing between them in kind and purpose was able to avoid the conclusion that secular power was derived from and subordinate to the spiritual in temporal matters. Indeed, secular power was only so subject in those (spiritual) matters in which God had specifically subordinated it.[22] Although there was an ultimately divine source of authority in church and state the choice of individual incumbents, whether episcopal or royal, lay with human beings, that is the people: the pope was thereby excluded as a medium between God and man, both as regards royal power, which derived 'from God and the people electing the king in person or in his dynasty', and as regards the jurisdiction of bishops, which came immediately from God and the people's consent.[23] John further assaulted hierocratic argumentation by pointing out that Pseudo-Dionysius' thesis that the lowest could not be led to the highest except through intermediaries suggested that, since bishops only had spiritual powers, the pope through his position in the hierarchy only had such powers as well.[24] John, following Augustine and Pseudo-Dionysius, also denied that cosmetic allegorical arguments, such as those of the two swords or the relationship of the sun to the moon, had in themselves, without scriptural support, any validity for determining matters of jurisdiction.[25]

John did not, however, completely separate secular and spiritual power, which is why his tract has been described as seeking a middle way. He maintained that the pope could indirectly (or 'accidentally') depose a secular ruler, just as the emperor could indirectly depose the pope. Through excommunication the pope could bring it about that a delinquent prince was deposed by the people; similarly the emperor could cause the people to depose the pope. The pontiff could act against a king not only in spiritual matters but also in temporal, if the barons and peers of the realm so begged him. Likewise the emperor could correct the pope, if he was delinquent in temporal matters; if the pope's offence was in spiritual ones, the cardinals could call in the secular arm of the emperor to depose him. There were problems with John's argument – not least in the vagueness of his terms. He referred somewhat indiscriminately to 'prince', 'emperor' and 'king'. It was also not clear who the people were. Furthermore, there was a definite inconsistency with his overall argument for a plurality of territorial states, when he referred to the universality of the emperor's jurisdiction as legitimising the latter's power indirectly to depose the pope. Certainly, John's modification of the separation of the powers illustrates the difficulty of applying the term 'dualist' to his ideas.[26]

On the question of property, John set out at great length to disprove the arguments in Giles of Rome's *De ecclesiastica potestate* (On Ecclesiastical Power). John denied to the pope any rights of dominion or jurisdiction over the temporal goods of the laity: Christ had not exercised such powers. Rather, lay property was acquired by individuals through their own skill, labour and industry. Church property was held by ecclesiastical communities; the pope could therefore only be the dispenser, not the lord, of the church's temporal goods.[27]

The cumulative effect of John's scholastic method, marshalling authorities for and against propositions, was to provide biblical, juristic, historical and Aristotelian arguments which could be used for the cause of the French crown. He gave a detailed refutation of the validity of the Donation of Constantine as the basis for any papal claim to sovereignty over France. He finished his argument by showing that, even if the Donation had been valid, the imperial claims to jurisdiction lying behind it did not apply to the Franks who were free from subjection to the Roman emperor. Not only that, the empire had been founded on force and there was no guarantee that it would last forever: even if it had been God's will that the Romans should have supplanted previous empires, God could equally will the demise of the Roman empire.[28] John's tract certainly reflected the reality of the emergence of territorial states and the contemporary weakness of the empire, but in the early fourteenth century it was a matter of opinion whether the idea of empire still had strength in it, and how much political reality could be given to imperial claims. Certainly, French pretensions to the crown of the empire were very much alive, as was shown in Pierre Dubois' *De recuperatione terrae sanctae* (The Recovery of the Holy Land) of 1305/7[29] and Philip IV's campaign for the election of his brother Charles of Valois in 1308. Nevertheless, the prime home for apologists for the Roman empire was in Italy.

Italy: scholastic ideas and the myth of Rome

The early fourteenth century in Italy was an especially fruitful period for political thought, which benefited from the spreading of scholastic ideas and methods by Italian scholars who had been students in Paris. Ptolemy of Lucca, who had studied there under Aquinas, his friend and fellow-Dominican, produced his continuation of the latter's *De regno* (On Kingship) by *c.* 1305. He did not, however, gain the credit for this work, since throughout the rest of the Middle Ages (and indeed until the twentieth century) Aquinas was accepted as the author of the whole treatise. Ptolemy argued on two levels. He accepted what may be termed a hierocratic relationship between the pope and secular rulers: 'Just as the body has its being through the soul ... so also has the temporal jurisdiction of princes [its being] through the spiritual jurisdiction of St Peter and his successors.'[30] Indeed, 'Kings and princes are in God's place on earth; through them God governs the world as through second causes.'[31] On the political level he used naturalistic Aristotelian arguments. He was an advocate for the republican regimes of Italian cities: for them a 'political regime' (*regimen politicum*) was suitable, that is rule by the many (*dominium plurium*) – 'This regime properly belongs to cities, as we mostly see in parts of Italy, and it once flourished at Athens.'[32] He devoted the whole of Book 4 to this topic, supporting his argument with a host of examples from the history of the Roman republic. His aim was to mirror political reality, to which end he adopted a relativistic approach; for larger territorial units he accepted that a 'royal regime' (*regimen regale*) was suitable.[33] Political rule was adapted to those of 'virile mind and daring heart', such as were found in Italy.[34] Regal rule was acceptable, but political was better: indeed, political rule had been the only one in mankind's state of innocence before the Fall, whereas royal rule was suited to his corrupt and fallen nature.[35]

Remigio de' Girolami (d. 1319), also a Dominican who had studied in Paris, was a central figure in the spread of scholasticism to Florence, where he taught for more than forty years. Dante was familiar with his ideas and probably heard him preach, although it is not safe to say that he was his student. Like Ptolemy of Lucca, Remigio argued on two levels. He held that secular power was derived ultimately from that of the pope, who would normally not act directly in the temporal sphere. He was by no means an extreme hierocrat, however, as his opposition to the Donation of Constantine showed.[36] Faction-fighting in Florence, the most noxious aspect of the reality of public life in city-republics, provided the context for his political tracts, *De bono communi* (On the Common Good) (1302) and *De bono pacis* (On the Good of Peace) (1304). In these he applied Aristotelian arguments to Italian city-states. The atmosphere of political crisis led him to articulate his solutions in an arresting and, indeed, extreme manner. Citizenship with its communal obligations was fundamental to what a human being was: 'If he is not a citizen, he is not a man, because man is by nature a civil animal, according to the Philosopher in Book 8 of the *Ethics* and Book 1 of the *Politics*.'[37] The achievement of the common good was the supreme aim of political life, because this was the only way in which peace could be attained. Remigio firmly subordinated the good of the individual to that of the community. To reinforce his argument he pushed it to rhetorical extremes: a citizen should love his city next to God and be prepared to be damned for his city if he could go to hell without sin.[38] In his *De bono communi* he also supported his thesis with examples from the history of the Roman republic.

Dante Alighieri (1265–1321), poet and political thinker, was a victim of this communal strife at Florence: he was one of the White Guelph party expelled in 1301 by the Black Guelphs, supported by Boniface VIII. He spent the rest of his life in exile. His experiences made him an opponent of the temporal claims of the papacy. The solution he proposed for the ills of Italy was the re-establishment of a strong Roman empire, to which end he became a fervent supporter of Henry VII during his invasion. Although much of Dante's language is idealistic (and especially so in some of his political letters written at that time), it is beside the point to describe his ideas as unrealistic. Dante's perception was that the emperor was the only person who could bring to the peninsula that peace which the warring republics, lordships (*signorie*) and the papacy had destroyed. In so doing the emperor would be making effective in reality the ultimate sovereignty which was his in law.

Dante wrote his scholastic tract *Monarchia* (Monarchy) between 1309 and 1313 to demonstrate the necessity for a strong imperial power in Italy. He divided his work into three parts. In the first he sought to show that one temporal monarchy was necessary for the well-being of the world. His approach was initially philosophical without any reference to the Roman empire as such. He was influenced by the Averroist contention that there was one intellect for the whole of humankind, although he would not have argued this idea through to exclude personal immortality. More exactly, Dante, following Averroes, envisaged a human intellectual potentiality which he called the 'possible intellect' (*intellectus possibilis*), and which could not be realised in its entirety by any one person:

> It is the proper task of the human race, understood as a whole, always to actuate the total potential of the possible intellect, in the first place by speculation and secondarily by action, as the result and application of speculation.[39]

For this to be achieved peace was necessary which could only be brought about by the rule of one monarch or emperor.[40] He supported his thesis with other arguments: justice is strongest under a monarch who does not suffer from cupidity, having nothing to desire, and who is the minister of all.[41] Although he held that the human race should be ruled by one supreme monarch and directed towards peace by a common law, he accepted that, within this overall framework, nations, kingdoms and cities had different laws in accordance with local conditions.[42]

In the second part Dante sought to show that the Roman people acquired world empire by right. In so doing he gave powerful expression to the myth of Rome, deploying a mass of republican and imperial examples drawn from Roman history and literature. He argued that the Roman people was the noblest, and that its empire was brought to perfection by miracles willed by God.[43] The Roman people sought the common good: indeed, 'The Roman people, in subjecting the world to itself, aimed at the public good.'[44] Nature had ordained that Rome would rule the world, and Roman victory in the contest for world-empire must have been in accordance with the judgement of God.[45] Dante's culminating arguments were religious ones. By being born into the Roman empire Christ recognised that it had been founded on right, and by becoming man had recognised the validity of the Emperor Tiberius' decree that the whole human race should be registered.[46] Dante finished with a truly ingenious argument. For the atonement to be accomplished Christ had to be punished for the sin of Adam and the subsequent ones of all humankind. For such a penalty to be a true punishment, it had to be inflicted by a judge who had jurisdiction over the whole human race, which was being punished in the flesh of Christ. Tiberius (whose representative Pontius Pilate was) would not have had such jurisdiction if the Roman empire had not been founded on right. The Roman empire was therefore necessary for the atonement.[47]

The third part of *Monarchia* was devoted to the relationship between pope and emperor: did imperial power derive from God directly or through the pope? Dante conducted a *tour d'horizon* of hierocratic arguments, rejecting the approach of the Decretalists on the grounds of their ignorance of theology and philosophy.[48] Having demolished to his own satisfaction the hierocratic interpretation of the sun–moon allegory, on the grounds that the moon did not depend for its existence on the sun, that it moved under its own power and shone by its own light, although it received more abundant light (and therefore greater power) from the sun, he concluded:

> Temporal government does not receive its existence from the spiritual, nor the power which is its authority, nor even its operation as such; but it does receive help from the

151

spiritual government to operate more powerfully by the light of grace with which the blessing of the supreme pontiff infuses it in heaven and on earth.[49]

Dante proceeded to maintain that, although Christ was lord and governor of both spiritual and temporal matters, it did not follow that his vicar was as well.[50] He denied that the papal power of binding and loosing applied to imperial decrees and that the allegorical interpretation of the two swords as symbolising two forms of government was legitimate.[51] There then followed an extensive refutation of the validity of the Donation of Constantine, principally on the grounds that such division and destruction of the imperial power was impossible.[52] The empire did not depend on the church: the papal coronation of Charlemagne involved usurpation of a right, and in any case the empire existed before the church.[53] Furthermore, Dante could find no support in the Old or New Testament for priests involving themselves in temporal affairs.[54] Since Christ's kingdom was not of this world, Dante concluded that 'The power to give authority to the kingdom of this world is contrary to the nature of the church.'[55]

In his final chapter Dante explained that temporal and spiritual authority existed in parallel:

> Ineffable Providence has set before man two ends to aim at: the happiness of this life, which consists in the exercise of his own powers, and is symbolised by the earthly paradise; and the happiness of eternal life, which consists in the enjoyment of the vision of God (to which his own powers cannot rise unless helped by the divine light), which is understood as the heavenly paradise.[56]

Two guides had been appointed to lead man to his two ends: the pope to bring him to eternal life through Revelation; the emperor to conduct him to temporal happiness through philosophical teachings. The task of the emperor was to bring his subjects safe to port in peace and freedom through the vicissitudes of this world. God alone elected and confirmed the emperor, and gave him his authority directly, yet, as Dante said in the last sentences of *Monarchia*:

> The truth of this last question is not to be so strictly interpreted as meaning that the Roman emperor is not in some way subject to the Roman pontiff, since this mortal happiness is in some way directed towards our immortal happiness. Let

Caesar therefore observe towards Peter that reverence which a first-born son should observe towards his father, so that, illuminated by the light of paternal grace, he may shine more powerfully on the world, over which he has been set by him alone, who is the ruler of all things spiritual and temporal.[57]

This statement should not be understood as undermining Dante's distinction between the two powers: he recognised the hierarchy of ends which they both served. Clearly his was by no means a secular approach but a Christian one, according to which temporal government (including that of the emperor), within its own this-worldly sphere of operation, in no way derived from the church, which had a purely spiritual function. There should, however, be a mutually benevolent and beneficial co-operation between temporal and spiritual authority because humankind's earthly happiness led on to its eternal bliss. Temporal government was strengthened by the operation of supernatural grace.

Dante's *Divine Comedy*, begun around 1313 and completed shortly before his death, was a massive poetic work of theological and scriptural allegory, expressed in the form of the poet's journey into Hell, through Purgatory and into Heaven, but was also a vehicle for his political ideas. There was essentially a continuity of political views between the poem and *Monarchia*.[58] Dante set forth the heavenly empire (with God as emperor) as a model for the earthly, and stressed the emperor's role in establishing justice and the ideal society in the form of the Roman empire. The obstacles lying in the way of the emperor were the church, and in particular the papacy with its temporal jurisdiction and wealth; the French monarchy; and Florence, the archetype of the corrupt and wealthy city. In the emperor's absence, Italy lay in a pitiable condition, a horse without a rider;[59] only with a strong empire could there be peace and concord. Dante was highly inventive and lavish in the condemnation which he heaped on the papacy: he lamented the way in which the papacy combined both temporal and spiritual power, the sword with the pastoral crook.[60] He condemned the Donation of Constantine extensively, envisaging Christ as lamenting how ill-laden his little ship had become.[61] Constantine was however saved despite his disastrous Donation.[62] Most telling was St Peter's speech regretting what had become of the church.[63] The church, for Dante, should be poor in terms of both possessions and jurisdiction.

Marsilius of Padua and William of Ockham

The most remarkable political writer of the Middle Ages was a product both of an Italian city-republic and the university of Paris. Marsilius dei Mainardini (1275/80–1342/3) was born in Padua. He studied medicine, quite probably in his native city which was pre-eminent for such studies, and moved to Paris where he was made rector of the university in 1313. In 1316 and 1318 he was promised ecclesiastical benefices by Pope John XXII, in the expectation of which he was to be disappointed. He also served the interests of two great north Italian lordships: those of the della Scala of Verona and the Visconti of Milan. His most famous political work, the *Defensor pacis* (Defender of Peace), was completed in 1324. At first the lengthy treatise circulated anonymously. When Marsilius was identified as its author in 1326, he fled from Paris, accompanied by his colleague Jean of Jandun, to the court of Lewis IV of Bavaria at Nuremberg. Thereafter he actively supported Lewis in his conflict with the papacy, and went with him on his invasion of Italy. It is not known whether Marsilius' brief text *De translatione imperii* (On the Translation of the Empire) was written before or after his departure from Paris. At the end of his life, he produced the short *Defensor minor* (Lesser Defender) (1339/42), a form of continuation and application of the *Defensor pacis*.

Marsilius confronted papal power head-on: in the *Defensor pacis* he focused on what he considered to be the true cause of the most real problem of his time – the disruption of the peace of Italy and Europe. He sought both to demonstrate that the papacy's claim to plenitude of power was the source of strife, and to destroy the theoretical basis of that claim. The papacy and the clergy in general, he considered, should not pursue temporal power but should follow a purely spiritual life free of possessions and jurisdiction. In order to support his thesis he argued on both political and theological levels. These two approaches differentiated Discourse I, which sought to establish a general political theory by the exercise of reason, from Discourse II, which attempted, by the interpretation of scripture, to confirm Marsilius' argument concerning the special case of the papal exercise of plenitude of power. Through this dual treatment Marsilius was following contemporary methods of intellectual debate at Paris, as, indeed, had Giles of Rome in the two tracts which we have considered. The extent to which Marsilius was or was not thereby reflecting an Averroist approach has been debated by historians.[64] Certainly, he was exploring two different ways of examining the overall question.

Marsilius' technique was to argue from first principles; in the process he drew considerably on Aristotle, but interpreted him in his own way. In order to demonstrate what powers the clergy could not possess, Marsilius began by examining the origin, purpose and structure of the civil community. In so doing he produced a model of general application on a naturalistic basis. The purpose of this community was the sufficient life;[65] for this end, tranquillity was necessary, which was found when the parts of the community worked in harmony like the members of the body of an animal, a biological image reflecting Marsilius' medical training.[66] The structure of government rested on the ultimate authority of the whole corporation of citizens (*universitas civium*) which was identified with the human legislator (*legislator humanus*), which in turn elected the executive or ruling part (*pars principans*) and could depose it.[67] The ruling part in turn established the other parts and offices of the community. This theoretical structure was very flexible and capable of being applied to a wide range of possible political communities. The *pars principans* could be one, few or more in number. Marsilius also habitually referred, unspecifically, to the corporation of citizens or its 'weightier part' (*valentior pars*), thereby raising the possibility that the legislator could be very restricted in number.[68] Furthermore, the legislator could always delegate its law-creating powers to one or more persons. The essence of Marsilius' approach was to concentrate on the efficient cause – the will of the citizen body.

At the centre of Marsilius' overall thesis stood his theory of law. Having examined the different meanings conventionally attributed to the term 'law' (*lex*), he concluded that in its proper sense it signified a coercive precept entailing punishment or reward in this world.[69] Marsilius' emphasis on command as the constitutive element of law has caused an unresolved debate among modern historians as to whether he was a legal positivist.[70] If he were such, he would have been unusual indeed in the Middle Ages. In the course of his discussion on the nature of law he said,

> Sometimes false understandings of what is just and beneficial become laws, when a command is given to observe them or they are made by means of a command, as appears

to be the case in the lands of some barbarians, who have it observed as just that a murderer be absolved from guilt and civil penalty, on payment of a fine for such a crime. This, however, is absolutely unjust, and as a result their laws are not absolutely perfect. For although they possess due form, that is a command enforcing their observance, they none the less lack due condition, that is the proper and true ordering of justice.[71]

It is possible that in these cases Marsilius was willing to accept such laws as facts and therefore valid. His overall view, however, was to understand law as conducive to justice and the common good. He had very great confidence that the human legislator, more than any individual wise man, would know and will those laws which were in fact best for it, just as an animal would pursue its own health and preservation.

Marsilius treated the civil community as a unity of order. To secure its survival, the government, he held, must also be a unity.[72] He saw clearly the characteristically medieval problem of competing jurisdictions. For Marsilius, the human legislator and the *pars principans* held the monopoly of the making and implementation of law. Although his model for the political community was naturalistic, he had in mind citizen-bodies which would in fact be composed of Christians. The human legislator had jurisdiction, including powers of appointment, over bishops, priests and clergy, and, indeed, control over all the externals of religion relating to the good of the community.[73] Since Marsilius was particularly sensitive to the way in which excommunication could be used as a weapon by the clergy to undermine secular government, he placed this penalty securely in the hands of the 'faithful human legislator'.[74]

The culmination of Marsilius' argument, and his great intellectual coup, was to deny the validity of canon law, and, indeed, the possibility of its very existence as law in the proper sense.[75] Papal decretals were merely 'oligarchic ordinances' (*ordinaciones oligarchicae*):[76] they had not been issued by the sole competent law-making authority, the human legislator. With this breathtaking destruction of canon law, the whole edifice of papal plenitude of power came tumbling down. Marsilius was truly innovative in insisting that every political community must be a jurisdictional unity: there was, according to him, no possibility that temporal and spiritual jurisdictions could exist parallel to each other. There was, in short, simply no such thing as spiritual jurisdiction. Furthermore, the whole hierarchical structure of the church was no more, and no less, than a human institution: the pope, for instance, was to be appointed by 'a general council or the faithful human legislator lacking a superior'; nor had Christ ordained that the pope should be the successor of St Peter.[77] Christ could have exercised coercive power, but chose not to, and certainly did not pass it on to his apostles: indeed, he forbade his apostles to have coercive power over one another and had subjected himself to Roman civil authority.[78] Marsilius was certain that the papacy was an historical product of human making, with its origins in Constantine's Donation.[79] Marsilius' insight was that the jettisoning of plenitude of power and all spiritual jurisdiction as dead lumber would signal liberation for both the church as well as the civil community: the priesthood could no longer purport to be able to free subjects from their oaths of allegiance, but, living a life of apostolic poverty, would be able to concentrate its efforts on its proper, spiritual mission.

Although Marsilius' crusade against papal plenitude of power was his driving obsession and prime motivation, modern historians have been most divided about a secondary aspect of his thought. Was he, in his political theory, at heart a republican or a pro-imperial apologist?[80] Discourse I of the *Defensor pacis*, taken on its own, could certainly appear republican and, in writing it, Marsilius doubtless drew on his experience of Padua in his youth. Yet it could equally well be argued that Discourse I was primarily treating the political community on an abstract level of general application. Certainly, monarchy was treated there as a valid form of rulership; and in both Discourses Marsilius referred favourably to the French kings (and notably Philip IV) at the expense of the papacy. The justification for the pro-imperial interpretation of Marsilius is more complex. Towards the beginning of the *Defensor pacis* there was a form of dedication to Lewis IV and a later statement that the papacy, by impeding the proper exercise of imperial jurisdiction, had helped destroy the peace of Italy.[81] In his pro-imperial *Defensor minor* and *De translatione imperii* Marsilius explained the origin of the empire with direct reference to his model for the establishment of governmental authority, as expounded in *DP* 1.12. The corporation of provinces had transferred to the Roman people the revocable authority to

make laws for the whole world. The Roman people, thus constituted as human legislator, had then transferred its authority to the
emperor (and could revoke it), with the result that 'according to
human law there is a legislator, that is the corporation of citizens
or its weightier part, or the supreme prince of the Romans called
the emperor'.[82] This overt identification of the human legislator
with the emperor was foreshadowed in the *Defensor pacis*.
Marsilius there referred in Discourse II to the 'human legislator or
the prince by its authority' (*legislator humanus vel ipsius auctoritate
principans*) and accepted that the legislator could be one or many.[83]
Although it is essential to study both tracts for a proper understanding of Marsilius' political thought, there are dangers in
arguing backwards from the *Defensor minor* to elucidate the
meaning of the *Defensor pacis*. The most likely explanation is that
his commitment to the imperial cause developed further during
his exile. In the *Defensor minor* he was, therefore, legitimately able
to interpret the *Defensor pacis* in a pro-imperial sense. There is
little justification however for maintaining that his intention,
when he wrote the *Defensor pacis*, was to produce a model which
could identify the human legislator with the emperor. The
Defensor pacis illuminates Marsilius' meaning in the *Defensor
minor*, but the *Defensor minor* does not clarify that of the *Defensor
pacis*. There was, however, a basic consistency between the republican and imperial aspects of Marsilius' thought: in both cases the
human legislator was the source of authority. The emperor, like
other rulers, was appointed immediately by the legislator, but
ultimately by God as remote cause.[84] Similarly, the seven imperial
princes exercised their power to elect the emperor by delegation
from the supreme human legislator of the Roman empire.[85] In any
case, the coexistence of republican and imperial aspects in
Marsilius' political thought could be explained in a different and
parallel way. He could also be reflecting the contemporary
constitutional position in Italy north of the papal patrimony. In
this area there existed a hierarchy of sovereignty, with the
emperor being the ultimate superior and the remaining city-
republics enjoying a range of freedom varying from autonomy to
de facto territorial sovereignty. This interpretation would in no
way derive the emperor's authority from such cities, but would
respect Marsilius' view that the Roman people was the historical
human source.

Marsilius' fellow-exile at the court of Lewis IV, the English theologian and philosopher, William of Ockham (c. 1285–c. 1347), was also obsessed with the problem of the papacy, but approached it in a different way. Ockham was convinced that the church was faced with actual papal heresy in the case of Pope John XXII. The issue, in the first place, was poverty. Ockham was amongst those Franciscans who believed that John's attack on the doctrine of the apostolic poverty of Christ and his apostles, most notably through the bull *Cum inter nonnullos* of 1324, was a rejection of the foundations of their order, as sanctioned by previous popes, and heretical. The nightmare, treated as a theoretical possibility by canonists, had become reality.

It is particularly difficult to assess Ockham's political ideas. He was originally an Oxford-trained academic who, until 1324, wrote and lectured on theology and philosophy. In the mid-1320s he went to Avignon, where, probably at the command of Michael of Cesena, the Minister-General of the Franciscan order, he became involved in the poverty dispute with John XXII. Ockham also came under suspicion of heresy himself and was examined by a papal commission which considered theses in his theological works. Although he was never formally condemned, he fled from Avignon in May 1328, together with Michael of Cesena and his followers, ending up at the court of Lewis IV, first at Pisa and finally at Munich, where he was to spend the rest of his life. After 1328 he wrote, directly or indirectly, both against John (together with his successor-popes, Benedict XII (1334–42) and Clement VI (1342–52)) and also in support of Lewis in the latter's struggles with the papacy. Amongst these works of the second stage of Ockham's career were the massive *Opus nonaginta dierum* (Work of Ninety Days) (1332–4), concerning the poverty dispute, and the even larger *Dialogus* (Dialogue), which in Part I (1334) treated papal heresy and in the second tract of Part III (1337–) dealt with the rights of the Roman empire. In his *Contra Benedictum* (Against Benedict) Ockham attacked John's successor for perpetuating his predecessor's errors, and devoted the *Breviloquium de principatu tyrannico* (Short Discourse on Tyrannical Government) to a discussion of the nature and limits of papal power. Historians have disagreed profoundly about Ockham's political thought, and notably about whether it is possible to relate his theological and philosophical ideas to his political views. Any assessment of Ockham's thought is also hindered by his writing technique:

it can be difficult to discern his opinions from the confusing mass of opposing arguments he presented in some of his works.[86]

Ockham's approach was radically different from that of Marsilius. In many ways Ockham was a non-political or even anti-political writer: he certainly did not think that politics was very important – to this extent he echoed the view of Augustine. Marsilius in contrast was a political theorist concerned with issues of peace and power, whose notions about the nature of the church and the parameters of its authority were the product of his political ideas combined with theological positions heavily influenced by the poverty movement. Ockham's fundamental attitude was to consider truth more important than human authority. He was, therefore, very cautious about all human institutions and the capacity of individuals to act in accordance with their perceptions of the truth. He had great reservations in the face of political structures based on the exercise of power. Ockham's watchword was the Gospel-liberty of the Christian; his contribution to developing notions of the rights of individuals, irrespective of status or rank was noteworthy.

Unlike Marsilius, Ockham did not deny the validity of papal jurisdiction, but sought to limit its scope. Ockham respected the papacy as a divine institution, but rejected papal plenitude of power as it had come to be exercised in his day. His view was that the pope's power was primarily pastoral, but he did accept the existence of both spiritual and temporal jurisdictions, with the proviso that the pope and the emperor could each interfere casually in the other's sphere – that is, in extraordinary cases of need or emergency. The tendency of his thought was to desacralise secular power, basing it normally on the original consent of the community, and to bolster the spiritual mission of the papal office. In effect, Ockham rejected Marsilius' subjection of the church to secular control: whereas Marsilius had reached this position as part of the structure of his political theory, Ockham had no such confidence in the competence and goodwill of any government. It was, however, on the question of general councils of the church that Ockham most notoriously disagreed with Marsilius. The latter, through applying his model for the governmental structure of political communities to the church, located ultimate ecclesiastical authority in the faithful human legislator, which could summon a general council. Such a council could define doctrinal matters infallibly.[87] Ockham, in contrast, had no confidence in a body of this kind. He was highly unusual amongst medieval writers in denying the doctrinal infallibility of general councils. This position was an application of his attitude to truth and human authority. He had no confidence that the fathers of any general council would in fact be able or willing to determine the truth, which might reside instead in perhaps one Christian, maybe a woman or even an infant. With such an attitude, Ockham should not be seen as a forerunner of the conciliar movement in the church, although conciliarists were to use some of his ideas about general councils.[88]

As a nominalist theologian, Ockham held that only individuals had any reality. This approach helped distance him from Marsilius' views and underlay his respect for individual rights; but it also led him to reject the corporation theory of the *ius commune*, the other great intellectual movement of his time.

JURISTIC THOUGHT

Fourteenth-century jurists of the *ius commune* sought above all to accommodate the texts of the Roman, canon and feudal law (as contained in the *Libri feudorum*) to their contemporary society. Their works reflected the whole range of existing forms of political organisation and government and, in particular, confronted the realities of power. In a specifically Roman law context, the school of the Commentators, originating in the late thirteenth century, developed further the application of Aristotelian methods of argument to the elucidation of the *Corpus iuris civilis* and was, as modern historians agree, the high-point of civilian jurisprudence in the Middle Ages. The school began in France: the works of Jacobus de Ravannis (d. 1296) and Petrus de Bellapertica (d. 1308), who both taught at Orleans, were particularly important in the early stages. The Italian jurist, poet and friend of Dante, Cynus de Pistoia (1270–1336/7), who studied partly in Bologna and partly in France, was influential in bringing the Commentators' methods into Italy. There, civilian jurisprudence was dominated by a form of apostolic succession: Cynus taught the great Bartolus of Sassoferrato (1313/14–57) who, in turn, taught his younger colleague at Perugia, Baldus de Ubaldis (1327–1400): both in their day became the most famous jurists in Europe. An assessment of the contribution of the canonists in this period is less certain. The long-held assumption of a decline in the quality of canonist scholarship after the death of Johannes Andreae in 1348 must be questioned because of the standing of jurists such as Baldus de Ubaldis and Johannes de Lignano (d. 1383) (both of whom were canonists and civilians) and of Petrus de Ancharano (*c.* 1330–1416), Franciscus Zabarella (1360–1417) and Panormitanus (1386–1445). From the point of view of political thought, the emergence of a new *genre* of juristic writing, that of expert opinions (*consilia*), was particularly important because these were concerned with particular cases or questions which had arisen in practice. The collection of the canonist and civilian Oldradus de Ponte (d. *c.* 1337) is the earliest that survives.

The ruler's will and the normative structure

Juristic writers in this period developed further the already established trend of enlarging the scope of the ruler's will in the making and application of law. In so doing they were emphasising the role of power. Yet, following previous juristic tradition, they retained the overall normative context for the exercise of the ruler's will but refined the details of his right to derogate from higher norms. The general requirement of the ruler to have just cause in any such derogation remained, but increasingly there was a presumption amongst civilians, in the ruler's favour, that he did have just cause. There was however some reluctance in canonist circles to accept such a presumption. On the thorny question of subjects' private property rights the common juristic opinion was that such rights, being the product of the *ius gentium*, could only be removed or transferred by the ruler with just cause. Jurists, such as Jacobus de Ravannis, Petrus de Bellapertica and Cynus recognised, however, that in practice rulers did brush aside such a limitation, but held that they sinned in so doing. There was, however, evidence of another strand of juristic opinion which held that the emperor at least, through the exercise of his will alone, could remove his subjects' property without cause, an opinion rejected by Bartolus as an infringement of justice but followed by Jacobus Butrigarius (*c.* 1274–1348) and Baldus.[89]

The normative limitations on the exercise of jurisdiction were not exhausted by the categories of natural law, divine law and the *ius gentium*: late medieval jurists also treated feudal custom as having the status of a fundamental legal norm. It became commonplace to treat custom, including feudal ones, as second nature. Indeed, jurists interpreted feudal law as providing a much more effective bridle on the will of the ruler than other norms. It is difficult to exaggerate just how deep-seated feudal attitudes had become amongst jurists and just how far legal relationships had, where relevant, become coloured by feudal characteristics.[90]

The academic jurists produced a systematic treatment of feudal relations through commentaries on the Lombard *Libri feudorum* which the Glossator Hugolinus (d. 1235) added after 1220 to the *Corpus iuris civilis* as a tenth collation of the *Authenticum*. This meant that the purely medieval phenomenon of feudal custom was henceforth firmly located within the structure of the *ius commune,* and came to be treated in a wide range of juristic discourse, including *consilia.* Although the scholarship of the *Libri feudorum* was academic law of a specific kind distinct from the differing legal expressions of feudal relations emerging in various parts of Europe and thus to some extent artificial, it nevertheless illustrated the tendency of medieval *ius commune* jurisprudence to address the needs of contemporary society.[91] Furthermore, the *Libri feudorum* was only one source for the influx of feudal notions into the *ius commune*: they seeped anyway into civilian and canonist discourse through the influence of late medieval socio-legal structures, deep mentalities and legislation, both secular and ecclesiastical.

The elements of contract, consent, and mutual rights and duties inherent in feudal relationships were accepted by jurists as axiomatic and therefore severely limiting the exercise of the ruler's will. The civilian Guido de Suzaria (d. *c.* 1290) was important in establishing the juristic common opinion that the *princeps* was bound by his contracts and privileges, including feudal ones, on the grounds that they were guaranteed by natural law and the *ius gentium.*[92] Baldus, who wrote a highly influential commentary on the *Libri feudorum,* said of the emperor in a feudal context: 'God subjected the laws to him, but did not subject contracts to him.'[93] Furthermore, according to Baldus, the emperor was bound by his predecessors' feudal contracts and privileges because they were made by virtue of the imperial office.[94] The tendency of the *ius commune* was to protect feudal rights once established. The feudalising of relationships was also revealed at the highest level – that between emperor and pope. Originally the bond of faith established in the papal creation of the emperor had nothing to do with feudal notions. By the thirteenth and fourteenth centuries, however, the papacy had come to see the coronation oath sworn by the emperor as being feudal in nature and thus imposing obligations on the emperor as a papal vassal. This view was encapsulated in Clement V's constitution *Romani principes* (Clem. 2.9.1) of 1314, but had been rejected by Henry VII. But because of the reciprocal nature of the feudal bond, Baldus was able to accord to the emperor a right of armed resistance against the pope, if the latter acted unjustly in feudal terms:

> The church has a reciprocal obligation to its vassal, and cannot harm him [i.e. the emperor] as regards his empire. Indeed the pope shows himself unsuited to his power if he does not render such justice to the emperor who swore fealty to him ... And the emperor can defend himself with his army.[95]

At a lower political level, Italian jurists had also to accommodate the way in which power relationships in Italy became increasingly feudalised, from the mid-thirteenth century onwards, through popes and emperors granting vicariates and other feudal titles to *signori*, the emerging class of lords drawn mainly from the feudal nobility, with the most notable case being that of the imperial dukedom of Milan, created by Wenceslas, as King of the Romans, for Giangaleazzo Visconti in 1395.

In the early fourteenth century, in one area in particular, notable advances were made in limitations on the power of the ruler: that of due legal process seen as a natural right. In 1303 Boniface VIII issued the decretal *Rem non novam* (Extrav. comm. 2.3.1), which decreed that a summons was valid even if the accused did not know of it. The summons was deemed to have been issued by being affixed to the door of the principal church where the curia resided. The pope had in mind cases in which it was either dangerous to deliver the summons or the accused would avoid receiving it. In his gloss on this decretal, Johannes Monachus (1240/50–1313) argued that a summons was a requirement of natural law: justice could not be served unless the accused were present in court. The jurist saw this right as part of the liberty of a Christian man. He was thus confronting a fundamental problem: the rights of the ruled in a hierarchical governmental structure. He was saying that the indigenous rights of a Christian imposed a normative limitation on the pope's freedom of action as a ruler: Johannes had clearly understood the enduring theme of medieval Christianity that all the baptised were children of the free woman not the slave-girl, and that they had rights of liberty by virtue of their baptism, as Gregory the Great had emphasised. To reinforce his point, Johannes turned to the Aristotelian categories of despotic and political rule: he likened the government of the church to the political, in that it was exercised over free subjects who possessed the right of resistance, as opposed to the despotic, which was that of a master over his slaves. It has been argued that this gloss formed part of Johannes' support for the reinstatement of the Colonna cardinals, curial opponents who had been deposed by Boniface VIII.[96]

Due process next became one of the questions at issue in the conflict between Henry VII and Robert of Naples (1309–43), the Angevin king of Sicily. In the course of his expedition to Italy, Henry attempted to impose his authority on Robert who held his kingdom in liege homage from the pope. In September 1312, Henry summoned Robert to stand trial for treason in his presence, but without having the summons delivered to the king in person, his excuse being that his messengers would have been in mortal danger. When Robert failed to present himself within the time prescribed, Henry summarily condemned him to death in February 1313. Henry then justified his actions with two decrees: *Ad reprimendum* which stated that anyone committing treason against the emperor or the king of the Romans could be condemned in his absence in summary judicial proceedings, and *Quoniam nuper est* which defined who rebels against the empire were. Henry's legislation was rapidly incorporated into the *Corpus iuris civilis*.

Oldradus de Ponte, since 1311 auditor and judge in the Rota at the papal court at Avignon, produced, for Clement V, two *consilia* (numbered 43 and 69 in the printed editions) concerning the juristic aspects of the dispute between Henry and Robert. In *Consilium* 43, Oldradus treated the issues of due process involved in the dispute. He argued that the accused had a natural right of self-defence which required a properly delivered summons. On these grounds, Oldradus was able to impugn the validity of Henry's citation of Robert.[97] In *Consilium* 69, he argued that the empire was territorially confined and that kings outside it, like the Sicilian, the Spanish or the French, were not subject to the emperor.[98] Clement V was selective in his use of Oldradus' arguments. In March 1314, he published the constitution *Pastoralis cura* (Clem. 2.11.2), in which he declared that Henry, through the way in which he had summoned Robert, had infringed due process by violating the accused's natural right of self-defence. The pope thereby incorporated into canon law the principles of due process which had been enunciated by jurists and which, by this initiative, were to become firmly entrenched in the development of the *ius commune*.[99] Furthermore, according to Clement, the summons was in any case invalid because Robert was ordinarily domiciled in the kingdom of Sicily which was outside the territory of the empire, and for which Robert was the pope's vassal and thus not subject to the emperor – a traditional papal argument.

The dispute between Henry and Robert also occasioned the papal constitution *Saepe* (Clem. 5.11.2). In *Ad reprimendum* and his subsequent definitive condemnation of Robert, Henry had applied the canonist procedure of summary jurisdiction encapsulated in the words 'simply, plainly, without clamour and the normal forms of procedure' (*simpliciter et de plano, ac sine strepitu et figura iudicii*). Clement's annulling of Henry's legislation and actions, on the grounds that they infringed due process, made it acutely necessary to define more closely what was meant by this formula in the interests of clarifying summary justice in canon law proceedings. Clement did this in *Saepe* which insisted on necessary proofs and legitimate defence, and stated that a summons was necessary. In juristic terms the long-term result of this dispute was the permanent canon law contribution to the *ius commune* doctrine of due process acting as a restraint on the power of princes.[100]

The remaining form of limitation on the exercise of the ruler's will was treated by fourteenth- and fifteenth-century jurists as having the status of a universally valid norm: the rights of the community, the *iura imperii* or *iura regni*. The jurists, in their discussions, were drawing on legal tradition underpinned by assumptions which were fundamental to medieval political ideas and which stretched back into late antiquity. These jurists stressed that emperorship and kingship were offices or dignities established with the specific purpose of securing the preservation and well-being of the communities which the ruler served. Such offices were immortal, as were the communities themselves, and were distinct from the mortal men who operated them. The power of monarchs was hedged round by the purposes for which monarchy existed, which could be summed up in the requirements of the common good. Two texts in particular served as a focus for the development of such ideas. A shortened version of the Donation of Constantine had been included in Gratian's *Decretum* (Dist. 96, c. 14) and, as a result of its discussion by canonists, had been introduced by Accursius into civilian jurisprudence in about 1220. A central aspect of juristic treatment of the Donation concerned the question of whether the emperor was infringing the duties of his office by alienating part of the empire to the papacy.[101] In his decretal *Intellecto* (X.2.24.33), Honorius III (1216–27) had declared that the king of Hungary, by virtue of his coronation oath, could not make alienations prejudicing his kingdom and the honour of his crown. This text became the *locus classicus* for juristic elaboration of the inalienability of the kingdom's rights.[102] Particular stress was laid on the king's tutorial function which succinctly expressed his role of conservation and protection.

Although fourteenth- and fifteenth-century jurists placed an increasing emphasis on the role of the ruler's will, the extent to which they elaborated this large range of limitations to his freedom of jurisdictional action underlined that they in no sense upheld a positivist theory of law. Although the language of absolute monarchy existed in the form of the distinction between the ruler's *potestas absoluta* and his *potestas ordinaria*, he remained hedged in by normative limitations. But the perennial problem remained. The jurists intended such limitations to be taken seriously, but could a limited monarch of this kind be controlled in practice? It was at this point that the weaknesses of the juristic approach became apparent. All were agreed on the evils of tyranny: Bartolus, in his *De tyranno*, wrote one of the most sophisticated medieval tracts on this subject.[103] No legal problem was seen in the removal of a tyrannical *signore* by his oppressed subjects. As regards kings, however, responses were more circumspect: Baldus, for instance, accepted that a people could expel its king for tyranny, but that he still retained his royal dignity – that is, his office.[104] There was, furthermore, no juristic consensus about the pope's claim to universal powers of judgement *ratione peccati* because of civilians' fears that secular jurisdiction would thereby be eroded. Jurists were realistic about the problems of enforcing normative limitations, but they considered them to have real value in defining the boundaries of legitimate power.

Territorial sovereignty

In the fourteenth century, jurists further developed ideas of territorial sovereignty, but whereas previously the focus had been on kingdoms, now it included Italian city-states as well. The problem in Roman law terms was that in the *Corpus iuris civilis* cities enjoyed the status of *municipia*, licit corporations subject to imperial confirmation for their legal rights. The Glossators had, therefore, understood sovereignty to lie with the cities' superior, the emperor. Even when Azo, for instance, admitted custom as the source for the full powers of jurisdiction of some Lombard cities, he had retained imperial consent through acquiescence as the ultimate validation. Amongst the early Commentators, Jacobus de Ravannis had admitted that some Italian cities recognised no superior, and Petrus de Bellapertica and Cynus had referred generally, but without approbation, to peoples who did not recognise the emperor's sovereignty. But none of this amounted to an articulated civilian theory of the sovereignty of independent city-*populi*. Furthermore, canonist tradition had not produced a theory of the sovereignty of cities to match its justifications for the sovereignty of kings. It was the achievement of Bartolus to elaborate a theory of popular sovereignty to accommodate the political reality of independent city-republics.[105]

Bartolus' argument, building on the work of earlier Commentators, drew the full implications from the element of consent in popular law-making in the form of statute and custom. He saw that in the creation of law the consent of the people could act as a complete alternative to the will of the superior. Bartolus began his argument with customary law, which, being made by consent, did not require the authorisation of a superior. But statutes, since they were the product of the people's express consent, were in consequence of the same force (*paris potentiae*) as their custom, which was their tacit consent: statutes also therefore did not need the authorisation of a superior.[106] Bartolus next took the crucial step of maintaining that consent as the constitutive element of the people's law led beyond this to the non-recognition of a superior, the fundamental requirement for sovereignty. He held that the city which did not recognise a superior (*civitas quae superiorem non recognoscit*) was in the position of a free people (*populus liber*), a daring use of this term because he was applying it to Italian cities, which for him were certainly within the empire,

168

whereas in the *Corpus iuris civilis* it signified an independent people outside the empire but possibly in alliance with it. To indicate the complete independence of such a city, Bartolus produced his masterstroke by attributing to it within its territory the same powers of jurisdiction which the emperor enjoyed in the empire as a whole: it was a city which was its own emperor (*civitas sibi princeps*). This completed the argument because the emperor, in civilian terms the model for sovereignty, was thereby supplanted. There was no clearer way of signifying the sovereignty of such cities in Roman law terms. Through his understanding of the power of consent Bartolus had adapted the established formula for a sovereign king, 'the king in his kingdom is the emperor of his kingdom', into a form suitable for a corporate entity, the city-*populus*. Bartolus' thesis should be seen within the context of the *de iure-de facto* dichotomy. His whole argument from consent justified the full legitimacy of *de facto* jurisdiction. For him the *de iure* and *de facto* structures of power existed in parallel. Cities could obtain jurisdiction *de iure* by imperial concession, which implied subjection to the emperor as superior; they could also exert their sovereignty by *de facto* non-recognition of the emperor as their superior, which would result in prescription or, in some cases, usurpation of imperial powers.

Baldus in his treatment of sovereign cities wrote in the context of Bartolus' argument, but had an even clearer understanding of the role of popular consent in the establishment of *de facto* sovereignty. Baldus' approach was distinguished by his integration of the ultimately Aristotelian concept of natural, political man into a jurisprudential structure. Previous and contemporary civilians had paved the way for this move. The entry of overtly political concepts into jurisprudence had been prepared by the community of terms such as *civis, civitas* and *civilis* in both legal and political science, and the way in which Roman and canon law had been seen as the subject-matter of political science before the reintroduction of Aristotle's *Politics*. Reference to political man was made in the commentaries on the Proem to the *Digest* by the southern French jurist Guilelmus de Cuneo (d. 1335), Cynus and Albericus de Rosciate (*c.* 1290–1360). Bartolus referred to political man in the sense of a freeman as opposed to a slave in a tract written at the end of his life, but, apart from one other use of the term 'political' in his commentary on the *Code*, otherwise used Aristotelian political categories only as a means of distinguishing between forms of government in his tract *De regimine civitatis* (On the Government of the City), where he went on to describe Aristotelian political terms as being not to the taste of jurists.[107] Baldus, in contrast, used the concept of natural political man in a systematic way to provide a philosophical foundation for the *de facto* argument. For him the *ius gentium*, being a product of natural reason in so far as it underwrote both the existence and sovereignty of city-states, was an expression of man's political nature. Thus the Bartolist justification of city-sovereignty on the basis of the efficacy of popular consent, an argument resting on the acceptance of legal facts, was given an ultimate philosophical foundation beyond the *ius gentium* itself.[108]

It is notable that neither Bartolus nor Baldus used the *lex regia* as the basis for their theories of the sovereignty of city-*populi*. It was a commonplace amongst late medieval jurists to discuss whether the *lex regia* had been revocable or irrevocable on the Roman people's part: to this extent the text provided a focus for discussions of popular sovereignty. But jurists had a choice about whether they extended the application of the *lex regia* beyond the relationship between the emperor and the Roman people. Both Bartolus and Baldus considered the *lex regia* to have been irrevocable: their arguments for the sovereignty of cities were legal interpretations of aspects of the political reality which confronted them and not extrapolations from a historical event which they understood to have taken place in antiquity.[109]

There were two main strands in the juristic treatment of kingdoms. In the first, there was further elaboration of the contention which denied the universal *de iure* sovereignty of the emperor. The Neopolitan jurist Andreas de Isernia (d. *c.* 1316), in his commentary on the *Libri feudorum* (*c.* 1300), argued that a king in his kingdom possessed the same power as the emperor in the empire, but in the sense that a kingdom and the empire were essentially the same kind of territorial body. The world, he maintained, had returned to its pristine condition before the conquests of Rome – that is, a plurality of kingdoms.[110] Oldradus in *Consilium* 69, justified the independence of kingdoms outside the territorially confined empire by arguing that the Roman emperor was not *de iure* lord of the world, because the Roman people, lacking any just title to dominion over other nations, could not through the *lex regia* have legally transferred any such authority to the emperor. For Oldradus, the *de iure* independence of kingdoms was based on the *ius gentium*. Indeed, that of the Sicilian and Spanish ones was further reinforced by the fact that their inhabitants had conquered their lands with their own blood. Similarly the king of France was subject to the emperor neither *de facto* nor *de iure*. Furthermore, Oldradus, giving considerable emphasis to biblical authorities, was unable to find any justification in the Old or New Testaments for the divine origin of the empire, and also rejected the papal claim to have transferred the empire: his grounds were that the church could not thereby have created a right which did not previously exist.[111]

The second strand was that of the Commentators' mainstream interpretation which retained the *de iure* sovereignty of the emperor. Jacobus de Ravannis had maintained that *de iure* sovereignty resided only with the emperor, whatever the claims of the king of France – a view supported by Petrus de Bellapertica.[112] Bartolus had neglected kingship in his commentaries, although, in his tract *De regimine civitatis* (On the Government of the City), he argued that different forms of government were suited to states of different magnitude, with monarchy being suited to one of the largest size. It was Baldus who treated kingdoms within the overall *de iure–de facto* structure which he had applied to cities. According to Baldus, peoples, deriving their origin from the *ius gentium*, could on this basis by the exercise of their natural reason establish, through election, their form of government – either republican in the case of cities or monarchical in that of kingdoms. The fully legitimate sovereignty of kings rested therefore on a *de facto* foundation.[113] Baldus accepted that the *de iure* and *de facto* structures coexisted in a peculiarly medieval form of hierarchy of sovereignty. For him the sovereignty of an independent king was of a higher kind than that of a city within the lands of the empire (*terrae imperii*) in Italy north of the papal lands, where it was always possible that the emperor might appear to exercise his rights.

As regards the other main form of territorial rulership prevalent in fourteenth-century Italy, that of the *signori*, there were marked differences of approach between Bartolus and Baldus. Bartolus was unsympathetic to them and tended to condemn them as tyrants. Baldus, in contrast, accepted that their existence was a political fact of life; indeed, for the last ten years of his career (from 1390) he served the greatest of them all, Giangaleazzo Visconti. Baldus accepted both *de facto* and *de iure* justifications for the rule of *signori*. He wrote several *consilia* in which he explored the legal implications of the *de iure* grant of an imperial dukedom to Giangaleazzo. Baldus held that his master exercised truly imperial powers and that in him the empire had risen from the dead.[114]

Corporation theory

The most significant contribution of fourteenth-century juristic thought, however, lay in the application of corporation theory to independent cities and kingdoms. The Commentators considered that a corporation (*universitas*) was at one and the same time a body composed of a plurality of human beings and an abstract unitary entity perceptible only by the intellect. The Glossators, in contrast, had almost universally identified the corporation with its members: as Accursius had said, 'the corporation is nothing other than the men who are there.'[115] The Commentators, however, saw the corporation's human components not as mere isolated individuals (*singuli*), but as corporate men (*universi*) – that is, men seen specifically as united in a corporate whole, a view anticipated to some extent by Johannes Bassianus, Azo and, indeed, Accursius himself. The Commentators also understood the corporation to be a legal person distinct from the individuals who composed it. Thirteenth-century jurists had invented the use of the term *persona* to denote a legal person, with a particularly important role being played by Innocent IV. Through a constructive use of fiction jurists had created a legal entity with legal capabilities and a purely legal existence: the corporation was, in short, a fictive person (*persona ficta*).[116]

Baldus, while following the same path as Bartolus, developed the political application of corporational thought further than did his master. In commenting on Accursius' definition of the corporation, Baldus explained how the two aspects of the city-*populus* as a corporation combined: it was a collection of men into a unitary entity understandable only by the intellect, a definition embracing both the abstraction and the men who formed the material basis for this abstraction. Like all corporations, the people in its abstract aspect was immortal. Furthermore, Baldus viewed the natural, political men who composed it as corporate men: to be a citizen was to be a member of such a corporation. For both Bartolus and Baldus the city-*populus* as a corporation acted through the instrumentality of its mortal members organised in a structure of councils and representative elected officials.[117]

Baldus also applied corporation theory to kingdoms in a highly effective manner. For him, the kingdom, quite apart from being a territorial entity, was identified with its members but was also distinct from them in that it possessed an abstract and perpetual aspect in the form of the *universitas* or 'republic' of the kingdom (*respublica regni*). This immortal corporation of the kingdom established a similarly undying legal person, the royal office, or *dignitas*, which it conferred on its mortal king for him to operate. This was the classic formulation of the doctrine of 'the king's two bodies': Baldus considered that there were two completely different kinds of person in the king – one was human and mortal and the other abstract, perpetual and legal (his *dignitas*). As he said, 'The person of the king is the organ and instrument of that intellectual and public person; and that intellectual and public person is the principal source of action.'[118] The individual king acted therefore as the personification of his dignity.

Bartolus and Baldus, in their political application of corporation theory, produced state concepts which were clearly different from those elaborated by writers within the tradition of Aristotelian-based political science, which tended to identify the state with its members. For instance, Aquinas, as we have seen, understood the state to be a unity of order of its members. Furthermore, the juristic corporational approach was not acceptable to nominalist theologians or philosophers: Ockham, for instance, expressly rejected the jurists' *persona ficta* concept because for him any group was identified with the individual human beings who composed it.[119] Baldus in particular, in so far as he treated territorially sovereign cities and kingdoms as transpersonal, abstract entities distinct from their members or government, made a crucial contribution to the development of what is generally seen as a hallmark of the early modern conception of the state. Yet his approach, in so far as he recognised a relationship between the corporation as an abstract entity and its material substratum of constituent human members, retained, like the Aristotelian tradition, an essentially organic conception of the state, although he could perhaps be credited with an abstract organic view. The step had yet to be taken to a fully early modern idea of the state as an abstract locus or apparatus of power entirely distinct from any human beings, whether its members or governors.

CONCILIAR IDEAS

Origins

The conciliar movement of the fourteenth and fifteenth centuries marked an outright assault on papal monarchy as it had developed in the high Middle Ages. Although a movement as such can only be discerned from the period of the institutional breakdown in the government of the church, caused by the Great Schism, there had been a sudden surge of conciliar ideas in the years from the pontificate of Boniface VIII to the death of Marsilius of Padua. These ideas, and the movement into which they coalesced, were very varied, and indeed eclectic in their sources, covering a broad spectrum of opinion, and had an ancient pedigree stretching back to the councils of the early church and to the original practice of election by consent to ecclesiastical office. Justifications for conciliar ideas were produced from the Bible and church history. The *ius commune*, and high medieval canon law in particular, also provided a major source, both in terms of the treatment of the problem of the heretical pope and corporation theory. Conciliar ideas could be seen as having both a purely ecclesiological significance and as also being a contribution to political thought since they were concerned with the government of the church. Aristotelian political science was also drawn upon.

The context for the recrudescence of conciliar ideas was provided by the conflict between Philip IV and Boniface VIII, and its aftermath. In 1297 the dissident Colonna cardinals had already called for a general council to be summoned to annul the pope's process against them. In March 1303, Philip's minister, Nogaret, at a council of French bishops, had demanded that a general council be called to judge and depose Boniface on grounds of heresy and usurpation; this demand was repeated at a meeting of the French Estates held in the following June. John of Paris in his *De regia potestate et papali* (On Royal and Papal Power) agreed that a general council could depose the pope on the grounds that it implicitly represented the Christian people.[120] He also held that the pope could not determine dubious matters concerning the faith without calling a general council, because 'the pope with the council is greater than the pope alone'.[121]

It was, however, the canonist Guilielmus Durantis the Younger (*c.* 1266–1330), bishop of Mende, who expressed the most strikingly original ideas concerning the relationship between the pope and general councils.[122] He developed his views in the context of the French crown's calls for a council to judge Boniface posthumously for heresy, simony and treason. In 1308, largely in response to the Templar crisis, Clement V did issue a bull of convocation of a council to take place at Vienne; in it he requested that bishops and archbishops should submit written reports of the reforms they judged to be necessary. Guilielmus wrote his *Tractatus maior* (Greater Tract) in response. In contrast to the Decretalists as a whole, whose works, before the Great Schism at least, showed little interest in the question of councils, Guilielmus manipulated a wealth of canon and Roman law knowledge to construct his theory. He proposed a fundamental change in the constitution of the church whereby councils should be regularly called every ten years: they would thus become a part of the church's normal governmental structure. This reform, if implemented, would in itself remove one of the pope's greatest prerogatives of power: that he alone could validly summon a general council. Further, Guilielmus proposed that all general legislation in the church should take place only in such a council, and that the pope should not be able to dispense from conciliar decrees unless a council had been convoked. In addition he placed the pope under conciliar budgetary control. Guilielmus described his proposals as 'reform in head and members' (*reformatio tam in capite quam in membris*), the first time this established formula had been applied to the whole church.[123] He was placing the tightest curbs on papal sovereignty, as he overtly applied the principle of 'what touches all must be approved by all'. His approach was essentially an episcopal one, reflecting the bishops' claims to their rights which they held to be guaranteed by the *status ecclesiae*. Finding the Decretalists uncongenial, because they were papal monarchists, Guilielmus turned rather to the *Decretum* as a more suitable source for ideas favouring the rights of councils. In so doing, he imagined that he was recreating the conditions in the primitive church. His ideas provoked the firm opposition of Clement V. When Vienne finally convened in 1311, the pope managed to avoid the posthumous condemnation of Boniface; pressurised Guilielmus into reneging on his ideas by composing his *Tractatus minor* (Lesser Tract) in which he supported traditional ideas of papal power; and left the council with the structure of papal monarchy intact. The council did, however, place the call for reform, in head and members, in the context of the whole church.

Canonists writing in the first half of the fourteenth century, such as Guido de Baysio (c. 1246/56–1313), Johannes Monachus and Johannes Andreae, although they considered papal monarchy to be limited and not arbitrary, did not envisage any thorough-going institutional checks on the monarchical authority of the pope: in this respect, Guilielmus was ahead of his time.

Marsilius of Padua, as we have seen in his treatment of general councils, applied his model of the sovereign human legislator to spiritual as well as temporal affairs: the council so established represented the faithful.[124] Certainly, some of Marsilius' ideas were to be used by subsequent conciliarists, but his destruction of the papal office in any meaningful sense distanced him from them because it was a distinctive characteristic of conciliarism to retain the office of pope while seeking to reform his relationship with the council, and thereby the church as a whole. According to Marsilius, the Roman bishop was to be set up by the faithful human legislator or the general council. In his *Defensor minor* Marsilius overtly rejected his opponent Ockham's view that a general council could err.[125] Ockham was conservative about the papacy and, unlike Marsilius, considered it to have been divinely instituted. Although Ockham's attacks on papal plenitude of power were to be used by conciliarists, he would only see general councils as being sometimes superior to the pope, in for instance the case of examination of a pope for heresy: for him such councils were not part of the normal governmental structure of the church.

The Great Schism and the Councils of Pisa and Constance

The Great Schism, from soon after its outbreak, stimulated a renewed interest in conciliar ideas as one of the ways (and ultimately the successful one) in which the crisis could be solved. This phase of conciliarism culminated, in an institutional sense, with the decrees *Haec sancta* (1415) and *Frequens* (1417), issued at the Council of Constance. In *Haec sancta* (sometimes referred to as *Sacrosancta*), the general council declared that it represented the Catholic church on earth; that it held power directly from Christ; that everyone, including the pope, was bound to obey it in matters concerning the faith, the ending of the Schism, and general reform of the church in head and members; and that anyone, even the pope, who disobeyed the decrees of this or any other legally convoked council on such matters was to be punished. *Frequens* sought permanently to change the church's constitution by decreeing that a general council should be held five years after Constance; that another should be called seven years after that one; and that such councils should thereafter be held every ten years in perpetuity. These decrees were the product of a massive debate which had been focused by the exchange of ideas at Pisa and Constance, and which could be divided into theological and juristic treatments.[126]

Theologians at Pisa and Constance had to confront the problem that in canon law only the pope could call a valid general council: at Pisa, because neither papal claimant would do so; at Constance, because the Pisan pope, John XXIII, who had called the council, soon fled it in March 1415 in an attempt to discredit it. The solution put forward was that the church had the right of self-assembly to ensure its own unity. At Pisa, the Parisian theologians, Pierre d'Ailly (1352–1420) and his greater pupil, Jean Gerson (1363–1429), both argued that the letter of the canon law, as positive law, could be transcended for the good of the church by the application of the Aristotelian principle of equity (*epieikeia*); and that, if necessary, the general council could assemble without the authorisation of the pope. As Gerson said, conciliar authority was based on divine and natural law, not canon. At Constance, in his sermon *Ambulate,* in which he rallied its members after John's flight, Gerson reasserted the council's right to assemble without papal consent.[127]

The overall theological tone of conciliarism at Constance was moderate. The general council was, indeed, held to be supreme because it represented the church; but the council did so in the sense that it contained within itself the church's hierarchical structure: it was representative because it comprised senior ecclesiastics who were understood to represent the church by virtue of their office. D'Ailly, in his *Tractatus de ecclesia* (Tract on the Church) (1416) held that the general council possessed plenitude of power through representing the church in its totality: the council had, however, an ultimately directing and regulatory role, whereas the pope's plenitude of power was of an executive and ministerial kind. Gerson had expressed much the same view in his sermon *Prosperum iter faciat nobis* (May he Have a Good Journey for Us) preached in 1415 when Sigismund, king of the Romans, had departed from Constance, for Spain, to try and bring about the abdication of the Avignon pope, Benedict XIII, or his

abandonment by the Spanish kingdoms: the council had delib-
erative and determinative authority and could depose the pope
whose plenitude of power was executive in nature – indeed, the
council had doctrinal supremacy and had to be obeyed by
the pope in all matters pertaining to the faith, ending the Schism
and reform in head and members. In *De ecclesiastica potestate*
(Concerning Ecclesiastical Power) (1416/17) Gerson gave the
most mature expression of his views. The general council was the
final seat of ecclesiastical authority because, being comprised of
the various members of the hierarchical structure of the church, it
enshrined all the church's legitimate power which was greater
than that of any individual member of the hierarchy; the pope
was therefore subordinate to the council. Fullness of power was
present in the church and therefore in the council which represented it and gave it form; the council could decide who was to
exercise plenitude of power as pope, and regulate how he was
to use it. The council could proceed without the pope and exercise
all papal powers of jurisdiction.

The Great Schism posed a massive problem for canonists,
precisely because the Decretalists had tended to develop ideas of
papal monarchy and had given very little attention to the role
of general councils. Canonists had a particular, professional
problem in trying to cope with the requirement that such a
council could only legitimately be called by the pope and that its
decrees, to be legally valid, had also to be papally ratified. They
became increasingly desperate as the Schism continued and,
under the pressure of the necessity of ending it, came to contem-
plate solutions they would not have originally entertained. The
intransigence of both popes made papal monarchy itself seem to
be no longer the means, but rather a hindrance, to achieving the
church's well-being. A significant advance towards a juristic
solution to the Schism occurred when the original rights and
wrongs over Urban VI's election in 1378 were seen as being no
longer relevant in the circumstances of a prolonged schism, which
had come to be perceived as a question of heresy and thus
susceptible to a more straightforward canon law resolution. To
bring about the deposition of the papal claimants for heresy it
would be necessary to demonstrate that the calling of a general
council did not depend on a pope.

Petrus de Ancharano represented this change in approach. In
his canon law commentaries Petrus supported papal monarchical

power. According to him, the pope did not have to rule with the cardinals and was supreme over a general council, except in matters of faith; indeed, such a council could only judge and punish the pope in the case of heresy. Between 1405 and 1409, however, Petrus wrote six *consilia* on ways to end the Schism. In the end, after initial reluctance, he came to support the Roman and Avignonese cardinals' initiative in calling the Council of Pisa. The factor which led him to change his mind was the papal electoral capitulations: at the conclaves which had elected them, both Benedict XIII and the Roman pope, Gregory XII (1406–15), had sworn to work for an end to the Schism – by their own resignations if necessary. Petrus de Ancharano came to believe that both Benedict and Gregory, through their procrastination, had become perjurors by breaking the oaths they had sworn in making these capitulations. In 1408 Petrus gave his support to the conciliar way of ending the Schism. He now argued that the power to convoke the council had devolved to the cardinals because of the failure of the head of the church. He was willing to go further in this emergency: if the cardinals would not fulfil this role, then it devolved on the bishops, and then progressively to the clergy, and finally to the Christian people. At the Council of Pisa he gave an address justifying its legitimacy. He made it clear that details of the original reasons why the Schism had broken out were transcended by the guilt of those now continuing it. Benedict and Gregory were, in short, heretics. Petrus had come to espouse these views in response to a state of emergency in which the council was the living law on earth. Basically, he remained a papal monarchist, while acknowledging the capacity of the council to end the Schism and, if necessary in some future crisis, to use plenitude of power again. Petrus supported the efforts of the Council of Pisa in order to restore a strong papacy.[128]

The final stage of the canonist response to the Great Schism was to be found in the development of a solution in terms of corporation theory.[129] Here the works of Franciscus Zabarella were of prime importance.[130] He had supported the cardinals at Pisa and played a leading role at Constance, where he had a hand in the drafting of *Haec sancta*.[131] Zabarella wrote an extensive commentary on the Clementines and a shorter one on the *Decretales*, together with some *repetitiones* and *consilia*.[132] From the point of view of the Schism, his most important work was his tract *De schismate* (On the Schism) which put forward legal arguments in favour of a general council. This tract was included in his commentary on the *Decretales* and was written between 1402 and 1408.[133]

Zabarella drew on the developments in corporation theory made by thirteenth- and fourteenth-century jurists. Particularly important were ideas concerning the relationship between head and members within the corporation and the question of the extent to which jurisdiction inhered in the corporation as a whole, when, for instance, the headship was vacant. Zabarella's ideas were consistent with the dominant stream of corporation theory which located jurisdiction within the *universitas* itself, understood as both head and members. He was not associated with that strand of juristic opinion which placed jurisdiction solely in the head. In *De schismate* Zabarella explained the relationship between the pope's authority and that of the church as a whole by applying corporation theory in a conciliarist way. Power lay 'as if fundamentally' (*tanquam in fundamento*) in the Christian community understood as a corporate body, and in the pope 'as the principal minister' (*tanquam principali ministro*) through whom this power was deployed. Zabarella held that the pope was made by the consent of the corporate body of Christians from which he derived his power. He maintained that, since the Schism had brought about a quasi-vacancy in the government of the church through the lack of a head, power lay with the congregation of the faithful. In this circumstance, the universal church as a corporate body was represented by a general council, a corporation itself within which the government of the church would be exercised by the weightier part of those present. Zabarella considered that it did not matter how a general council came into being: it was legitimate, once it existed, by the very fact that it represented the congregation of the faithful. It derived its legitimacy from that congregation, not from those who summoned it. At a stroke, this argument cut through the canon law requirement that the pope had to call the general council for it to be valid. The canon law rule derived from a view of church government whereby legitimacy was derived from the pope as monarch, to whose care the church had been committed by Christ. Conciliarist corporation theory provided a completely different model according to which Christ had given to the church, as a whole, authority and power which it in turn delegated to the pope: the physical expression of the universal church, for governmental purposes, was the congregated general council.

For Zabarella, the general council possessed the widest powers, because it represented the whole church: it could not err and had the task of correcting the pope if he fell into error. The inerrancy of the church was therefore focused on the council. Within his very wide definition of heresy, Zabarella included responsibility for continuing the Schism. He was certain that the council, as guardian of the faith, could judge the pope for heresy: in matters of faith the council was greater than the pope. The objection that the pope's power derived from God posed no problem in Zabarella's view, because he held that the council also acted by divine power and that, since the choice of which individual should be Pope was a human one, human beings could also depose individual popes: this constituted no threat to the divinely created institution of the papacy itself.

Zabarella also proposed a corporate headship of the Roman church, which he considered to be comprised of the pope and the cardinals together as head and members. Thus plenitude of power inhered in pope and cardinals as representing the Roman church. As a result, without the co-operation of the cardinals, the pope could issue no general legislation concerning the *status ecclesiae*: he had to consult them on all major matters. Zabarella held that the cardinals had the full powers of the apostolic see during a papal vacancy; when they elected a pope they acted in the name of the whole church. If a general council was to be called, the cardinals represented the universal church in the administration of matters leading up to its convening. But only a general council could depose a pope, not the cardinals on their own. As parts of the pope's body, the cardinals ultimately derived their authority from the whole church: they represented the universal church and took its place.

Zabarella perceived that all ecclesiastical power, and most notably that of the pope, existed for the sake of the church and was limited for the sake of its overall spiritual objective. His analysis in terms of corporation theory was designed to reveal the most suitable governmental structure for the church: the superiority of the general council was the best means to bring the congregation of the faithful back to health and to keep it in that condition. According to him, the root cause of the church's evils lay in not calling councils.

In the event, the lasting achievement of the Council of Constance was the ending of the Schism. In May 1415 it deposed John XXIII; in July of the same year Gregory XII resigned. It deposed Benedict XIII in July 1417, although he never accepted the council's decision. In November of that year the required two-thirds' majority of the twenty-three cardinals present at the council, together with six representatives of each of the five nations into which it was divided, elected Cardinal Oddo Colonna, who took the name of Martin V (1417–31).

The Council of Basel

The Council of Basel opened in 1431, seven years after that of Pavia–Siena in accordance with the requirements of *Frequens*. The pope, Eugenius IV (1431–47), was never happy with the council and tried unsuccessfully to dissolve it rapidly. The first phase of Basel lasted until 1437, when Eugenius declared it dissolved and transferred it to Ferrara in order to conduct negotiations for union with the Greek Orthodox church. The Council of Ferrara in turn was transferred to Florence, where in 1439 an ill-fated act of union between the Latin and Greek churches was made. The moderate elements (including virtually all the higher clergy) abandoned Basel for Ferrara–Florence. The radical majority remained at Basel: in 1438 they suspended Eugenius and in 1439 declared him deposed, thus creating a schism between the pope and the council. Even before Eugenius' dissolution, the council had begun encroaching on aspects of the Roman curia's powers of administration and jurisdiction.

The tone of the Council of Basel was different from that of Constance. In an attempt to demonstrate continuity, Basel swiftly reissued *Haec sancta*. But whereas membership of Constance was determined by office, that of Basel was far more egalitarian: the council decided its own membership by incorporation into itself, as an *universitas*, and voted by numerical majorities. The presence of a large number of lower clergy at Basel in part accounted for the fact that its conciliarism, especially after 1437, was more radical than that of Constance. Basel developed further the principle of conciliar supremacy: the council was the church's sovereign body because it represented the congregation of the faithful which was the ultimate source of authority. The council, as the primary recipient of Christ's authority, exercised plenitude of power over all Christians, including the pope, who was no more than the council's executive minister. There was, however, a problem as regards Basel's claim to represent the whole church. If the members of the council did not represent the church because of the offices they held, and if they were not elected delegates, how could their claim to be the assembled church through incorporation amount to true representation of the whole congregation of the faithful?

Two writers in particular exemplified the conciliarism of Basel. John of Segovia (1393–1458), sent as the university of Salamanca's representative in 1433, served the council until its dissolution in 1449. John was the most typical and effective spokesman for Basel; with the departure of so many leading prelates in 1437 he rose to the front rank of practical and intellectual influence within the council. He produced a large number of speeches and tracts, and wrote his most famous work, *Historia actorum generalis synodi Basiliensis* (A History of the Acts of the General Synod of Basel), between 1449 and 1453. John held that conciliar supremacy had a scriptural basis whereas papal sovereignty was founded on human rather than divine law. Nevertheless he expressed his model for the government of the church in terms of a corporation theory which owed much to juristic thought, including the treatment of city-communes. For John, the relationship of the pope to the church was like that of a *rector* to an *universitas*: the pope was the chief executor of conciliar decrees – he acted as a public person so long as he served the public good. John located supreme power ultimately in the community of the faithful, and by delegation in the council: the pope's power was derived from the sovereignty of the ecclesiastical community.[134]

Nicholas of Cusa (1401–64), a German who had studied canon law at Padua, was incorporated into the Council of Basel in 1432 and submitted his lengthy work of political and ecclesiological theory, *De concordantia catholica* (Catholic Concordance), to the council at the end of 1433 or the beginning of 1434. In the early years of Basel he was a conciliarist, but changed over to the papal side in 1437. In the *De concordantia catholica* Nicholas argued that consent was the basis of all law and authority, because of man's natural freedom and equality – hence his advocacy of the election of rulers and other representatives. Nicholas gave particularly subtle explanations of how all legitimate authority derived from both God and the people. All ecclesiastical rulership was instituted by Christ through the agency of human consent. The free submission of naturally free people was essential for the establishment of legitimate authority. This natural freedom was implanted in men by God with the result that all authority, which also derived from God, was recognised as divine when it resulted from the common consent of subjects. Nicholas held that, within the church, the union of the faithful, or the universal council representing it, was superior to the pope, the church's minister. Nicholas's consent argument was expressed within the overall structure of a harmoniously and hierarchically differentiated society in which authority was derived ultimately from God. His shift from a conciliarist to a papalist position was easily accomplished.[135]

In the event, Basel turned out to be the last general council of the conciliar epoch. The death-knell was sounded for Basel as successive secular rulers abandoned it during the 1440s. Papal diplomacy was particularly effective in this respect because it presented conciliarism as having political implications in that it constituted a general threat to monarchy as such.[136] Conciliar ideas indeed survived, but the movement as such collapsed: Basel ended up by dissolving itself. At Constance, the church's future had seemed to lie with conciliarism as the only practical solution to the reality of schism. In the process, fundamental changes in the structure of the church's government had been enunciated; but once unity had been achieved with the election of Martin V the deep-seated momentum had left the movement.

CONCLUSION

The fifteenth century witnessed the gradual transition from the medieval to the early modern world in Europe, a transition marked by a subtle change in atmosphere for political ideas. The Great Schism and the conciliar movement marked the end of the medieval papal monarchy. Although the papacy survived, it had been badly damaged by the loss of prestige brought about through schism and by the conciliar challenge to its authority. The Renaissance papacy that emerged from this crisis was different in profound respects from what had gone before. The popes concentrated on reconstructing their temporal state in central Italy at the expense of their universalist claims. Secular monarchies in Europe also suffered many vicissitudes, but by the last part of the century a consolidation in monarchy could be perceived.[1] Early modern monarchical states were beginning to emerge with a greater concentration of power around the ruler than had existed in the Middle Ages. Furthermore, a fundamental change in intellectual *milieu* and sensibility resulted from the cumulative effect of the spread of Renaissance humanism from its beginnings in Italy in the early fourteenth century. This movement may most conveniently be defined as a group of disciplines based on the study of the literature of the ancient world and concentrating on grammar, rhetoric, history and moral philosophy. It sought to understand the culture of antiquity within its original historical context, and with its emphasis on classical Latin philology produced political writings of a markedly different tone from medieval ones. Humanism was as much a style as anything else.

Viewed from the perspective of continuity, however, there was no clear dividing-line between the political thought of the Middle Ages and that of the Renaissance: scholasticism, for instance, was as much a Renaissance phenomenon as was humanism. Well into at least the seventeenth century, the juristic, theological and overtly political works of medieval scholastics continued to be prime sources for the discussion of political thought: their ideas were quoted, followed, emended and rejected. The writings of, for instance, Francisco de Vitoria (c. 1485–1546), Jean Bodin (1529/30–96), Francisco Suárez (1548–1617) and Hugo Grotius (1583–1645), amongst very many others, illustrated this trend.[2] The juristic legacy was, perhaps, the most important, because so many of those involved in government had received a legal education. For the practice of law on the Continent, scholastic jurisprudence remained the staple training: it was in no sense superseded by humanist jurisprudence. Medieval jurists retained a predominant influence in sixteenth-century Italy, as was also the case in Germany through the reception of Roman law; they also enjoyed considerable renown in French legal circles. As regards theology, the sixteenth-century revival of Thomism was particularly important for the development of early modern natural-law theories of the state. This is not to underestimate, however, the level of opposition that scholastic thought attracted and the denigration of Aristotelian methods that accompanied such attacks.

The Middle Ages made distinctive, long-term contributions to political thought. Most obviously, the notion of theocratic monarchy provided the basis for the later development of kingship by the grace of God into that by divine right, and, indeed, was the ultimate foundation of theories of kingship under the *ancien régime*. The medieval belief that all power in its nature and exercise existed within a normative context contributed to the elaboration of constitutionalist ideas and rights theories. The perception that absolute power, itself a medieval coinage, was nevertheless limited was to underlie early modern conceptions of absolute monarchy and to distinguish them from later and more totalitarian ideas of absolutism. Medieval treatments of government by the people as well as of monarchy were to provide material for later republican and royal theorists, as for instance in the French wars of religion in the sixteenth century.[3] In the Middle Ages, jurists made particularly important contributions to ideas of popular and monarchical sovereignty; they also, through their corporation theory, aided the development of ideas of the territorial state, whether city or kingdom, as an abstract entity. In some areas, medieval political ideas retained a particularly tenacious influence. Thomism remained a viable theological system into the twentieth century; the *Corpus iuris canonici* was only replaced as the law of the Catholic church in 1918; and medieval formulations of kingship by the grace of God still cause a distant echo in Britain today. In other areas the world passed on from the concerns which troubled the Middle Ages. So much of this book, for instance, has been devoted to conflicts and relationships between spiritual and temporal power. These questions were characteristic of the period because of the public position of the church in European power structures. Although such questions remained crucial in the sixteenth and seventeenth centuries, the changed position of the papacy in the context of the Protestant and Catholic Reformations, and the consolidation of territorial states of both confessions, meant that medieval notions on the subject became less and less relevant.

Although so much has been written by modern historians on aspects of medieval political ideas, and although the literature on the subject has been greatly increased in scope and sophistication in even the last decade, there is still a tendency, when treating the history of European political ideas as a whole, to give relatively scant attention to the Middle Ages. This book will have succeeded in its purpose if it has shown that an approach which, typically, concentrates on Greece and Rome, and then, after bidding farewell to Augustine, skips over the Middle Ages using Aquinas and Marsilius as stepping-stones to reach Machiavelli, omits a substantial part of Europe's political thought. The Middle Ages were the seed-time of European civilisation: without a knowledge of them, it is not possible fully to understand political thought in later centuries.

NOTES

1 THE ORIGINS OF MEDIEVAL POLITICAL IDEAS, c. 300–c. 750

1 This was known as the *Corpus iuris civilis* from the sixteenth century, but in the Middle Ages as the *Corpus iuris*.
2 John 18:36.
3 Matthew 22:21.
4 1 Peter 2:17.
5 Romans 13:1–2.
6 The Donatists were a heretical sect which regarded the church as apostate through having compromised with secular authority.
7 Constantine's description of himself is ambiguous. *Ton ektos* could either be neuter case ('of exterior matters') and thus be understood to refer to his jurisdiction over the externals of Christianity; or the phrase could be masculine ('of people who are exterior', i.e. pagans). I have accepted the arguments of D. de Decker and G. Dupuis-Masay, 'L' "épiscopat" et l'empereur Constantin', *Byzantion*, L (1980), pp. 118–57. For the scholarly dispute over the interpretation of *ton ektos* see especially F. Dvornik, *Early Christian and Byzantine Political Philosophy: Origins and Background*, Dumbarton Oaks Studies 9, 2 vols (Washington, DC: The Dumbarton Oaks Center for Byzantine Studies, 1966), II, pp. 752–4, who adopts the contrary view.
8 See H.J. Scheltema, 'Byzantine Law', in *The Cambridge Medieval History*, IV: *The Byzantine Empire*, eds J.M. Hussey, D.M. Nicol and G. Cowan (Cambridge: Cambridge University Press, 1967), II, p. 62. G. Ostrogorsky, *History of the Byzantine State*, trans. J. Hussey (Oxford: Basil Blackwell, 1956), p. 134, favours 726.
9 'Deo auctore nostrum gubernantes imperium, quod nobis a caelesti maiestate traditum est.'
10 'Nutu divino imperiales suscepimus infulas' (C.7.37.3).
11 See for instance C. Const. 'De emendatione codicis'; C.1.14.9.
12 D. Const., 'Omnem', 11; D. Const., 'Tanta', 23.
13 D.14.2.9: 'tou kosmou kurios' in the original Greek.
14 D.1.4.1; Inst. 1.2, 6. This passage from Ulpian (d. 223) probably originally meant that the emperor's interpretation must prevail

NOTES

where there was doubt about the law. Here the passage is interpreted in the context of the *Corpus iuris*.

15 'Omnibus enim a nobis dictis imperatoris excipiatur fortuna, cui et
ipsas deus leges subiecit, legem animatam eum mittens hominibus'
(Auth. Coll. 4.3, 2, 4 = Nov. 105, 2, 4). See A. Steinwenter, 'Νόμος
ἔμψυχος: zur Geschichte einer politischen Theorie', *Anzeiger der
Akademie der Wissenschaften in Wien*, phil.–hist. Kl., CXXXIII (1946),
250–68.

16 D.1.3.31 (Ulpian).

17 See K. Pennington, *The Prince and the Law, 1200–1600* (Berkeley:
University of California Press, 1993), pp. 77–90.

18 See W. Ullmann, *Law and Politics in the Middle Ages: An Introduction to
the Sources of Medieval Political Ideas* (London: The Sources of History,
1975), p. 56; and F. Lucrezi, *Leges super principem: la 'monarchia
costituzionale' di Vespasiano* (Naples: Jovene, 1982), p. 178.

19 The classic treatment of this view is in T. Mommsen, *Römisches
Staatsrecht*, 3rd edn (Leipzig: S. Hirzel, 1887), II, 2, pp. 876–9; but
see Lucrezi, *Leges super principem*, pp. 179–84 for a rejection of
this argument.

20 'Lege antiqua, quae regia nuncupabatur, omne ius omnisque
potestas populi Romani in inperatoriam translata sunt potestatem'
(D. Const., 'Deo auctore', 7 and C.1.17.1, 7).

21 'Vtpote cum lege regia, quae de imperio eius lata est, populus ei et in
eum omne suum imperium et potestatem conferat' (D.1.4.1; see also
Inst. 1.2, 6).

22 *Römisches Staatsrecht*, II, 2, p. 876, n. 2.

23 'Quid interest suffragio populus voluntatem suam declaret an rebus
ipsis et factis? quare rectissime etiam illud receptum est, ut leges non
solum suffragio legis latoris, sed etiam tacito consensu omnium per
desuetudinem abrogentur' (D.1.3.32). See also Inst. 1.2, 11: 'Ea vero
[iura], quae ipsa sibi quaeque civitas constituit, saepe mutari solent
vel tacito consensu populi vel alia postea lege lata.'

24 C.8.52.2.

25 C.1.14.12.

26 C.5.59.5, 2.

27 See for instance G. Post, 'A Romano-canonical maxim, "Quod omnes
tangit", in Bracton', *Traditio* IV (1946), pp. 197–251.

28 C.1.14.4 (*l. Digna vox*). See also C.6.23.3.

29 D.1.1.1, 3–4.

30 D.1.1.9.

31 'Naturalia quidem iura, quae apud omnes gentes peraeque servan-
tur, divina quadam providentia constituta semper firma atque
immutabilia permanent.'

32 Inst. 1.2, 2. See also Inst. 1.3, 2 and D.1.1.4 (Ulpian).

33 'Ius civile est, quod neque in totum a naturali vel gentium recedit
nec per omnia ei servit' (D.1.1.6). Ulpian may be identifying the *ius
naturale* with the *ius gentium* here.

34 'Maxima quidem in hominibus sunt dona dei a superna collata
clementia sacerdotium et imperium, illud quidem divinis ministrans,

189

hoc autem humanis praesidens ac diligentiam exhibens; ex uno eodemque principio utraque procedentia humanam exornant vitam.'

35 'Ideoque nihil sic erit studiosum imperatoribus, sicut sacerdotum honestas, cum utique et pro illis ipsis semper deo supplicent. Nam si hoc quidem inculpabile sit undique et apud deum fiducia plenum, imperium autem recte et competenter exornet traditam sibi rempublicam, erit consonantia quaedam bona, omne quicquid utile est humano conferens generi. Nos igitur maximam habemus sollicitudinem circa vera dei dogmata et circa sacerdotum honestatem, quam illis obtinentibus credimus quia per eam maxima nobis dona dabuntur a deo, et ea, quae sunt, firma habebimus, et quae nondum hactenus venerunt, adquirimus.'

36 'Publicum ius est quod ad statum rei Romanae spectat ... publicum ius in sacris, in sacerdotibus, in magistratibus consistit' (D.1.1.1, 2).

37 'Cum nec multo differant ab alterutro sacerdotium et imperium, et sacrae res a communibus et publicis, quando omnis sanctissimis ecclesiis abundantia et status ex imperialibus munificentiis perpetuo praebetur' (Auth. Coll. 2.1, 2, 1 = Nov. 7, 2, 1).

38 Auth. Coll. 9.6, 1 = Nov. 131, 1; see also Auth. Coll. 1.6, 1, 8 = Nov. 6, 1, 8.

39 Nov. 42.

40 See, for instance, W. Ullmann, *A History of Political Thought: The Middle Ages* (Harmondsworth: Penguin Books, 1965), pp. 35–6.

41 See E. Herman, 'The secular church', in *Cambridge Medieval History*, IV, 2 (1967), pp. 105–6; H. Grégoire, 'The Amorians and Macedonians 842–1025', *Cambridge Medieval History*, IV, 1 (1966), pp. 133–4; and D.M. Nicol, 'Byzantine political thought', in J.H. Burns (ed.), *The Cambridge History of Medieval Political Thought c. 350–c. 1450* (Cambridge: Cambridge University Press, 1988), pp. 67–8.

42 As Marcian, for instance, had been at the Council of Chalcedon.

43 This is not to suggest that a formal, legal distinction between *potestas ordinis* and *potestas jurisdictionis* was made at this time. See S. Chodorow, *Christian Political Theory and Church Politics in the Mid-Twelfth Century: The Ecclesiology of Gratian's Decretum* (Berkeley: University of California Press, 1972), p. 155, for the scholarly debate whether this distinction is found in the work of the twelfth-century canonist, Gratian, or appears later.

44 Auth. Coll. 9.6, 2 = Nov. 131, 2.

45 Herman, 'The secular church', p. 109.

46 The Vulgate contains about 520 references to *regnum* without pejorative overtones – about 70 to *regnum dei* and 30 to *regnum caelorum*. See W. Suerbaum, *Vom antiken zum frühmittelalterlichen Staatsbegriff: über Verwendung und Bedeutung von Res publica, regnum, imperium und status von Cicero bis Jordanis*, Orbis antiquus, 16/17 (Münster: Aschendorff, 1977), pp. 288–9.

47 O. von Gierke, *Das deutsche Genossenschaftsrecht*, III (Berlin: Weidmann, 1881); F. Kern, *Kingship and Law in the Middle Ages*, trans. S.B. Chrimes (Oxford: Basil Blackwell, 1939), pp. 12–13, 85–97; and Ullmann, *History of Political Thought*, pp. 12–13.

48 *Germania*, 7: 'Reges ex nobilitate, duces ex virtute sumunt.'

49 For the argument that the thesis of Germanic kingship is a myth see P.D. King, 'The barbarian kingdoms', in J.H. Burns (ed.), *The Cambridge History of Medieval Political Thought c. 350–c. 1450* (Cambridge: Cambridge University Press, 1988), pp. 147–53.

50 *Historia Francorum*, 2.38, p. 102.

51 See, for instance, W. Ullmann, *Principles of Government and Politics in the Middle Ages* (London: Methuen, 1961), p. 118. For Svinthila see Isidore of Seville, *Historia Gothorum, Wandalorum, Sueborum*, ch. 62, p. 292.

52 Victor of Vita, *Historia persecutionis africanae provinciae sub Geiserico et Hunirico regibus Wandalorum*, 2.39, p. 22, and 3.14, p. 43.

53 'Gratia autem dei sum id quod sum.'

54 'Non potest homo accipere quidquam, nisi fuerit ei datum de caelo.'

55 'Non haberes potestatem adversum me ullam, nisi tibi datum esset desuper.'

56 'Ipsi regnaverunt, et non ex me; principes extiterunt, et non cognovi.'

57 For Ullmann's thesis of theocratic monarchy see, especially, *Principles of Government*, pp. 117–37.

58 'Dei enim minister est tibi, in bonum ... Dei enim minister est ... Ministri enim Dei sunt' (Romans 13:4–6).

59 See, for instance, *Moralia*, 26.26.45, p. 1300.

60 See Gregory I, *Regula pastoralis*, 2.6.

61 See M. Reydellet, *La royauté dans la littérature latine de Sidonie Apollinaire à Isidore de Seville* (Ecole française de Rome, 1981), pp. 554–606.

62 *Etymologiae*, 9.3.4, col. 342: 'Rex eris si recte facies, si non facias, non eris.' See also Horace, *Epistulae*, 1.1.59–60.

63 See *Sententiae*, 3.48–51, cols 718–24; *Differentiae*, 2.156 and 158, col. 95.

64 'Obedite praepositis vestris et subiacete eis; ipsi enim pervigilant, quasi rationem pro animabus vestris reddituri.'

65 Cicero, *De officiis*, 1.25.

66 *Sententiae*, 3.49.3, col. 721.

67 In 528: see W. Ullmann, *The Individual and Society in the Middle Ages* (London: Methuen, 1967), p. 21, n. 41.

68 *Formulae*, 1.24, p. 58.

69 See W. Ullmann, *The Carolingian Renaissance and the Idea of Kingship* (London: Methuen, 1969), pp. 177–87; Ullmann, 'A note on inalienability in Gregory VII', *Studi Gregoriani* IX (1972), pp. 117–40; and Ullmann, 'Juristic obstacles to the emergence of the concept of the state in the Middle Ages', *Annali di storia del diritto* XII–XIII (1968–9), pp. 49–51.

70 See J.L. Nelson, 'National synods, kingship as office, and royal anointing: an early medieval syndrome', in her collected essays: *Politics and Ritual in Early Medieval Europe* (London: Hambledon Press), p. 264.

71 See J.L. Nelson, 'On the limits of the Carolingian Renaissance', in *Politics and Ritual*, pp. 58–9, and King, 'The barbarian kingdoms', p. 139.

72 See P.D. King, *Law and Society in the Visigothic Kingdom*, Cambridge Studies in Medieval Life and Thought, third series, 5 (Cambridge: Cambridge University Press, 1972), pp. 16–18; and King, 'The alleged territoriality of Visigothic Law', in B. Tierney and P. Linehan (eds), *Authority and Power. Studies on Medieval Law and Government Presented to Walter Ullmann on his Seventieth Birthday* (Cambridge: Cambridge University Press, 1980), pp. 1–11.

73 See P. Wormald, '*Lex scripta* and *Verbum regis*: legislation and Germanic kingship from Euric to Cnut', in P.H. Sawyer and I.N. Wood (eds), *Early Medieval Kingship* (Leeds: School of History, University of Leeds, 1977), pp. 108–9.

74 See Wormald, '*Lex scripta*', p. 107; Ullmann, *Law and Politics*, pp. 196–7.

75 Augustine, *De vera religione*, 31, col. 148 (also quoted in *Decr. Grat.*, Dist.4.c.3): 'In istis temporalibus legibus, quanquam de his homines iudicent cum eas instituunt tamen cum fuerint institutae atque firmatae, non licebit iudici de ipsis iudicare, sed secundum ipsas'; Isidore, *Sententiae*, 3.51.1–2, col. 723.

76 See *Kingship and Law, passim* and especially pp. 149–65. This thesis is still used by A. Wolf in 'Die Gesetzgebung der entstehenden Territorialstaaten', in H. Coing (ed.), *Handbuch der Quellen und Literatur der neueren europäischen Privatrechtsgeschichte*, I: *Mittelalter (1100–1500)* (Munich: C.H. Beck, 1973), p. 534; and by R. van Caenegem, 'Government, law and society', in J.H. Burns (ed.), *The Cambridge History of Medieval Political Thought c. 350–c. 1450* (Cambridge: Cambridge University Press, 1988), p. 182.

77 See Ullmann, *Principles of Government*, pp. 20–1; and *Law and Politics*, pp. 30–1 and 193.

78 See *Politics and Ritual*, p. 62.

79 See Ullmann, *Law and Politics*, p. 30, n. 1; and K. Kroeschell, '"Rechtsfindung". Die mittelalterlichen Grundlagen einer modernen Vorstellung', in *Festschrift für Hermann Heimpel* III (Göttingen: Vandenhoeck & Ruprecht, 1972), p. 516.

80 See Nelson, 'Limits of Carolingian Renaissance', p. 62; and Kroeschell, 'Rechtsfindung', p. 512.

81 See Wormald, '*Lex scripta*', p. 111.

82 Ammianus Marcellinus, *Res gestae*, 28.5.14 (see below, p. 28). See K. Bund, *Thronsturz und Herrscherabsetzung im Frühmittelalter*, Bonner Historische Forschungen 4 (Bonn: Ludwig Röhrscheid Verlag, 1979), pp. 132–8, 143 and 787ff.

83 See King, *Law and Society*, pp. 122–58; and King, 'The barbarian kingdoms', p. 144.

84 'Principes seculi nonnumquam intra ecclesiam potestatis adeptae culmina tenent, ut per eamdem potestatem disciplinam ecclesiasticam muniant. Caeterum, intra ecclesiam potestates necessariae non essent, nisi ut, quod non prevalet sacerdos efficere per doctrinae sermonem, potestas hoc imperet per disciplinae terrorem' (*Sententiae*, 3.51.4, col. 723); see also ibid., 3.47.1, col. 717.

85 See H.-J. Diesner, *Isidor von Sevilla und seine Zeit* (Stuttgart: Calwer, 1973), p. 58.

86 See n. 43 above.

87 *Sententiae*, 3.51.6, col. 723–4.

88 *Historia Francorum*, 9.21, p. 379 ('rex acsi bonus sacerdos'); see also Council of Orleans of 511 (*MGH, Conc.* 1, p. 2) for mention of the 'sacerdotalis mentis' of Clovis.

89 *Carmina*, 2.10.21–2: 'Melchisedech noster merito rex atque sacerdos conplevit laicus religionis opus', p. 40; see also Genesis 14:18.

90 See King, 'The barbarian kingdoms', p. 144.

91 See Nelson, 'National synods', p. 250.

92 See Nelson, 'National synods', p. 249; and R. Collins, 'Julian of Toledo and the royal succession in late seventh-century Spain', in P.H. Sawyer and I.N. Wood (eds), *Early Medieval Kingship* (Leeds: School of History, University of Leeds, 1977), p. 44.

93 See King, *Law and Society*, pp. 48–9.

94 J.M. Wallace-Hadrill, *Early Germanic Kingship in England and on the Continent* (Oxford: Clarendon Press, 1971), pp. 48–50.

95 W.A. Chaney, *The Cult of Kingship in Anglo-Saxon England: The Transition from Paganism to Christianity* (Manchester: Manchester University Press, 1970), especially p. 64.

96 The classic treatment is O. Höfler, 'Der sakralcharakter des germanischen Königtums', in T. Mayer (ed.), *Das Königtum. Seine geistigen und rechtlichen Grundlagen*, Vorträge und Forschungen III (Constance: Jan Thorbecke Verlag, 1956), pp. 75–104.

97 See I.N. Wood, 'Kings, kingdoms and consent', in P.H. Sawyer and I.N. Wood (eds), *Early Medieval Kingship* (Leeds: School of History, University of Leeds, 1977), p. 27.

98 'Ritu veteri potestate deposita removetur, si sub eo fortuna titubaverit belli, vel segetum copiam negaverit terra' (*Res gestae*, 28.5.14, p. 479). See King, 'The barbarian kingdoms', pp. 151–2.

99 *Romana et Getica*, 78, p. 76: 'Proceres suos, quorum quasi fortuna vincebant, non puros homines, sed semideos id est Ansis vocaverunt.' See King, 'The barbarian kingdoms', p. 152.

100 See D.N. Dumville, 'Kingship, genealogies and regnal lists', in P.H. Sawyer and I.N. Wood (eds), *Early Medieval Kingship* (Leeds: School of History, University of Leeds, 1977), pp. 78–9 and 96.

101 King in 'The barbarian kingdoms', p. 152, argues that it was a 'badge of legitimism' throughout.

102 *PL*, 13, col. 1131–47.

103 'Tu es Petrus et super hanc petram aedificabo ecclesiam meam, et portae inferi non praevalebunt adversus eam. Et tibi dabo claves regni caelorum, et quodcumque ligaveris super terram, erit ligatum et in caelis, et quodcumque solveris super terram, erit solutum et in caelis.'

104 'Pasce agnos meos ... Pasce oves meas.'

105 In Greek there is a play on words, *Petros* being the masculine form of *petra* (rock).

106 See W. Ullmann, 'The significance of the *Epistola Clementis* in the Pseudo-Clementines', *Journal of Theological Studies*, new series XI (1960), 295–317.

107 'Portamus onera omnium qui gravantur: quin immo haec portat in nobis beatus apostolus Petrus, qui nos in omnibus, ut confidimus, administrationis suae protegit et tuetur heredes' (*PL*, 13, col. 1133).

108 See W. Ullmann, 'Leo I and the theme of papal primacy', *Journal of Theological Studies*, new series XI (1960), 25–51.

109 *Sermo* 3.4, col. 147: 'Ille [i.e. beatus Petrus] honoretur ... cuius dignitas etiam in indigno haerede non deficit.'

110 *Sermo* 3.4, col. 147: 'ipsum [i.e. beatum Petrum] vobis, cuius vice fungimur, loqui credite.'

111 1 Corinthians 12:4; Ephesians 1:23; Romans 12:5.

112 See *Principles of Government*, p. 39, and *Gelasius I. (492–496): Das Papsttum an der Wende der Spätantike zum Mittelalter*, Päpste und Papsttum, 18 (Stuttgart: Hiersemann, 1981), pp. 70 and 75.

113 See *PL*, 54, col. 671 (letter to the papal vicar of Thessalonika): 'Vices enim nostras ita tuae credidimus charitati , ut in partem sis vocatus sollicitudinis, non in plenitudinem potestatis.' See K. Pennington, *Pope and Bishops. The Papal Monarchy in the Twelfth and Thirteenth Centuries* (Philadelphia: University of Pennsylvania Press, 1984), p. 59; Ullmann, *Gelasius*, p. 70 n. 33; R.L. Benson, 'Plenitudo potestatis: evolution of a formula from Gregory IV to Gratian', *Collectanea Stephan Kuttner, Studia Gratiana* XIV (1967), 195–217; J.A. Watt, *The Theory of Papal Monarchy in the Thirteenth Century. The Contribution of the Canonists* (London: Burns & Oates, 1965), p. 76.

114 For the history of this formula see S. Vacca, *Prima sedes a nemine iudicatur: genesi e sviluppo storico dell'assioma fina al Decreto di Graziano*, Miscellanea historiae pontificiae 61 (Rome: Editrice Pontificia Università Gregoriana, 1993).

115 See H.F. Dondaine, *Le Corpus Dionysien de l'Université de Paris au XIIIe siècle* (Rome: Edizioni di storia e letteratura, 1953); S. Gersh, *From Iamblichus to Eriugena. An Investigation of the Prehistory and Evolution of the Pseudo-Dionysian Tradition* (Leiden: Brill, 1978).

116 See T. Struve, *Die Entwicklung der organologischen Staatsauffassung im Mittelalter*, Monographien zur Geschichte des Mittelalters 16 (Stuttgart: Hiersemann, 1978), pp. 67–71.

117 See Ullmann, *History of Political Thought*, pp. 49–52; and J. Richards, *Consul of God: The Life and Times of Gregory the Great* (London: Routledge, 1980), pp. 64–6.

118 See G. O'Collins, *The Easter Jesus* (London: Darton, Longman & Todd, 1973), p. 83.

119 *Liber de incarnationis dominicae sacramento*, 4, 32, col. 826: 'Hic [i.e. Petrus], inquam, ubi audivit, "Vos autem quid me dicitis?" [Matthew 16:15], statim loci non immemor sui, primatum egit: primatum confessionis utique, non honoris; primatum fidei, non ordinis.' See Ullmann, *Gelasius*, p. 20.

120 *Epistola* 5 (*PL*, 50, col. 437). See Ullmann, *Principles of Government*, p. 134.

121 'Duo quippe sunt, imperator auguste, quibus principaliter mundus hic regitur, auctoritas sacrata pontificum et regalis potestas' (*Epistola* 12, c. 2, A. Thiel (ed.), *Epistolae Romanorum pontificum genuinae et quae*

ad eos scriptae sunt a S. Hilaro usque ad Pelagium II., I (Braunsberg: Edward Peter, 1868), pp. 350–1).

122 Also *rex* is the direct translation of *Basileus*.

123 In *Epistolae*, ed. A. Thiel, pp. 567–8.

124 'Quod si dixeris, "Sed imperator catholicus est," salva pace ipsius dixerimus, filius est, non praesul ecclesiae, quod ad religionem competit, discere ei convenit, non docere' (ibid., *Epistola* 1, c. 10, pp. 292–3: letter of Gelasius while deacon of Pope Felix III).

125 'Nosti etenim, fili clementissime, quod licet praesideas humano generi dignitate, rerum tamen praesulibus divinarum devotus colla submittis, atque ab eis causas tuae salutis exspectas, inque sumendis coelestibus sacramentis eisque ut competit disponendis, subdi te debere cognoscis religionis ordine potius quam praeesse, itaque inter haec ex illorum te pendere judicio, non illos ad tuam velle redigi voluntatem' (ibid., *Epistola* 12, c. 2, p. 351).

126 Ibid., *Epistola* 12, c. 2, pp. 351–2.

127 'Christus memor fragilitatis humanae, quod suorum saluti congrueret, dispensatione magnifica temperavit, sic actionibus propriis dignitatibusque distinctis officia potestatis utriusque discrevit ... ut et Christiani imperatores pro aeterna vita pontificibus indigerent, et pontifices pro temporalium cursu rerum imperialibus dispositionibus uterentur' (ibid., *Tractatus* IV, c. 11, p. 568); see ibid., *Epistola* 12, c. 2, p. 351.

128 Ibid., *Epistola* 26, c. 11, pp. 407–8. See W. Ullmann, *The Growth of Papal Government in the Middle Ages*, 3rd edn, (London: Methuen, 1970), p. 27; and R.L. Benson, 'The Gelasian doctrine: uses and transformations', in G. Makdisi, D. Sourdel and J. Sourdel-Thomine (eds), *La notion d'autorité au Moyen Age. Islam, Byzance, Occident* (Paris: Presses universitaires de France, 1982), p. 18.

129 'In quibus tanto gravius est pondus sacerdotum, quanto etiam pro ipsis regibus hominum in divino reddituri sunt examine rationem' (*Epistola*, 12, c. 2, ed. A. Thiel, p. 351).

130 *Growth of Papal Government*, pp. 20–8, and *Gelasius*, pp. 198–212.

131 See Benson, 'Gelasian doctrine', p. 15.

132 See Ullmann, *Gelasius*, p. 13.

133 See pp. 12–13.

134 'Sacerdotalem namque et apostolicum tuae pietatis animum', *PL*, 54, col. 1131.

135 See Benson, 'Gelasian doctrine', p. 20.

136 See n. 117; also R.A. Markus, 'Gregory the Great's Europe,' *Transactions of the Royal Historical Society*, 5th series, XXXI (1981), pp. 21–36; and J. Herrin, *The Formation of Christendom* (Oxford: Blackwell, 1987), p. 182.

137 'Si quis vero regum, sacerdotum iudicum atque saecularium personarum, hanc constitutionis nostrae paginam agnoscens contra eam venire temptaverit, potestatis honorisque sui dignitate careat reumque se iudicio divino existere de perpetrata iniquitate cognoscat et, nisi vel ea quae ab illo sunt male ablata restituerit vel digna paenitentia inlicite acta defleverit, a sacratissimo corpore ac sanguine Dei domini

redemptoris nostri Iesu Christi alienus fiat atque in aeterno examine districtae ultionis subiaceat' (*Registrum* XIII, 12, p. 380).

138 After 684/5 this imperial approbation was in the hands of the Exarch of Ravenna.

139 The doctrine that Christ as God and man had one will.

140 See Herrin, *Formation*, pp. 284–7. These decrees included denunciations of the Roman church for practices dissimilar to those of Constantinople in matters of fasting and clerical celibacy, and a renewal of canon 28 of the Council of Chalcedon asserting the equality of status of the two churches.

141 For the patristic doctrine of the relationship between the Fall and the establishment of government, and the influence of that thesis on the Middle Ages, the best modern study is W. Stürner, *Peccatum und potestas. Der Sündenfall und die Entstehung der herrscherlichen Gewalt im mittelalterlichen Staatsdenken*, Beiträge zur Geschichte und Quellenkunde des Mittelalters, ed. H. Fuhrmann (Sigmaringen: Jan Thorbeke Verlag, 1987): see especially pp. 38–102 and 264–6.

142 See R.A. Markus, *Saeculum: History and Society in the Theology of St Augustine* (Cambridge: Cambridge University Press, 1970); and Markus, 'Two conceptions of political authority: Augustine, *De civitate dei*, XIX.14–15, and some thirteenth-century interpretations', *The Journal of Theological Studies*, new series XVI (1965), pp. 68–100.

143 'Fecerunt itaque civitates duas amores duo, terrenam scilicet amor sui usque ad contemptum Dei, celestem vero amor Dei usque ad contemptum sui' (*De civitate dei*, XIV.28).

144 'Coetus multitudinis iuris consensu et utilitatis communione sociatus' (*De republica*, 1.25.39).

145 'Remota itaque iustitia quid sunt regna nisi magna latrocinia?'

146 'Populus est coetus multitudinis rationalis rerum quas diligit concordi communione sociatus.'

147 'Quantum enim pertinet ad hanc vitam mortalium, quae paucis diebus ducitur et finitur, quid interest sub cuius imperio vivat homo moriturus, si illi qui imperant ad impia et iniqua non cogant?' (5.17).

148 'Vera autem iustitia non est nisi in ea re publica, cuius conditor rectorque Christus est … in ea certe civitate est vera iustitia, de qua scriptura sancta dicit, "Gloriosa dicta sunt de te, civitas Dei".'

149 *L'Augustinisme politique. Essai sur la formation des théories politiques du moyen-âge*, L'Eglise et l'Etat au moyen-âge, 2, 2nd edn (Paris: J. Vrin, 1955), p. 19.

150 *De civitate dei* V.12, 15–17, 21, 24–6.

2 THE GROWTH OF SPECIFICALLY MEDIEVAL POLITICAL IDEAS, *c.* 750–*c.* 1050

1 Decrees divided into articles (*capitula*) and issued by the monarch aided by the advice of his advisers or an assembly. They were mostly administrative in nature. See F.L. Ganshof, 'Wat waren de capitularia?', *Verhandelingen van de Koninklijke Vlaamse Academie voor Wetenschappen, Letteren en schone Kunsten van Belgie*, Kl. Letteren XXII

(Brussels, 1955, with French résumé). But see also P. Geary's article on capitularies in J. Strayer (ed.), *Dictionary of the Middle Ages* (New York: Charles Scribners' Sons, 1983), pp. 91–2.

2 See H.H. Anton, *Fürstenspiegel und Herrscherethos in der Karolingerzeit*, Bonner historische Forschungen 32 (Bonn: Ludwig Röhrscheid Verlag, 1968); and W. Berges, *Die Fürstenspiegel des hohen und späten Mittelalters* (Stuttgart: Hiersemann, 1938).

3 See J.L. Nelson, 'On the limits of the Carolingian Renaissance' in her collected essays, *Politics and Ritual in Early Medieval Europe* (London: Hambledon Press, 1986), pp. 49–67.

4 'Et Zacharias papa mandavit Pippino, ut melius esset illum regem vocari, qui potestatem haberet, quam illum, qui sine regali potestate manebat; ut non conturbaretur ordo per auctoritatem apostolicam iussit Pippinum regem fieri' (*Annales regni Francorum* (for the year 749), p. 8).

5 'Praecelsus Pippinus electione totius Francorum in sedem regni cum consecratione episcoporum et subiectione principum una cum regina Bertradane, ut antiquitus ordo deposcit, sublimatur in regno' (Continuator of Fredegar, *Chronicle*, IV, ed. J.M. Wallace-Hadrill (London: Nelson, 1960), c. 33, p. 102).

6 For the older view see, for instance, F. Kern, *Kingship and Law in the Middle Ages* (Oxford: Blackwell, 1939), pp. 35–36; and W. Ullmann, *A Short History of the Papacy in the Middle Ages* (London: Methuen, 1972), p. 76.

7 On these questions see H. Wolfram, *Intitulatio*, I: *Lateinische Königs- und Fürstentitel bis zum Ende des 8. Jahrhunderts*, Mitteilungen des Instituts für Österreichische Geschichtsforschung 21 (Graz–Vienna–Cologne: Böhlau Verlag, 1967), p. 213.

8 'Memor esto ergo semper, rex mi, dei regis tui cum timore et amore, quod tu es in vice illius super omnia membra eius custodire et regere, et rationem reddere in die iudicii etiam per te. Et episcopus est in secundo loco, in vice Christi tantum est. Ergo considerate inter vos diligenter legem dei constituere super populum dei' (*MGH, Epp.*, IV, p. 503).

9 *MGH, Conc.*, II, 1, p. 142.

10 See preface to the *Libri carolini* (*MGH, Conc.*, II, Suppl.), p. 2.

11 *MGH, Epp.*, IV, n. 171, p. 282. See W. Levison, 'Die mittelalterliche Lehre von den beiden Schwerten', *Deutsches Archiv für Erforschung des Mittelalters* IX (1952), pp. 25–8; H. Hoffman, 'Die beiden Schwerter im hohen Mittelalter', *Deutsches Archiv für Erforschung des Mittelalters* XX (1964), p. 78; Anton, *Fürstenspiegel*, p. 113.

12 See Anton, *Fürstenspiegel*, pp. 111–12.

13 Ibid., p. 94.

14 See P. Godman, *Poets and Emperors. Frankish Politics and Carolingian Poetry* (Oxford: Clarendon Press, 1987), p. 65.

15 See W. Ullmann, *The Carolingian Renaissance and the Idea of Kingship* (London: Methuen, 1969), p. 44.

16 'Principaliter itaque totius sanctae dei ecclesiae corpus in duas eximias personas, in sacerdotalem videlicet et regalem, sicut a

sanctis patribus traditum accepimus, divisum esse novimus. De qua re Gelasius Romanae sedis venerabilis episcopus ad Anastasium imperatorem ita scribit: "Duae sunt quippe", inquit, "imperatrices augustae, quibus principaliter mundus hic regitur, auctoritas sacrata pontificum et regalis potestas, in quibus tanto gravius pondus est sacerdotum, quanto etiam pro ipsis regibus hominum in divino reddituri sunt examine rationem"' (*MGH, Conc.*, II, 2:1.3, p. 610). See above, pp. 35–6, for the Gelasian passage, which has 'imperator auguste', not 'imperatrices augustae'.

17 See the critical text contained in J. Reviron, *Les idées politico-religieuses d'un évêque du IXᵉ siècle. Jonas d'Orleans et son 'De institutione regia'. Etude et texte critique*, L'Eglise et l'Etat au Moyen Age 1 (Paris: J. Vrin, 1930), p. 134; and the discussion by R.L. Benson, 'The Gelasian doctrine: uses and transformations', in G. Makdisi, D. Sourdel and J. Sourdel-Thomine (eds), *La notion d'autorité au Moyen Age. Islam, Byzance, Occident* (Paris: Presses universitaires de France, 1982).

18 See H. Fuhrmann, *Einfluss und Verbreitung der pseudoisidorischen Fälschungen*, 3 vols, Schriften der MGH 24 (Stuttgart: Hiersemann, 1972–4).

19 *MGH, Epp.*, V, n. 17: 'Neque ignorare debueratis maius esse regimen animarum, quod est pontificale quam imperiale, quod est temporale' (p. 228), and 'Sic enim ipsis imperatoribus loquitur [Gregorius Nazanzenus] dicens, "Suscipitisne libertatem verbi, libenter accipitis, quod lex Christi sacerdotali vos nostrae sibicit potestati atque istis tribunalibus subdit?"' (p. 229).

20 'Universitas credentium ab hac sancta Romana ecclesia, quae caput omnium est ecclesiarum, doctrinam exquirit, integritatem fidei deposcit' (*MGH, Epp.*, VI, *Ep.* 86, p. 447); 'Nos divinitus … constituti … principes super omnem terram, id est, super universam ecclesiam' (*Ep.* 88, p. 475); 'Non autem vobis licet clericos iudicare, cum vos magis ab ipsis conveniat iudicari' (*Ep.* 99, c. 83, p. 595).

21 'Regale ministerium specialiter est populum dei gubernare et regere cum equitate et iustitia et, ut pacem et concordiam habeant, studere' (*MGH, Conc.*, II, 2:2.2, p. 651); *De institutione regia*, c. 4 (Reviron edn, p. 145).

22 'Fac [mitissime rex] quidquid potes pro persona quam gestas, pro ministerio regali quod portas, pro nomine Christiani quod habes, pro vice Christi qua fungeris' (*Via regia, PL*, 102, col. 958).

23 'Ut sanctae suae ecclesiae et regni huius curam gereremus' (*MGH, Cap.*, I, n. 150, c. 2, p. 303).

24 'Sed quamquam summa huius ministerii in nostra persona consistere videatur, tamen et divina auctoritate et humana ordinatione ita per partes divisum esse cognoscitur, ut unusquisque vestrum in suo loco et ordine partem nostri ministerii habere cognoscatur; unde apparet, quod ego omnium vestrum admonitor esse debeo, et omnes vos nostri adiutores esse debetis' (*MGH, Cap.*, I, n. 150, c. 3, p. 303); see also c. 8 (p. 304) and c. 14 (p. 305).

25 See Anton, *Fürstenspiegel*, pp. 293–4, 318.

26 See J. Devisse, *Hincmar, Archevêque de Reims 845–882*, 3 vols (Geneva: Droz, 1976), II, pp. 677 and 696; and Benson, 'Gelasian doctrine', p. 23.

27 See J.L. Nelson, 'The earliest surviving royal *Ordo*: some liturgical and historical aspects', in B. Tierney and P. Linehan (eds), *Authority and Power. Studies on Medieval Law and Government Presented to Walter Ullmann on his Seventieth Birthday* (Cambridge: Cambridge University Press, 1980), pp. 33–5.

28 For Carolingian coronation *ordines* see, especially, J.L. Nelson, *Politics and Ritual in Early Medieval Europe* (London: Hambledon Press, 1986), pp. 133–71, 239–57, 259–81, 283–307, 329–39, 361–74.

29 See P. Schramm, *Kaiser, Könige und Päpste*, 4 vols (Stuttgart: Hiersemann, 1968), II, pp. 140–248.

30 See 'Earliest surviving', p. 48.

31 See J.L. Nelson, 'National synods, kingship as office, and royal anointing: an early medieval syndrome', in *Politics and Ritual in Early Medieval Europe* (London: Hambledon Press, 1986), p. 250.

32 'Deus omnipotens, te, o clarissime rex, quando voluit, et ubi voluit, de regali nobilique genere nobiliter procreavit, et misericorditer ad lavacrum regenerationis perduxit: caput tuum oleo sacri chrismatis linivit, et diganter in filium adoptavit. Constituit te regem populi terrae, et proprii Filii sui in caelo fieri iussit haeredem' (*Via regia, PL*, 102, col. 933). The best modern discussion of this passage is in O. Eberhardt, *Via Regia. Der Fürstenspiegel Smaragds von St. Mihiel und seine literarische Gattung*, Münstersche Mittelalter-Schriften 28 (Munich: Wilhelm Fink Verlag, 1977), pp. 536ff. (see pp. 537–8 for a summary of the range of conflicting scholarly opinion).

33 'Coronet te Dominus corona gloriae in misericordia et miserationibus suis et ungat te in regni regimine oleo gratiae Spiritus sancti sui, unde unxit sacerdotes, reges, prophetas et martyres, qui per fidem vicerunt regna et operati sunt iustitiam atque adepti sunt promissiones; eisdemque promissionibus gratia Dei dignus efficiaris, quatenus eorum consortio in caelesti regno perfrui merearis. Amen ... Et pace in diebus tuis concessa cum palma victoriae te ad perpetuum regnum perducat. Amen. Et qui te voluit super populum suum constituere regem, et in praesenti seculo felicem et aeternae felicitatis tribuat esse consortem. Amen. Clerum ac populum, quem sua voluit opitulatione tuae subdere ditioni, sua dispensatione et tua administratione per diuturna tempora te faciat feliciter gubernare; quo divinis monitis parentes, adversitatibus omnibus carentes, bonis omnibus exuberantes, tuo ministerio fideli amore obsequentes et in praesenti seculo pacis tranquillitate fruantur et tecum aeternorum civium consortio potiri mereantur' (*MGH, Cap.*, II, p. 457).

34 See Ullmann, *Carolingian Renaissance*, pp. 73–4.

35 See ibid., p. 95.

36 'Mediator Dei et hominum te mediatorem cleri et plebis in hoc regni solio confirmet et in regnum eternum secum regnare faciat': for the text of this *ordo* see C. Erdmann, *Forschungen zur politischen Ideenwelt des Frühmittelalters* (Berlin: Akademie Verlag, 1951), pp. 87ff.

37 'Et unicuique in suo ordine secundum sibi competentes leges tam ecclesiasticas quam mundanas legem et iustitiam conservare' (MGH, Cap., II, n. 276, p. 339).

38 'Polliceor etiam me servaturum leges et statuta populo qui mihi ad regendum misericordia dei committitur' (MGH, Cap., II, n. 283, p. 364).

39 See 'Kingship, law and liturgy in the political thought of Hincmar of Rheims', in Politics and Ritual in Early Medieval Europe (London: Hambledon Press, 1986), p. 142.

40 'Accipe coronam regni, quae licet ab indignis ... capiti tuo imponi-tur ... intelligas per hanc te participem ministerii nostri non ignores, ita ut, sicut nos in interioribus pastores rectoresque animarum intelligimur, tu quoque in exterioribus verus Dei cultor strenuus contra omnes ... coronatus.'

41 'A qua consecratione ... proici a nullo debueram, saltem sine audientia et iudicio episcoporum, quorum ministerio in regem sum consecratus' (Libellus adversus Wenilonem, c. 3, MGH, Cap., II, p. 451).

42 The best study is J. Hannig, Consensus fidelium. Frühfeudale Interpretationen des Verhältnisses von Königtum und Adel am Beispiel des Frankenreiches, Monographien zur Geschichte des Mittelalters 27 (Stuttgart: Hiersemann, 1982).

43 See F. Graus, 'Über die sogennante germanische Treue', Historia I (1959), pp. 71–121; and Graus, 'Herrschaft und Treue. Betrachtungen zur Lehre von der germanischen Kontinuität', Historia XII (1966), pp. 5–44.

44 See E.A.R. Brown, 'The tyranny of a construct: feudalism and historians of medieval Europe', American Historical Review LXXIX (1974), pp. 1063–88, for the classic and highly influential attack on the concept of feudalism.

45 See, for instance, D.E. Luscombe, 'Introduction: the formation of political thought in the west (c. 750–c. 1150)' in J.H. Burns (ed.) The Cambridge History of Medieval Political Thought c. 350–c. 1450 (Cambridge: Cambridge University Press, 1988), pp. 159–60; and R. van Caenegem, 'Government, law and society (c. 750–c. 1150)', in J.H. Burns (ed.) The Cambridge History of Medieval Political Thought c. 350–c. 1450 (Cambridge: Cambridge University Press, 1988), pp. 198–210.

46 There was, for instance, the case of Tassilo, duke of Bavaria, who in 757 became Pippin's vassal (Annales regni Francorum, pp. 14–16).

47 See E. Magnou-Nortier, Foi et fidélité. Recherches sur l'évolution des liens personnels chez les Francs du VIIᵉ au IXᵉ siècle, Publications de l'Université de Toulouse-Le Mirail, série A, 28 (Association des publications de l'Université de Toulouse-Le Mirail, 1976), p. 120.

48 'Ego Hludowicus misericordia domini Dei nostri et electione populi rex constitutus' (MGH, Cap., II, n. 283, p. 364).

49 See Nelson, 'Kingship, law and liturgy', p. 153.

50 MGH, Cap., II, n. 254, pp. 253–5.

51 MGH, Cap., II, n. 269, p. 296.

52 See Nelson, 'Kingship, law and liturgy', p. 150.

53 'Lex consensu populi et constitutione regis fit' (*MGH, Cap.*, II, n. 273, p. 313). See also Hincmar, *De ordine palatii*, c. 8 (*MGH, Cap.*, II, p. 520): 'Habent enim reges et reipublicae ministri leges ... habent capitula christianorum regum ac progenitorum suorum, quae generali consensu fidelium suorum tenere legaliter promulgaverunt.'

54 'Wat waren de capitularia?', pp. 96–7.

55 See Hannig, *Consensus fidelium*, pp. 166–95.

56 See Ullmann, *Carolingian Renaissance*, pp. 178–9.

57 'Karolus gratia dei rex regnique Francorum rector et devotus ecclesiae defensor et adiutor' (*MGH, Cap.*, II, n. 19, p. 44): see T. Mayer, 'Staatsauffassung in der Karolingerzeit', in *Das Königtum. Seine geistigen und rechtlichen Grundlagen* (Lindau and Constance: Jan Thorbecke Verlag, 1956), pp. 170–71.

58 '[Tractare] de regis ac regni stabilitate et utilitate ... et suum atque totius populi communem profectum': see K.F. Werner, 'Hludowicus augustus: gouverner l'empire chrétien – idées et réalités', in P. Godman and R. Collins, *Charlemagne's Heir. New Perspectives on the Reign of Louis the Pious (814–840)* (Oxford: Clarendon Press, 1990), p. 89.

59 See F. Crosara, 'Respublica e respublicae. Cenni terminologici dall' età romana all' XI secolo', in G. Moschetti (ed.), *Atti del Congresso Internazionale di Diritto Romano e di Storia del Diritto, Verona 1948* (Milan: Giuffré, 1953), IV, p. 257; W. Wehlen, *Geschichtsschreibung und Staatsauffassung im Zeitalter Ludwigs des Frommen*, Historische Studien 418 (Lübeck and Hamburg: Matthiesen Verlag, 1970); E. Boshof, 'Einheitsidee und Teilungsprinzip in der Regierungszeit Ludwigs des Frommen', in P. Godman and R. Collins, *Charlemagne's Heir. New Perspectives on the Reign of Louis the Pious (814–840)* (Oxford: Clarendon Press, 1990), p. 165.

60 See T. Struve, *Die Entwicklung der organologischen Staatsauffassung im Mittelalter*, Monographien zur Geschichte des Mittelalters 16 (Stuttgart: Hiersemann, 1978), pp. 87–91; and J. Fried, 'Der Karolingische Herrschaftsverband im 9. Jh. zwischen "Kirche" und "Königshaus"', *Historische Zeitschrift* CCXXXV (1982), pp. 1–43.

61 See Struve, *Entwicklung*, p. 87.

62 'Interea nostis ... quibus ordinibus Christi constat ecclesia? Certum quippe quod secundum singulorum officia requirendus est ordo disciplinae et status rei publicae. Vnde primum considerari oportet intus divina, tum exterius humana, quia proculdubio his duobus totius ecclesiae status administratur ordinibus ... Habeat igitur rex rempublicam libere in usibus militiae suae ad dispensandum, habeat et Christus res ecclesiarum, quasi alteram rempublicam, omnium indigentium et sibi servientium usibus, suis commissam ministris fidelibus' (II, c. 2, p. 548).

63 The literature on the coronation of Charlemagne is vast. See, for instance, R. Folz, *The Concept of Empire in Western Europe from the Fifth to the Fourteenth Century* (London: Edward Arnold, 1969), pp. 19–23; P. Classen, 'Karl der Grosse, das Papsttum und Byzanz. Die Begründung des Karolingischen Kaisertums', in H. Beumann

(ed.), *Karl der Grosse* (Düsseldorf: Verlag L. Schwann, 1968), I, pp. 537–608; and K.F. Werner, 'L'empire carolingien et le Saint Empire', in M. Duverger (ed.), *Le concept d'empire* (Paris: Presses universitaires de France, 1980), pp. 151–98.

64 'Et tunc venerabilis et almificus presul manibus suis propriis pretiosissima corona coronavit eum. Tunc universi fideles Romani videntes tanta defensione et dilectione quam erga sanctam Romanam ecclesiam et eius vicarium habuit, unanimiter altisona voce, Dei nutu atque beati Petri clavigeri regni caelorum, exclamaverunt: "Karolo, piissimo Augusto a Deo coronato, magno et pacifico imperatori, vita et victoria." Ante sacram confessionem beati Petri apostoli, plures sanctos invocantes, ter dictum est: et ab omnibus constitutus est imperator Romanorum.' See *Liber pontificalis*, ed. L. Duchesne (Paris: Boccard, 1955), II, p. 7.

65 'Ablato patricii nomine imperator et augustus est appellatus' (*MGH, SS rer. Germ.*, VI, p. 112).

66 'Ipsa die sacratissima natalis Domini, cum rex ad missam ante confessionem beati Petri apostoli ab oratione surgeret, Leo Papa coronam capiti eius imposuit et a cuncto Romanorum populo adclamatum est: Carolo augusto, a Deo coronato magno et pacifico imperatori Romanorum, victoria et vita. Et post laudes ab apostolico more antiquorum principum adoratus est' (ibid.).

67 'Karolus serenissimus augustus a Deo coronatus magnus pacificus imperator Romanum gubernans imperium, qui et per misericordiam Dei rex Francorum et Langobardorum' (as, for instance, in *MGH, Cap.*, I, c. 45, p. 126).

68 'Quo tempore imperatoris et augusti nomen accepit. Quod primo in tantum aversatus est ut adfirmaret se eo die ... ecclesiam non intraturum si pontificis consilium praescire potuisset.' See Einhard, *Vita Karoli Magni*, O. Holder-Egger (ed.), *MGH, Scriptores rerum Germanicarum in usum scholarum*, 25, c. 28, p. 32 (1911).

69 See P. Classen, 'Romanum gubernans imperium. Zur Vorgeschichte der Kaisertitulatur Karls des Grossen', *Deutsches Archiv für Erforschung des Mittelalters* IX (1952), 103–21; and Classen, 'Karl der Grosse', p. 588.

70 Erdmann, *Forschungen zur politischen Ideenwelt*, pp. 1–51.

71 See his *Vom antiken zum frühmittelalterlichen Staatsbegriff: über Verwendung und Bedeutung von Res publica, regnum, imperium und status von Cicero bis Jordanis*, Orbis antiquus 16/17 (Münster: Aschendorff, 1977), p. 298.

72 Above, p. 16.

73 See, for instance, Folz, *Concept of Empire*, p. 17; Classen, 'Karl der Grosse', p. 592.

74 *MGH, Conc.*, 2: Supplementum, 1.6, pp. 20–2. See Folz, *Concept of Empire*, p. 19.

75 See Classen, 'Karl der Grosse', p. 587; Werner, 'L'empire carolingien', pp. 168–70.

76 'Karolus divina largiente gratia imperator et augustus idemque rex Francorum et Langobardorum dilecto et honorabili fratri Michaeli

glorioso imperatori et augusto aeternam in Domino nostro Jesu Christo salutem' (*MGH, Epp.*, 4, p. 556).

77 See J.L. Nelson, 'Kingship and Empire', in J.H. Burns (ed.), *The Cambridge History of Medieval Political Thought c. 350–c. 1450* (Cambridge: Cambridge University Press, 1988), p. 232.

78 'Sed quamvis haec admonitio devote ac fideliter fieret, nequaquam nobis nec his qui sanum sapiunt visum fuit, ut amore filiorum aut gratia unitas imperii a Deo nobis conservati divisione humana scinderetur, ne forte hac occasione scandalum in sancta ecclesia oriretur' (*MGH, Cap.*, I, n. 136, p. 270). For this transpersonal interpretation see E. Boshof, 'Einheitsidee', pp. 165, 178–80.

79 'Ita quoque nobis propter bonam opinionem, orthodosiam, regimen imperii Romani suscepimus: Graeci propter kacodosiam, id est malam opinionem, Romanorum imperatores existere cessaverunt' (*MGH, Epp.*, VII, p. 390).

80 'Excellentiam tuam ad honorem et exaltationem sanctae Romanae ecclesiae et ad securitatem populi Christiani eligendam esse speravimus' (from John's offer of the crown to Charles: *MGH, Epp.*, VII, n. 59, p. 311).

81 See Erdmann, *Forschungen zur politischen Ideenwelt*, p. 30.

82 See, for instance, H. Fuhrmann, 'Konstantinische Schenkung und abendländisches Kaisertum. Ein Beitrag zur Überlieferungsgeschichte des Constitutum Constantini', *Deutsches Archiv für die Erforschung des Mittelalters* XXII (1966), pp. 65–6.

83 'Quoniam, ubi principatus sacerdotum et christianae religionis caput ab imperatore caelesti constitutum est, iustum non est, ut illic imperator terrenus habeat potestatem' (*Constitutum Constantini*, c. 18, ed. H. Fuhrmann, *MGH, Fontes iuris Germanici antiqui in usum scholarum* X (Hanover, 1968), pp. 94–5).

84 'Et pontifex, qui pro tempore ipsius sacrosanctae Romanae ecclesiae extiterit, celsior et princeps cunctis sacerdotibus totius mundi existat' (c. 12, ibid., pp. 82–3).

85 See Fuhrmann, 'Konstantinische Schenkung und abendländisches Kaisertum', pp. 121–2.

86 See W. Ullmann, 'The origins of the *Ottonianum*', *The Cambridge Historical Journal* XI(1) (1952), pp. 114–28.

87 Widukind of Corvey, *Rerum gestarum Saxonicarum libri tres*, Paul Hirsch and H.-E. Lohmann (eds), *MGH, Scriptores rerum Germanicarum in usum scholarum*, LX (Hanover, 1935), 1.39 (p. 58) and 3.49 (p. 128).

88 Widukind, ibid., 3.76, p. 154. See Erdmann, *Forschungen zur politischen Ideenwelt*, pp. 44–7.

89 See Nelson, 'Kingship and empire', p. 245.

90 DO III.389, *MGH, Diplomata*, II, ii, 818–20.

91 DH II.284, *MGH, Diplomata*, III, 336.

92 See W. Ullmann, *The Growth of Papal Government in the Middle Ages*, 3rd edn (London: Methuen, 1970), p. 250; and Folz, *Concept of Empire*, p. 68.

93 See M. Maccarrone, 'Il sovrano "vicarius dei" nell'alto medio evo', in *The Sacral Kingship*. Contributions to the Central Theme of the VIIIth

International Congress for the History of Religions, Rome, April, 1955 (Leiden: E.J. Brill, 1959), pp. 590–1; R. Deshman, 'Christus rex et magi reges: Kingship and Christology in Ottonian and Anglo-Saxon art', *Frühmittelalterliche Studien. Jahrbuch des Instituts für Frühmittelalterforschung der Universität Münster* X (1976), pp. 387–9.

94 See E.H. Kantorowicz, *The King's Two Bodies: A Study in Medieval Political Theology* (Princeton: Princeton University Press, 1957), pp. 61–78; Deshman, 'Christus rex et magi reges'.

95 See K.J. Leyser, *Rule and Conflict in an Early Medieval Society: Ottonian Saxony* (London: Edward Arnold, 1979), pp. 102–3; and Leyser, *Medieval Germany and its Neighbours, 900–1250* (London: Hambledon Press, 1982), pp. 76–9. For the itinerant nature of this monarchy see John W. Bernhardt, *Itinerant Kingship and Royal Monasteries in Early Medieval Germany, c. 936–1075*, Cambridge Studies in Medieval Life and Thought, fourth series, 21 (Cambridge: Cambridge University Press, 1993), pp. 45–70.

96 See J. Gillingham, *The Kingdom of Germany in the High Middle Ages (900–1200)*, Historical Association Pamphlet 77 (London, 1971), pp. 9–11.

97 See H. Keller, 'Zum Charakter der "Staatlichkeit" zwischen karolingischer Reichsreform und hochmittelalterlichem Herrschaftsausbau', *Frühmittelalterliche Studien* XXIII (1989), p. 250.

98 'Si rex periit, regnum remansit, sicut navis remanet, cuius gubernator cadit. Aedes publicae fuerant, non privatae' – *Gesta Chuonradi imperatoris*, H. Bresslau (ed.), *MGH, Scriptores rerum Germanicarum in usum scholarum* 61 (Hanover, 1915), c. 7, p. 30.

99 See H. Beumann, 'Zur Entwicklung transpersonaler Staatsvorstellungen', in T. Mayer (ed.), *Das Königtum. Seine geistigen und rechtlichen Grundlagen*, Vorträge und Forschungen III (Lindau and Constance: Jan Thorbecke Verlag, 1956), pp. 193, 199.

100 See B. Paradisi, 'Formule di sovranità e tradizione biblica', in *Studi sul Medioevo giuridico*, Istituto storico italiano per il medio evo, Studi storici, fasc. 163–73, 2 vols (Rome, 1987), I, p. 494.

101 See B. Schneidmüller, *Karolingische Tradition und frühes französisches Königtum. Untersuchungen zur Herrschaftslegitimation der westfrankisch-französischen Monarchie im 10. Jahrhundert*, Frankfurter historische Abhandlungen 22 (Wiesbaden: Franz Steiner Verlag, 1979), pp. 67–8.

102 See K.F. Werner, 'Das hochmittelalterliche imperium im politischen Bewusstsein Frankreichs (10.–12. Jahrhundert)', *Historische Zeitschrift* CC (1965), pp. 16–18; Schneidmüller, *Karolingische Tradition*, pp. 177–8; J. Dunbabin, 'What's in a name? Philip, King of France', *Speculum* LXVIII(4) (1993), pp. 967–8.

103 See Werner, 'Hochmittelalterliche imperium', p. 16, n. 2; Schneidmüller, *Karolingische Tradition*, p. 67.

104 *Collectio canonum*, c. 7, *PL*, 139, col. 480.

105 Ibid., c. 9, *PL*, 139, col. 482; see M. Mostert, *The Political Theology of Abbo of Fleury. A Study of the Ideas about Society and Law of the Tenth-Century Monastic Reform Movement*, Medieval Studies and Sources 2 (Hilversum: Verloren Publishers, 1987), pp. 110, 130–2.

106 *Epitoma vitae regis Roberti pii*, R.-H. Bautier and G. Labory (eds), in Institut de recherche et d'histoire des textes, *Sources d'histoire médiévale*, I (Paris: Editions du Centre National de la Recherche Scientifique, 1965), p. 80.

107 See Werner, 'Hochmittelalterliche imperium', p. 16, n. 1.

108 *Cartularium Saxonicum*, W. de G. Birch (ed.) (London: Whiting & Co., 1893), III, nos. 1259, 1201, 1319, 1044; for assessment of the authenticity of charters see P.H. Sawyer, *Anglo-Saxon Charters: An Annotated Guide and Bibliography*, Royal Historical Society Guides and Handbooks (London: Royal Historical Society, 1968); see also J.L. Nelson, 'Inauguration rituals', in *Politics and Ritual in Early Medieval Europe* (London: Hambledon Press, 1986), pp. 301–3.

109 See discussion in E.E. Stengel, 'Imperator und imperium bei den Angelsachsen. Eine wort- und begriffsgeschichtliche Untersuchung', *Deutsches Archiv für die Erforschung des Mittelalters* XVI (1960), pp. 32–5.

110 *Historia ecclesiastica gentis Anglorum*, eds Bertram Colgrave and R.A.B. Mynors (Oxford: Clarendon Press, repr. 1991), 2.5, pp. 148–50; for this passage see also J.M. Wallace-Hadrill, *Bede's Ecclesiastical History of the English People. An Historical Commentary* (Oxford: Clarendon Press, 1988), pp. 57–8.

111 *Life of Alfred*, ed. W.H. Stevenson (Oxford: Clarendon Press, 1904).

112 For Spain see Erdmann, *Forschungen zur politischen Ideenwelt*, pp. 33–6; Folz, *Concept of Empire*, pp. 40–1; J.F. O'Callaghan, *A History of Medieval Spain* (Ithaca: Cornell University Press, 1975), pp. 121, 136, 164; R. Collins, *Early Medieval Spain. Unity in Diversity, 400–1100* (London: Macmillan, 1983), pp. 235–6.

113 See H. Löwe, 'Kaisertum und Abendland in Ottonischer und Frühsalischer Zeit', *Historische Zeitschrift* CXCVI (1963), p. 562; Werner, 'Hochmittelalterliche imperium', pp. 49–53.

3 POLITICAL IDEAS IN THE HIGH MIDDLE AGES, *c.* 1050–*c.* 1290

1 See his *Ep.*, 167 (*PL*, 54, col. 1203).

2 See R. Schieffer, *Die Entstehung des päpstlichen Investiturverbots für den deutschen König*, Schriften der MGH 28 (Stuttgart: Anton Hiersemann Verlag, 1981), p. 11, n. 16.

3 *Epistola*, VII, 3 (*PL*, 144, col. 440).

4 'Splendidae memoriae pater eius magnificus imperator sublimiter exaltavit ecclesiam' (ibid., col. 441).

5 *MGH, Libelli de lite*, I, 225.

6 See Schieffer, *Entstehung*, pp. 48–95.

7 'Salvo debito honore et reverentia dilecti filii nostri Henrici, qui inpresentiarum rex habetur et futurus imperator Deo concedente speratur, sicut iam sibi concessimus, et successorum illius, qui ab hac apostolica sede personaliter hoc ius impetraverint' (*MGH, Const.*, I, no. 382, c. 6, p. 540).

8 For papal use of these texts see above, p. 30. See also B. Szabó-Bechstein, 'Libertas ecclesiae: Ein Schlüsselbegriff des Investiturstreits

und seine Vorgeschichte, 4.–11. Jahrhundert', *Studi Gregoriani* XII (Rome, 1985), p. 5 (this is the best study of the concept of *libertas ecclesiae*).

9 *Reg.*, II, 55a (*MGH, Epistolae selectae in usum scholarum*, II, 2nd edn (Berlin: Weidmann, 1955), pp. 201–8).

10 As in I.S. Robinson, *The Papacy 1073–1198. Continuity and Innovation* (Cambridge: Cambridge University Press, 1990), at for instance p. 18.

11 'Quod illi liceat imperatores deponere'; 'Quod solus possit uti imperialibus insigniis'; 'Quod a fidelitate iniquorum subiectos potest absolvere.'

12 'Pape omnis potestas mundi subdi debet ... Regna mutare potest' (c. 10), quoted in Caspar's notes to Dictate XII, p. 204.

13 *Reg.* I, 21, p. 35.

14 *Reg.* III, 10, pp. 263–4.

15 For a translation of this letter see T.E. Mommsen and K.F. Morrison (trans.) and R.L. Benson (ed.), *Imperial Lives and Letters of the Eleventh Century* (with a historical introduction by K.F. Morrison), The Records of Civilization Sources and Studies, 67 (New York and London: Columbia University Press, 1962), pp. 150–1.

16 *Reg.* III, 10a, pp. 270–1.

17 See Schieffer, *Entstehung*, pp. 159–73: he argues that Gregory condemned lay investiture as a result of the crisis of 1076.

18 'Maior potestas exorciste conceditur, cum spiritualis imperator ad abiciendos demones constituitur, quam alicui laicorum causa secularis dominationis tribui possit' (*Reg.* VIII, 21, p. 555).

19 After quoting Gregory I's statement (for the text of which see p. 38, n. 137), Gregory VII added, 'Beatus Gregorius ... reges, qui statuta sua ... violarent, non modo deponi sed etiam excommunicari atque in eterno examine dampnari decrevit' (*Reg.* VIII, 21, pp. 550–1).

20 'Duo sunt quippe, imperator auguste, quibus principaliter mundus hic regitur, auctoritas sacrata pontificum et regalis potestas; in quibus tanto gravius pondus est sacerdotum, quanto etiam pro ipsis regibus hominum in divino reddituri sunt examine rationem; *et paucis interpositis* inquit: Nosti itaque inter hec illorum te pendere iudicio, non illos ad tuam velle redigi voluntatem' (*Reg.* VIII, 21, p. 553). For the section which Gregory omitted from Gelasius' text see p. 36, n. 125.

21 'In terra imperia regna principatus ducatus marchias comitatus et omnium hominum possessiones pro meritis tollere unicuique et concedere' (*Reg.* VII, 14a, p. 487).

22 'Quis nesciat reges et duces ab iis habuisse principium, qui Deum ignorantes superbia rapinis perfidia homicidiis postremo universis pene sceleribus mundi principe diabolo videlicet agitante super pares, scilicet homines, dominari ceca cupidine et intollerabili presumptione affectaverunt?' (*Reg.* VIII, 21, p. 552).

23 'Quis dubitet sacerdotes Christi regum et principum omniumque fidelium patres et magistros censeri?' (*Reg.* VIII, 21, p. 553); ibid., p. 562, he refers to 'oculos illius, videlicet Domini sacerdotes magistros et patres'.

24 'Quos sancta ecclesia sua sponte ad regimen vel imperium deliberato consilio advocat non pro transitoria gloria, sed pro multorum salute, humiliter obediant' (ibid., p. 561).

25 *Reg.* IX, 3, pp. 575–6.

26 See p. 37.

27 See, for instance, B. Tierney, 'The continuity of papal political theory in the thirteenth century. Some methodological considerations', *Mediaeval Studies* XXVII (1965), pp. 227–45.

28 'Quod absentes papa possit deponere' (*Reg.* II, 55a, Dictate, V).

29 See Robinson, *Papacy*, pp. 179–80.

30 'Quod nullus audeat condemnare apostolicam sedem apellantem' (*Reg.* II, 55a, Dictate, XX).

31 'Quod illius precepto et licentia subiectis liceat accusare' (ibid., Dictate, XXIV).

32 'Quod a nemine ipse iudicari debeat' (ibid., Dictate, XIX).

33 'Quod nullum capitulum nullusque liber canonicus habeatur absque illius auctoritate' (ibid., Dictate, XVII); 'Quod nulla synodus absque precepto eius debet generalis vocari' (ibid., Dictate, XVI).

34 'Quod illi soli licet pro temporis necessitate novas leges condere' (ibid., Dictate, VII).

35 See C. Morris, *The Papal Monarchy. The Western Church from 1050 to 1250* (Oxford: Clarendon Press, 1991), p. 131.

36 'Sanctam Romanam ecclesiam omnium ecclesiarum matrem et magistram' (H.E.J. Cowdrey, ed. and trans., *The 'Epistolae vagantes' of Pope Gregory VII* (Oxford: Clarendon Press, 1972), p. 134).

37 *MGH, L de L*, I, pp. 571–620.

38 *MGH, L de L*, I, p. 385 (c. 43).

39 'Ergo rex a Christi sacerdotibus, qui veri aecclesiae principes sunt, est constituendus; consensus tantum laicorum requirendus. Igitur quia sacerdotium iure regnum constituit, iure regnum sacerdotio subiacebit' (*MGH, L de L*, III, p. 73 (c. 22)).

40 'Regnum et sacerdotium deo nesciente sibi usurpavit. In quo piam dei ordinationem contempsit, que non in uno, sed in duobus, duo, id est regnum et sacerdotium, principaliter consistere voluit, sicut ipse salvator in passione sua de duorum gladiorum sufficientia typica intelligi innuit. Cui cum diceretur: 'domine, ecce duo gladii hic,' respondit, 'satis est,' significans hac sufficienti dualitate spiritualem et carnalem gladium in ecclesia esse gerendum, quibus omne nocivum foret amputandum, videlicet sacerdotali ad obedientiam regis pro deo, regali vero gladio ad expellendos Christi inimicos exterius, et ad obedientiam sacerdotii interius' (C. Erdmann (ed.), *Die Briefe Heinrichs IV.* (Leipzig: Hiersemann Verlag, 1937), p. 19).

41 See pp. 49–50.

42 See I.S. Robinson, *Authority and Resistance in the Investiture Contest. The Polemical Literature of the Late Eleventh Century* (Manchester: Manchester University Press, 1978), p. 136. For Peter Damian, see W. Levison, 'Die mittelalterliche Lehre von den beiden Schwerten', *Deutsches Archiv für die Erforschung des Mittelalters* IX (1952), pp. 28–9.

43 *In Cantica canticorum et de sancta Maria tractatus ad Comitissam Matildam,* eds B. Bischoff and B. Traeger, Spicilegium Friburgense, 19 (Freiburg, Schweiz: Universitätsverlag, 1973), p. 52.

44 *MGH, Epp.,* VI, 327, 502, 641.

45 Letter 17, *Die Briefe Heinrichs IV.,* ed. Erdmann, p. 25 (written in 1082).

46 'Et ita de alio in alium caritate tenderetur, dum nec sacerdotii regnum nec sacerdotium regni honore privaretur' (*Die Briefe Heinrichs IV.,* ed. Erdmann, p. 19).

47 'Ego H. dei gratia rex cum omnibus episcopis nostris tibi dicimus: descende, descende!' (*Die Briefe Heinrichs IV.,* ed. Erdmann, p. 17). See p. 90, n. 15.

48 *MGH, L de L,* I, pp. 435–7 (c. 2). For *Cunctos populos* see p. 5. *Placuit* was Constantius' decree of 354 closing down pagan temples.

49 *MGH, L de L,* I, pp. 438–9 (c. 4).

50 *MGH, Scriptores,* XI, pp. 591–681, at 598, 602, 609 and 671 (for *vicarius conditoris*). For the theme of Romanism and the Salians see especially T. Struve, 'Kaisertum und Romgedanke in salischer Zeit', *Deutsches Archiv für die Erforschung des Mittelalters* XLIV (1988), pp. 424–54.

51 'His duobus ecclesiae capitibus discordantibus, omnia sive animae sive corpori profectura turbantur et ad interitum inclinantur' (*MGH, L de L,* I, p. 470).

52 *MGH, L de L,* I, pp. 466–7.

53 'Quamvis rex a numero laicorum merito in huiusmodi separetur, cum oleo consecrationis inunctus sacerdotalis ministerii particeps esse cognoscitur' (*MGH, L de L,* I, p. 467).

54 *MGH, L de L,* II, pp. 184–5 (Liber I, c. 1).

55 'Igitur, sive sit ille Gregorius, sive Hildebrant, vel alius quisquam, qui praeest parti, non ecclesiae, non potuit Henrichum regem damnare, qui certe hoc studet, hoc optat et maxime laborat, ut fiat unum corpus ecclesiae, quatinus perinde etiam possit fieri unum corpus rei publicae' (*MGH, L de L,* II, p. 228 (Liber II, c. 15)).

56 'Qui, cum pro pontificali dignitate non deberent vel negotiis saecularibus sese implicare, usurpaverunt sibi ordinationem regiae dignitatis contra Dei ordinationem' (*MGH, L de L,* II, p. 226 (Liber II, c. 15)).

57 *MGH, L de L,* II, p. 199 (Liber I, c. 11); ibid., p. 227 (Liber II, c. 15). See p. 92, n. 19.

58 *MGH, L de L,* II, p. 188 (Liber I, c. 3).

59 'Quis poterit discernere causam regni a causa sacerdotii?' (*MGH, L de L,* II, p. 462 (c. 11).

60 'Ergo concordia principis pontifex ordinetur, ut eius obsequio in rebus temporalibus eclesia fulceatur' (*MGH, L de L,* II, p. 538 (c. 6)).

61 See G.H. Williams, *The Norman Anonymous of 1100 A.D. Toward the Identification and Evaluation of the So-called Anonymous of York,* Harvard Theological Studies 18 (Cambridge, Mass.: Harvard University Press, 1951). For a critical text see K. Pellens (ed.), *Die Texte des normannischen Anonymus. Neu aus des HS 415 des Corpus Christi College Cambridge,* Veröffentlichungen des Instituts für Europäische Geschichte Mainz, 42 (Wiesbaden: Franz Steiner Verlag, 1966).

62 'In una quippe erat naturaliter individuus homo, in altera per gratiam christus, id est, deus-homo' (*Die Texte des normannischen Anonymus*, ed. Pellens, p. 130).

63 See Williams, *Norman Anonymous*, p. 166.

64 'Manifestum est reges habere sacrosanctam potestatem ecclesiastici regiminis super ipsos etiam pontifices Domini et imperium super eos, ut et ipsi pie fideliterque regant sanctam ecclesiam' (see Pellens' discussion in *Die Texte des normannischen Anonymus*, p. xxxvi).

65 *MGH, L de L*, I, pp. 391–2 (c. 47).

66 See Robinson, *Authority and Resistance*, p. 128. See also H. Fuhrmann, ' "Volkssouveränität" und "Herrschaftsvertrag" bei Manegold von Lautenbach', in S. Gagnér *et al.* (eds), *Festschrift für Hermann Krause* (Cologne/Vienna: Böhlau Verlag, 1975), pp. 21–42.

67 See p. 30.

68 'They all drank from the spiritual rock that followed them as they went, and that rock was Christ.'

69 See Robinson, *Authority and Resistance*, p. 172. For Cyprian see G. Haendler, 'Die drei grossen nordafrikanischen Kirchenväter über Mt 16, 18–19', in *Die Rolle des Papsttums in der Kirchengeschichte bis 1200. Ein Überblick und achtzehn Untersuchungen* (Göttingen: Vandenhoeck & Ruprecht, 1993), pp. 126–8.

70 See F. Gillmann, 'Zur scholastischen Auslegung von Mt 16, 18', *Archiv für katholisches Kirchenrecht* CIV (1924), pp. 41–53. See also Matthew 18:18 for Christ's grant of powers of binding and loosing to all the apostles.

71 See W. Ullmann, *The Growth of Papal Government in the Middle Ages*, 3rd edn (London: Methuen, 1970), p. 408.

72 *MGH, L de L*, II, pp. 644–5.

73 See M.J. Wilks, '*Ecclesiastica* and *Regalia*: Papal investiture policy from the Council of Guastalla to the First Lateran Council, 1106–23', *Studies in Church History* VII (1971), pp. 69–85.

74 'Quanto autem vita spiritualis dignior est quam terrena, et spiritus quam corpus, tanto spiritualis potestas terrenam sive saecularem potestatem honore, ac dignitati praecedit. Nam spiritualis potestas terrenam potestatem et instituere habet, *ut sit*, et iudicare habet si bona non fuerit' (2.2.4, *PL*, 176, col. 418).

75 See M. Maccarrone, ' "Potestas directa" e "potestas indirecta" nei teologi del XII e XIII secolo', in *Sacerdozio e regno da Gregorio VII a Bonifacio VIII*, Miscellanea Historiae Pontificiae XVIII (1954), pp. 29–31. For a hierocratic interpretation see J.A. Watt, 'Spiritual and temporal powers', in J.H. Burns (ed.), *The Cambridge History of Medieval Political Thought c. 350–c. 1450* (Cambridge: Cambridge University Press), pp. 368–9. For Hugh's political ideas see also F.-W. Witte, 'Die Staats- und Rechtsphilosophie des Hugo von St Viktor', *Archiv für Rechts- und Sozialphilosophie* XLIII (1957), pp. 555–74; F. Merzbacher, 'Recht und Gewaltenlehre bei Hugo von St. Viktor', *Zeitschrift der Savigny Stiftung für Rechtsgeschichte*, Kan. Abt. XLIV (1958), pp. 181–208; and J. Ehlers, *Hugo von St. Viktor. Studien zum Geschichtsdenken und zur Geschichtsschreibung des 12.*

Jahrhunderts, Frankfurter historische Abhandlungen 7 (Wiesbaden: Steiner Verlag, 1973).

76 'Et quidem quotidie perstrepunt in palatio leges, sed Iustiniani, non Domini. Iustene etiam istud?' (*De consideratione*, 1.4.5, p. 399).

77 'Alii in partem sollicitudinis, tu in plenitudinem vocatus es. Aliorum potestas certis artatur limitibus: tua extenditur et in ipsos, qui potestatem super alios acceperunt' (*De consideratione*, 2.8.16, p. 424).

78 'Tuus ergo et ipse, tuo forsitan nutu, etsi non tua manu, evaginandus. Alioquin, si nullo modo ad te pertineret et is, dicentibus apostolis: "Ecce gladii duo hic," non respondisset Dominus: "Satis est," sed: "Nimis est." Vterque ergo ecclesiae, et spiritualis scilicet gladius, et materialis, sed is quidem pro ecclesia, ille vero et ab ecclesia exserendus: ille sacerdotis, is militis manu, sed sane ad nutum sacerdotis et iussum imperatoris' (*De consideratione*, 4.3.7, p. 454).

79 *Epistola* CCLVI, *Opera omnia*, VIII, p. 163. For Stickler's views see, for instance, his 'Sacerdozio e regno nelle nuove ricerche attorno ai secoli XII e XIII nei Decretisti e Decretalisti fino alle decretali di Gregorio IX', in *Sacerdozio e regno da Gregorio VII a Bonifacio VIII*, Miscellanea Historiae Pontificiae XVIII (1954), pp. 1–26. For a useful discussion of Stickler's interpretation see S. Chodorow, *Christian Political Theory and Church Politics in the Mid-Twelfth Century: The Ecclesiology of Gratian's Decretum* (Berkeley: University of California Press, 1972), pp. 223–8 and 245–6.

80 For a hierocratic interpretation see, for instance, Ullmann, *Growth of Papal Government*, pp. 426–37. See also E. Kennan, 'The "De consideratione" of St Bernard and the papacy in the mid-twelfth century: a review of scholarship', *Traditio* XXIII (1967), pp. 73–115.

81 See, for instance, T. Gregory, 'L'idea di natura nella filosofia medievale prima dell' ingresso della fisica di Aristotele – il secolo XII', in *La filosofia della natura nel medioevo. Atti del Terzo Congresso internazionale di filosofia medioevale* (Passo della Mendola, Trento, 31 agosto – 5 settembre 1964) (Milan: Società editrice Vita e Pensiero, 1966), pp. 27–65; and T. Gregory, 'La nouvelle idée de nature et de savoir scientifique au XIIᵉ siècle', in J.E. Murdoch and E.D. Sylla (eds), *The Cultural Context of Medieval Learning* (Proceedings of the First International Colloquium on Philosophy, Science and Theology in the Middle Ages, September 1973), Boston Studies in the Philosophy of Science 26 (Dordrecht/Boston: D. Reidel Publishing Co., 1975), pp. 193–218. See also G. Post, *Studies in Medieval Legal Thought, Public Law and the State, 1100–1322* (Princeton: Princeton University Press, 1964), pp. 499–521.

82 See B. Tierney, '*Natura id est deus*: a case of juristic pantheism', *Journal of the History of Ideas* XXIV (1963), pp. 307–22.

83 See C.J. Nederman, 'Nature, sin and the origins of society: the Ciceronian tradition in medieval political thought', *Journal of the History of Ideas* XLIX (1988), pp. 3–26.

84 *Policraticus*, 1.4, 3.6, 4.1, 4.5, 6.21 (bees).

85 *Policraticus*, 4.1.

86 See p. 32; also M. Kerner, *Johannes von Salisbury und die logische Struktur seines Policraticus* (Wiesbaden: Franz Steiner Verlag, 1977), pp. 170–6.

87 'Princeps vero capitis in re publica optinet locum uni subiectus Deo et his qui vices illius agunt in terris, quoniam et in corpore humano ab anima vegetatur caput et regitur. Cordis locum senatus optinet, a quo bonorum operum et malorum procedunt initia. Oculorum aurium et linguae officia sibi vendicant iudices et praesides provinciarum. Officiales et milites manibus coaptantur. Qui semper adsistunt principi, lateribus assimilantur. Quaestores et commentarienses … ad ventris et intestinorum refert imaginem. Quae, si immensa aviditate congesserint et congesta tenacius reservaverint, innumerabiles et incurabiles generant morbos, ut vitio eorum totius corporis ruina immineat. Pedibus vero solo iugiter inherentibus agricolae coaptantur, quibus capitis providentia tanto magis necessaria est, quo plura inveniunt offendicula, dum in obsequio corporis in terra gradiuntur, eisque iustius tegumentorum debetur suffragium, qui totius corporis erigunt sustinent et promovent molem. Pedum adminicula robustissimo corpori tolle, suis viribus non procedet sed aut turpiter inutiliter et moleste manibus repet aut brutorum animalium ope movebitur' (*Policraticus*, 5.2).

88 See Kerner, *Johannes von Salisbury*, pp. 176–81; and T. Struve, *Die Entwicklung der organologischen Staatsauffassung im Mittelalter*, Monographien zur Geschichte des Mittelalters 16 (Stuttgart: Hiersemann, 1978), pp. 126–30; but see also D.E. Luscombe, 'John of Salisbury in recent scholarship', in M. Wilks (ed.), *The World of John of Salisbury*, Studies in Church History, Subsidia 3 (Oxford: Basil Blackwell, 1984), p. 24, for the debate about whether John derived his organic analogy from William of Conches.

89 'Publicae ergo utilitatis minister et aequitatis servus est princeps' (*Policraticus*, 4.2). For John's contribution to the theme of the common good see P. Hibst, *Utilitas publica – Gemeiner Nutz – Gemeinwohl. Untersuchungen zur Idee eines politischen Leitbegriffs von der Antike bis zum späten Mittelalter*. Europäische Hochschulschriften, Reihe III. Geschichte und ihre Hilfswissenschaften, Series III, vol. 497 (Frankfurt, Bern, New York, Paris: Peter Lang, 1991), pp. 179–84.

90 'Est ergo tirannus, ut eum philosophi depinxerunt, qui violenta dominatione populum premit, sicut qui legibus regit princeps est. Porro lex donum Dei est, aequitatis forma, norma iustitiae, divinae voluntatis imago' (*Policraticus*, 8.17).

91 'Tirannus, pravitatis imago, plerumque etiam occidendus' (*Policraticus*, 8.17).

92 See R.H. and M.A. Rouse, 'John of Salisbury and the doctrine of tyrannicide', *Speculum* XLII (1967), pp. 693–709; but see also C.J. Nederman, 'A duty to kill: John of Salisbury's theory of tyrannicide', *Review of Politics* L (1988), pp. 365–89.

93 'Secundum quam decet vivere omnes qui in politicae rei universitate versantur' (*Policraticus*, 4.2).

94 'Hunc ergo gladium de manu Ecclesiae accipit princeps, cum ipsa tamen gladium sanguinis omnino non habeat. Habet tamen et istum, sed eo utitur per principis manum, cui cohercendorum corporum contulit potestatem, spiritualium sibi in pontificibus auctoritate reservata. Est ergo princeps sacerdotii quidem minister et qui sacrorum officiorum illam partem exercet quae sacerdotii manibus videntur indigna. Sacrarum namque legum omne officium religiosum et pium est, illud tamen inferius, quod in poenis criminum exercetur et quandam carnificii repraesentare videtur imaginem' (*Policraticus*, 4.3).

95 'Merito in eum omnium subditorum potestas confertur, ut in utilitate singulorum et omnium exquirenda et facienda sibi ipse sufficiat, et humanae rei publicae status optime disponatur, dum sunt alter alterius membra' (*Policraticus*, 4.1).

96 *Policraticus*, 5.2, 4.2.

97 'Omnium legum inanis est censura si non divinae legis imaginem gerat; et inutilis est constitutio principis si non est ecclesiasticae disciplinae conformis' (*Policraticus*, 4.6). See G. Micza, *Das Bild der Kirche bei Johannes von Salisbury*, Bonner historische Forschungen 34 (Bonn: Ludwig Röhrscheid Verlag, 1970), pp. 78–9.

98 'In terris quaedam divinae maiestatis imago' (*Policraticus*, 4.1).

99 See D.1.1.1: 'Ius est ars boni et aequi. Cuius merito quis nos sacerdotes appellet: iustitiam namque colimus ... veram nisi fallor philosophiam, non simulatam affectantes' (Ulpian).

100 See pp. 11–12, for Roman law ideas; and for a magisterial treatment of Decretist and Glossatorial doctrines concerning natural law see R. Weigand, *Die Naturrechtslehre der Legisten und Dekretisten von Irnerius bis Accursius und von Gratian bis Johannes Teutonicus*, Münchener Theologische Studien III. Kanonistische Abteilung 26 (Munich: Max Huebler Verlag, 1967).

101 *Decr. Grat.*, Dist.1, c. 1: 'Nomine vero legis humanae mores iure conscripti et traditi intelligantur'; ibid., Dist.4, c. 3: 'Leges instituuntur, cum promulgantur, firmantur, cum moribus utentium approbantur.'

102 See K. Pennington, 'Law, legislative authority, and theories of government, 1150–1300', in J.H. Burns (ed.), *The Cambridge History of Medieval Political Thought, c. 350–c. 1450* (Cambridge: Cambridge University Press, 1988), p. 425. For the contradictions in the *Corpus iuris civilis* see above, pp. 9–10.

103 See K. Pennington, *Pope and Bishops. The Papal Monarchy in the Twelfth and Thirteenth Centuries* (Philadelphia: University of Pennsylvania Press, 1984), pp. 17–20.

104 See S. Kuttner, 'Sur les origines du terme "droit positif"', *Revue historique de droit français et étranger*, 4ième série XV (Paris, 1936), pp. 728–40.

105 See p. 11 (discussion of *l. Digna vox*).

106 See B. Tierney, '"The prince is not bound by the laws." Accursius and the origins of the modern state', *Comparative Studies in Society and History* V(4) (July 1963), pp. 378–400.

107 See Pennington, *Pope and Bishops*, pp. 65–73, and *The Prince and the Law* (Berkeley: University of California Press, 1993), pp. 54–75.

108 See p. 32.
109 See J.A. Watt, 'The use of the term "plenitudo potestatis" by Hostiensis', in S. Kuttner and J.J. Ryan (eds), Proceedings of the Second International Congress of Medieval Canon Law (Boston College, 12–16 August, 1963), Monumenta Iuris Canonici, Series C: Subsidia I (Vatican City, 1965), pp. 161–87.
110 See B. Tierney, 'Tuck on rights: some medieval problems', History of Political Thought IV(3) (Winter 1983), pp. 429–41; B. Tierney, 'Origins of natural rights language: texts and contexts, 1150–1250', History of Political Thought X(4) (Winter 1989), pp. 615–46.
111 See L. Fowler-Magerl, Repertorien zur Frühzeit der gelehrten Rechte: Ordo iudiciorum vel ordo iudiciarius. Ius commune, Sonderhefte 19 (Frankfurt-am-Main: Klostermann, 1984).
112 Decr. Grat., Dist.40, c. 6.
113 For the text of Huguccio's gloss on the words 'nisi deprehendatur a fide devius', see B. Tierney, Foundations of the Conciliar Theory. The Contribution of the Medieval Canonists from Gratian to the Great Schism (Cambridge: Cambridge University Press, 1955), pp. 248–50.
114 On Decr. Grat., Dist.22, c. 1, ed. H. Singer (Paderborn: F. Schoningh, 1902), p. 47.
115 See W.P. Müller, Huguccio: The Life, Works and Thought of a Twelfth-Century Jurist, Studies in Medieval and Early Modern Canon Law 3 (Washington, DC: Catholic University of America Press, 1994).
116 See A.M. Stickler, 'Alanus Anglicus als Verteidiger des monarchischen Papsttums', Salesianum XXI (1959), pp. 361–3.
117 See K. Pennington, 'The legal education of Pope Innocent III', and 'Further thoughts on Pope Innocent III's knowledge of law' in his Popes, Canonists and Texts, 1150–1550 (Aldershot: Variorum, 1993).
118 See W. Imkamp, Das Kirchenbild Innocenz' III. (1198–1216), Päpste und Papsttum 22 (Stuttgart: Anton Hiersemann Verlag, 1983).
119 X.1.6.34.
120 Regestum super negotio Romani imperii, 29, ed. F. Kempf (Rome: Pontificia Universitas Gregoriana, 1947), p. 43.
121 X.4.17.13.
122 X.2.1.13.
123 X.2.2.10.
124 'Constitui te super gentes et regna, ut evellas et destruas, et dissipes, et aedifices, et plantes.'
125 Registrum, 1, 401, p. 600 (ed. O. Hageneder and A. Haidacher).
126 X.4.17.13.
127 See, for instance, A Short History of the Papacy in the Middle Ages (London: Methuen, 1972), p. 223.
128 See, for instance, his Vicarius Christi. Storia del titolo papale (Rome: Facultas Theologica Pontificii Athenaei Lateranensis, 1952), pp. 110–16.
129 See his Pope and Bishops, pp. 67–74.
130 See B. Tierney, The Crisis of Church and State, 1050–1300 (Englewood Cliffs, N.J.: Prentice-Hall, 1964), p. 150.
131 Sext., 2.14.2. For Innocent IV's political and ecclesiological ideas see A. Melloni, Innocenzo IV. La concezione e l'esperienza della cristianità come regimen unius personae (Genoa: Marietti, 1990).

132 But see Pennington, *Prince and Law*, p. 75.
133 See K. Pennington, 'Bartholomé de Las Casas and the tradition of medieval law', *Church History* XXXIX (1970), pp. 149–61; and J. Muldoon, *Popes, Lawyers and Infidels: The Church and the Non-Christian World, 1250–1500* (Philadelphia: University of Pennsylvania Press, 1979).
134 See S. Mochi Onory, *Fonti canonistiche dell'idea moderna dello stato – imperium spirituale, iurisdictio divina, sovranità*, Publ. dell'Università Cattolica del Sacro Cuore, n.s., 38 (Milan: Società editrice 'Vita e Pensiero', 1951), and B. Tierney's criticisms of this in 'Some recent works on the political theories of the medieval canonists', *Traditio* X (1954), pp. 612–19.
135 For a discussion and the text of this *quaestio* see W. Ullmann, 'Arthur's homage to King John', *English Historical Review* XCIV (1979), pp. 356–64.
136 See Ullmann, 'Arthur's homage', p. 362, n. 1. For a survey of the modern literature on both formulae see H.G. Walther, *Imperiales Königtum, Konziliarismus und Volkssouveränität. Studien zu den Grenzen des mittelalterlichen Souveränitätsgedankens* (Munich: Wilhelm Fink Verlag, 1976), pp. 65–111.
137 See E.M. Meijers, *Etudes d'histoire du droit*, eds R. Feenstra and H.F.W.D. Fischer, III (Leiden: Universitaire Pers, 1959), pp. 192–3; and R. Feenstra, 'Jean de Blanot et la formule "Rex Franciae in regno suo princeps est"', in *Etudes d'histoire de droit canonique dédiées à Gabriel Le Bras*, II (Paris: Sirey, 1965), pp. 885–95.
138 See his *Super libro constitutionum*, Proem, 3–7 (ed. F. Calasso, *I Glossatori e la teoria della sovranità: studio di diritto comune pubblico*, 3rd edn (Milan: Giuffrè, 1957), pp. 180–6).
139 See G. Verbeke, 'Moerbeke, traducteur et interprète; un texte et une pensée', in J. Brams and W. Vanhamel (eds), *Guillaume de Moerbeke. Recueil d'Etudes à l'occasion du 700ᵉ anniversaire de sa mort (1286)* (Louvain: University Press, 1989), pp. 6, 10, 20.
140 For medieval Latin translations of Aristotle see B.G. Dod, 'Aristoteles latinus', in N. Kretzmann *et al.* (eds), *The Cambridge History of Later Medieval Philosophy* (Cambridge: Cambridge University Press, 1982), pp. 45–79.
141 See C. Flüeler, *Rezeption und Interpretation der Aristotelischen Politica im späten Mittelalter*, 2 vols (Amsterdam and Philadelphia: B.R. Grüner, 1992), I, pp. 4–6.
142 See, for instance, from the Carolingian period, Rhabanus Maurus' letter to Abbot Brunward (*MGH, Epp.*, V, 23, p. 528); and Pope Stephen VI's letter to Emperor Basil I (885) (*MGH, Epp.*, VII, 107, p. 372). See also John of Salisbury, *Policraticus*, 4.2, 5.2 and 7.23.
143 *Politics*, 1253a.
144 For the dating of these works see Flüeler, *Rezeption*, I pp. 22–30 and 119–20.
145 'Gratia non tollit sed perficit naturam' (*ST* Ia, 8, 2).
146 *ST* Ia, 96, 4.

147 'Quia homo vivendo secundum virtutem ad ulteriorem finem
ordinatur, qui consistit in fruitione divina ... oportet eumdem finem
esse multitudinis humanae, qui est hominis unius. Non est ergo
ultimus finis multitudinis congregatae vivere secundum virtutem,
sed per virtuosam vitam pervenire ad fruitionem divinam' (De
regno, 1, 15, p. 274).
148 See Hibst, Utilitas publica, p. 185.
149 ST Ia IIae, 91–5.
150 'Quaedam rationis ordinatio ad bonum commune, ab eo qui curam
communitatis habet, promulgata' (ST Ia IIae, 90, 4).
151 ST Ia IIae, 95, 2.
152 ST Ia IIae, 94, 5.
153 'Omne autem naturale regimen ab uno est. In membrorum enim
multitudine unum est quod omnia movet, scilicet cor ... Est etiam
apibus unus rex, et in toto universo unus Deus factor omnium et
rector' (De regno 1.3, p. 259).
154 'Hoc igitur officium rex suscepisse cognoscat, ut sit in regno sicut in
corpore anima et sicut Deus in mundo' (De regno, 1, 13, p. 272). See D.E.
Luscombe, 'Conceptions of hierarchy before the thirteenth century', in
A. Zimmermann (ed.), Soziale Ordnungen im Selbstverständnis des
Mittelalters (Berlin and New York: Walter de Gruyter, 1979), pp. 1–19;
D.E. Luscombe, 'Thomas Aquinas and conceptions of hierarchy in the
thirteenth century', in A. Zimmermann (ed.), Thomas von Aquin. Werke
und Wirkung im Licht neuerer Forschungen (Berlin and New York:
Walter de Gruyter, 1988), pp. 261–77.
155 ST Ia IIae, 90, 1; Ia IIae, 96, 5; Ia IIae, 97, 3.
156 In octo libros politicorum Aristotelis expositio, 1.1.13.
157 ST Ia IIae, 95, 4; Ia IIae, 105, 1. See J.M. Blythe, Ideal Government
and the Mixed Constitution in the Middle Ages (Princeton: Princeton
University Press, 1992), pp. 39–59.
158 'Condere legem vel pertinet ad totam multitudinem, vel pertinet ad
personam publicam quae totius multitudinis curam habet' (ST Ia
IIae, 90, 3).
159 'Si enim sit libera multitudo, quae possit sibi legem facere, plus est
consensus totius multitudinis ad aliquid observandum quem
consuetudo manifestat, quam auctoritas principis, qui non habet
potestatem condendi legem, nisi inquantum gerit personam
multitudinis' (ST Ia IIae, 97, 3).
160 'Experimento videtur quod una civitas per annuos rectores adminis-
trata, plus potest interdum quam rex aliquis, si haberet tres vel
quatuor civitates' (De regno, 1, 5, p. 262).
161 'Relinquitur simpliciter magis esse expediens sub rege uno vivere,
quam sub regimine plurium' (De regno, 1, 6, p. 263).
162 De regno, 1, 1 (pp. 257–8) and 4 (p. 260).
163 'Nisi forte potestati spirituali etiam secularis potestas coniungatur,
sicut in Papa, qui utriusque potestatis apicem tenet scilicet spiritualis et saecularis, hoc illo disponente qui est sacerdos et rex,
sacerdos in aeternum secundum ordinem Melchisedech, Rex regum,
et Dominus dominantium' (Distinctio, 44, 3, 4), as quoted in A.P.

d'Entrèves (ed.) and J.G. Dawson (trans.), *Aquinas Selected Political Writings* (Oxford: Basil Blackwell, 1970), p. 186.

164 See Watt, 'Spiritual and temporal powers', p. 380.

165 'Et praecipue Summo Sacerdoti, successori Petri, Christi Vicario, Romano Pontifici, cui omnes reges populi Christiani oportet esse subditos, sicut ipsi Domino Iesu Christo. Sic enim ei, ad quem finis ultimi cura pertinet, subdi debent illi, ad quos pertinet cura antecedentium finium, et eius imperio dirigi' (*De regno*, 1, 15, p. 275).

166 *ST* IIa IIae, 10–12.

167 *De regimine principum* 3.2:2, 3 and 5, pp. 453–8 and 461–5.

168 See J. Miethke, 'Politische Theorien im Mittelalter', in H.J. Lieber (ed.), *Politische Theorien von der Antike bis zur Gegenwart* (Munich: Olzog Verlag, 1991), pp. 92–3.

169 'Sciendum est regem et quemlibet principantem esse medium inter legem naturalem et positivam; nam nullus recte principatur nisi agat ut recta ratio dictat: nam ratio debet esse regula humanorum operum' (*De regimine principum* 3.2:29, p. 532).

4 POLITICAL IDEAS IN THE LATE MIDDLE AGES, *c.* 1290–*c.* 1450

1 See J.R. Strayer, *The Reign of Philip the Fair* (Princeton: Princeton University Press, 1980), p. 267.

2 For an English translation of this bull see B. Tierney, *The Crisis of Church and State, 1050–1300* (Englewood Cliffs, N.J.: Prentice-Hall, 1964), pp. 185–6.

3 'Spiritualis potestas terrenam potestatem instituere habet, et iudicare, si bona non fuerit' (Extrav. comm. 1.8.1). For Hugh of St Victor see p. 108. For a discussion of the intellectual context of *Unam sanctam* see W. Ullmann, 'Boniface VIII and his contemporary scholarship', *Journal of Theological Studies*, n.s., XXVII(1) (1976), pp. 58–87.

4 'Porro subesse Romano Pontifici omni humanae creaturae declaramus, dicimus, diffinimus et pronunciamus omnino esse de necessitate salutis'; see Aquinas, *Contra errores Graecorum*, 2.27, 'Ostenditur quod subesse Romano pontifici sit de necessitate salutis' (as quoted in Ullmann, 'Boniface VIII', p. 82, n. 4).

5 Extrav. comm. 5.7.2.

6 'Quadraginta anni sunt quod nos sumus experti in iure et scimus quod duae potestates ordinatae a Deo' (P. Dupuy, *Histoire du differend d'entre le pape Boniface VIII et Philippes le Bel roy de France* (Paris, 1655), *Preuves*, p. 77): response to ambassadors of French Estates (June 1302). See J. Muldoon, 'Boniface VIII's forty years of experience in the law', *The Jurist* XXXI (1971), pp. 449–77.

7 For an edition and translation of the text see N.N. Erikson, 'A dispute between a priest and a knight', *Proceedings of the American Philosophical Society* CXI(5) (1967), pp. 288–309.

8 'Sed temporalia et spiritualia sunt omnino distincta nec sub eodem genere continentur nec communicant in materia, ergo temporalis et

spiritualis potestates sunt distincte non dependentes ad invicem' (text in G. Vinay, 'Egidio Romano e la cosidetta "Quaestio in utramque partem" con testo critico', *Bullettino dell'Istituto Storico Italiano per il Medio Evo e Archivio Muratori* LIII (1939), p. 94). See J.A. Watt, 'The "Quaestio in utramque partem" reconsidered', *Studia Gratiana* XIII (1967), pp. 411–53.

9 'Sine freno et sine capistro' (3.7, p. 181). For an English translation of the tract, with an introduction, see R.W. Dyson, *Giles of Rome on Ecclesiastical Power. The De ecclesiastica potestate of Aegidius Romanus* (Woodbridge, Suffolk: Boydell Press, 1986).

10 'Magis itaque erit ecclesia domina possessionis tue, quam tu ipse' (2.7, p. 74).

11 See M.J. Wilks, *The Problem of Sovereignty in the Later Middle Ages. The Papal Monarchy with Augustinus Triumphus and the Publicists,* Cambridge Studies in Medieval Life and Thought, second series, 9 (Cambridge: Cambridge University Press, 1963).

12 For a critical text with introduction see his *Le plus ancien traité de l'Eglise, Jacques de Viterbe, De regimine christiano (1301–2), Etudes des sources et édition critique* (Paris: Gabriel Beauchesne, 1926). For an English translation see R.W. Dyson, *James of Viterbo, On Christian Government* (Woodbridge, Suffolk: Boydell & Brewer, 1995).

13 For Gregory I see *Decr. Grat.*, Dist.89, c. 7 (referred to by James of Viterbo, 1.3, p. 116).

14 'Potest accipi via media ... ut dicatur quod institutio potestatis temporalis materialiter et inchoative habet esse a naturali hominum inclinatione, ac per hoc, a Deo in quantum opus nature est opus Dei; perfective autem et formaliter habet esse a potestate spirituali, que a Deo speciali modo derivatur. Nam gratia non tollit naturam sed perficit eam et format ... Vnde quia potestas spiritualis gratiam respicit, temporalis vero naturam: ideo spiritualis temporalem non excludit sed eam format et perficit. Imperfecta quidem et informis est omnis humana potestas, nisi per spiritualem formetur et perficiatur. Hec autem formatio est approbatio et ratificatio' (2.7, pp. 231–2).

15 'Duplex potestas propter respectum ad actus diversos' (2.8, p. 248).

16 See the critical edition of F. Bleienstein in his *Johannes Quidort von Paris über königliche und päpstliche Gewalt (De regia potestate et papali)* (Textkritische Edition mit deutscher Übersetzung), Frankfurter Studien zur Wissenschaft von der Politik 4 (Stuttgart: Ernst Klett Verlag, 1969); and English translation in A.P. Monahan, *John of Paris on Royal and Papal Power* (New York and London: Columbia University Press, 1974).

17 For an edition of Henry's text see R. Scholz, *Die Publizistik zur Zeit Philipps des Schönen und Bonifaz' VIII. Ein Beitrag zur Geschichte der politischen Ausschauungen des Mittelalters,* Kirchenrechtliche Abhandlungen 6/8 (Stuttgart: Ferdinand Enke, 1903), pp. 459–71.

18 They follow Jean Rivière, *Le problème de l'Eglise et de l'Etat au temps de Philippe le Bel,* Etudes et documents 8 (Louvain: Spicilegium sacrum Lovaniense, 1926), pp. 281–300.

19 'Patet homini necessarium et utile in multitudine vivere et maxime in multitudine quae sufficere potest ad totam vitam, ut est civitas vel regio, et praecipue sub uno principante propter bonum commune qui rex dicitur. Et patet etiam quod hoc regimen derivatur a iure naturali, ex eo scilicet quod homo naturaliter est animal civile seu politicum et sociale' (c. 1, p. 77). For John's use of Aristotle for his theory of monarchy see T. Renna, 'Aristotle and the French monarchy, 1260–1303', *Viator* IX (1978), pp. 309–24.

20 'Sacerdotium est spiritualis potestas ministris ecclesiae a Christo collata ad dispensandum fidelibus sacramenta' (c. 2, p. 80).

21 c. 3, pp. 80–4.

22 c. 5, pp. 88–9.

23 'A Deo et a populo regem eligente in persona vel in domo' (c. 10, p. 113); see T. Renna, 'The populus in John of Paris' theory of monarchy', *Tijdschrift voor Rechtsgeschiedenis* XLII (1974), pp. 243–68.

24 c. 18, pp. 165–6.

25 c. 18, pp. 167–8.

26 See pp. 94–5.

27 See J. Coleman, 'Property and poverty', in J.H. Burns (ed.), *The Cambridge History of Medieval Political Thought, c. 350–c. 1450* (Cambridge: Cambridge University Press, 1988), p. 639.

28 c. 21, p. 191.

29 For an English translation with an introduction see W.I. Brandt, *Pierre Dubois, The Recovery of the Holy Land* (New York: Columbia University Press, 1956).

30 'Sicut ergo corpus per animam habet esse, virtutem et operationem … ita et temporalis iurisdictio principum per spiritualem Petri et successorum eius' (3.10, p. 309).

31 'Reges et principes vices dei gerunt in terris, per quos Deus mundum gubernat sicut per causas secundas' (2.15, p. 293).

32 'Hoc regimen proprie ad civitates pertinet, ut in partibus Italiae maxime videmus, et olim viguit apud Athenas' (4.1, p. 325). For Ptolemy's republicanism see C.T. Davis, 'Ptolemy of Lucca and the Roman Republic', *Proceedings of the American Philosophical Society* CXVIII (1974), pp. 30–50. See also N. Rubinstein, 'The history of the word *politicus* in early-modern Europe', in A. Pagden (ed.), *The Languages of Political Theory in Early-Modern Europe* (Cambridge: Cambridge University Press, 1987), pp. 44–5.

33 4.2 (p. 327).

34 'Quaedam etiam [provinciae sunt] virilis animi et in audacia cordis et in confidentia suae intelligentiae sunt, tales regi non possunt nisi principatu politico' (4.8, p. 336).

35 2.9, pp. 286–7.

36 See C.T. Davis, 'An early Florentine political theorist: Fra Remigio de' Girolami', *Proceedings of the American Philosophical Society* CIV (1960), pp. 662–76.

37 'Si non est civis non est homo, quia homo est naturaliter animal civile secundum Philosophum in octavo Ethicorum et in primo Politicorum' (as quoted from *De bono communi* in L. Minio-Paluello,

'Remigio Girolami's *De bono communi*: Florence at the time of Dante's banishment and the philosopher's answer to the crisis', *Italian Studies* XI (1956), p. 60).

38 See C.T. Davis, 'Remigio de' Girolami and Dante: a comparison of their conceptions of peace', *Studi Danteschi* XXXVI (1959), pp. 115–16 (referring to the *De bono communi*). See also P. Hibst, *Utilitas publica – Gemeiner Nutz – Gemeinwohl. Untersuchungen zur Idee eines politischen Leitbegriffs von der Antike bis zum späten Mittelalter*, Europäische Hochschulschriften, Reihe III, Geschichte und ihre Hilfswissenschaften, Series III, vol. 497 (Frankfurt, Bern, New York, Paris: Peter Lang, 1991), pp. 190–3.

39 'Proprium opus humani generis totaliter accepti est actuare semper totam potentiam intellectus possibilis, per prius ad speculandum et secundario propter hoc ad operandum per suam extensionem' (1.4, p. 143). For an English translation of *Monarchia* see that of D. Nicholl: *Dante. Monarchy and Three Political Letters* (London: Weidenfeld & Nicolson, 1954).

40 1.4–5 (pp. 143–7).

41 1.11 (pp. 155–7) and 1.12 (p. 160).

42 1.14 (pp. 164–6).

43 2.3–4 (pp. 176–84).

44 'Romanus populus subiciendo sibi orbem bonum publicum intendit' (2.5, p. 191).

45 2.6 (pp. 193–5) and 2.8 (pp. 199–204).

46 2.10 (p. 214).

47 2.11 (pp. 214–17).

48 3.3 (p. 228).

49 'Regnum temporale non recipit esse a spirituali, nec virtutem que est eius auctoritas, nec etiam operationem simpliciter; sed bene ab eo recipit ut virtuosius operetur per lucem gratie quam in celo et in terra benedictio summi Pontificis infundit illi' (3.4, p. 239).

50 3.7 (pp. 245–7).

51 3.8–9 (pp. 248–55).

52 3.10 (pp. 256–61).

53 3.10 (pp. 260–1) and 3.12 (p. 266).

54 3.13 (p. 268).

55 'Colligitur quod virtus auctorizandi regnum hoc sit contra naturam Ecclesie' (3.14, p. 271).

56 'Duos igitur fines providentia illa inenarrabilis homini proposuit intendendos: beatitudinem scilicet huius vite, que in operatione proprie virtutis consistit et per terrestrem paradisum figuratur; et beatitudinem vite eterne, que consistit in fruitione divini aspectus ad quam propria virtus ascendere non potest, nisi lumine divino adiuta, que per paradisum celestem intelligi datur' (3.15, p. 273).

57 'Que quidem veritas ultime questionis non sic stricte recipienda est, ut romanus Princeps in aliquo romano Pontifici non subiaceat, cum mortalis ista felicitas quodammodo ad inmortalem felicitatem ordinetur. Illa igitur reverentia Cesar utatur ad Petrum qua primo-genitus filius debet uti ad patrem: ut luce paterne gratie illustratus

virtuosius orbem terre irradiet, cui ab Illo solo prefectus est, qui est omnium spiritualium et temporalium gubernator' (3.15, p. 275).

58 See the discussion of scholarly views in J.M. Ferrante, *The Political Vision of the Divine Comedy* (Princeton: Princeton University Press, 1984), pp. 4–7.

59 *Purgatorio*, 6.88–92.

60 *Purgatorio*, 16.109–11.

61 *Purgatorio*, 32.127–9.

62 *Paradiso*, 20.55–60.

63 *Paradiso*, 27.40–66.

64 See for instance M. Grabmann, 'Studien über den Einfluss der aristotelischen Philosophie auf die mittelalterlichen Theorien über das Verhältnis von Kirche und Staat', *Sitzungsberichte der Bayerischen Akademie der Wissenschaften*, Phil.-hist. Abteilung, II (1934), pp. 41–60; A. Gewirth, *Marsilius of Padua: The Defender of Peace*, I: *Marsilius of Padua and Medieval Philosophy* (New York: Columbia University Press, 1951), pp. 42–4; L. Schmugge, *Johannes von Jandun (1285/89). Untersuchungen zur Biographie und Sozialtheorie eines lateinischen Averroisten*, Pariser Historische Studien, Herausgegeben vom Deutschen Historischen Institut in Paris, 5 (Stuttgart: Hiersemann, 1966), p. 118; J. Quillet, 'L'Aristotélisme de Marsile de Padoue et ses rapports avec l'Averroisme', *Medioevo. Rivista di storia della filosofia medievale* V (1979), pp. 81–123; M. Grignaschi, 'L'ideologia marsiliana si spiega con l'adesione dell'autore all'uno o all'altro dei grandi sistemi filosofici dell'inizio del trecento?', *Medioevo. Rivista di storia della filosofia medievale*, V (1979), pp. 201–22; and M. Damiatta, *Plenitudo potestatis e universitas civium in Marsilio da Padova* (Florence: Edizioni 'Studi Francescani', 1983), p. 233.

65 *DP* 1.4.5 (p. 19): Latin text ed. R. Scholz (Hanover, 1932). For an English translation see Gewirth, *Marsilius of Padua*, II.

66 *DP* 1.2.3 (pp. 11–12). See J. Miethke, 'Marsilius von Padua. Die politische Philosophie eines lateinischen Aristotelikers des 14. Jahrhunderts', in H. Boockmann *et al.* (eds), *Lebenslehren und Weltentwürfe im Übergang vom Mittelalter zur Neuzeit*, Abhandlungen der Akademie der Wissenschaften in Göttingen, Phil.-Hist. Klasse, Dritte Folge, CLXXIX (Göttingen: Vandenhoeck & Ruprecht, 1989), pp. 56–8.

67 *DP* 1.12 (pp. 62–9) and 15 (pp. 84–94).

68 See, for example, *DP* 1.12.3 (pp. 63–4); see M.J. Wilks, 'Corporation and representation in the Defensor Pacis', *Studia Gratiana* XV (1972), pp. 253–92.

69 *DP* 1.10.4 (pp. 49–50).

70 For the view that Marsilius was a positivist see, especially, Gewirth, *Marsilius of Padua*, I, pp. 132–75. For the contrary opinion see, for instance, the most recent discussion in C.J. Nederman, *Community and Consent. The Secular Political Theory of Marsiglio of Padua's Defensor Pacis* (Lanham, Md.: Rowman & Littlefield, 1995), pp. 79–83. See also E. Lewis, 'The "positivism" of Marsiglio of Padua', *Speculum* XXXVIII (1963), pp. 541–82.

71 'Quandoque false cogniciones iustorum et conferencium leges fiunt, cum de ipsis datur observacionis preceptum, seu feruntur per modum precepti; sicut apparet in regionibus barbarorum quorundam, qui tanquam iustum observari faciunt homicidam absolvi a culpa et pena civili reale aliquod precium exhibentem pro tali delicto, cum tamen hoc simpliciter sit iniustum, et per consequens ipsorum leges non perfecte simpliciter. Est enim quod formam habeant debitam, preceptum scilicet observacionis coactivum, debita tamen carent condicione, videlicet debita et vera ordinacione iustorum' (*DP* 1.10.5, pp. 50–1).

72 *DP* 1.17 (pp. 112–21).

73 *DP* 2.8 (pp. 221–31) and 2.17.9 (p. 363).

74 *DP* 2.6.12 and 13 (pp. 209–15).

75 See, for instance, *DP* 2.4 (pp. 158–77).

76 *DP* 2.5.5 (p. 189).

77 For this role of the *generale concilium aut fidelis legislator humanus superiore carens* see *DP* 2.22.9 (p. 428); see also *DP* 2.28.13 (pp. 544–5).

78 See *DP* 2.4.3 (pp. 160–1); 2.4.12 (pp. 172–4); 2.5.9 (pp. 196–7).

79 *DP* 2.22.10 (pp. 429–30).

80 For the republican interpretation see, for instance, Gewirth, *Marsilius of Padua*, I, pp. 167–225 (on Discourse I); W. Ullmann, *Principles of Government and Politics in the Middle Ages* (London: Methuen, 1961), pp. 268–79; and Q. Skinner, *Foundations of Modern Political Thought* (Cambridge: Cambridge University Press: 1978), I, pp. 61–5. For the pro-imperial interpretation see Wilks, *Problem of Sovereignty*, pp. 109–17, and J. Quillet, *La philosophie politique de Marsile de Padoue* (Paris: Vrin, 1970). For Marsilius' views in the context of Italian politics see N. Rubinstein, 'Marsilius of Padua and Italian Political Thought of his Time', in J.R. Hale *et al.* (eds), *Europe in the Late Middle Ages* (London: Faber & Faber, 1965), pp. 44–75; but see also D. Sternberger, 'Die Stadt und das Reich in der Verfassungslehre des Marsilius von Padua', *Sitzungsberichte der Wissenschaftlichen Gesellschaft an der Johann Wolfgang Goethe-Universität, Frankfurt-am-Main*, XVIII (Wiesbaden: Franz Steiner Verlag, 1981), pp. 89–149.

81 *DP* 1.1.6 (pp. 7–8); 1.19.12 (pp. 135–6); also 2.22.20 (pp. 438–40).

82 'Est etiam similiter secundum legem humanam legislator, ut civium universitas aut eius pars valentior, vel Romanus princeps summus imperator vocatus' (*DM* 13.9, p. 280); see also *DM* 12.1, p. 254 (Latin text and French translation in C. Jeudy and J. Quillet, *Marsile de Padoue. Oeuvres mineures: Defensor minor, De translatione imperii* (Paris: Editions du Centre National de la Recherche Scientifique, 1979)). For an English translation see C.J. Nederman (ed.), *Marsiglio of Padua. Writings on the Empire. Defensor minor and De translatione imperii* (Cambridge: Cambridge University Press, 1993).

83 *DP* 2.17.9 (p. 363); 2.18.8 (p. 384); 2.20.2 (p. 393); 2.21.1–8 (pp. 402–10).

84 *DP* 1.9.2 (pp. 39–40); 2.30.4–9 (pp. 592–5).

85 *DP* 2.30.8 (p. 601).

86 The best treatment of Ockham's political ideas remains A.S. McGrade, *The Political Thought of William of Ockham*, Cambridge

Studies in Medieval Life and Thought, third series, 7 (Cambridge: Cambridge University Press, 1974). See also his editions with English translations by J. Kilcullen of Ockham, *A Short Discourse on the Tyrannical Government* (Cambridge: Cambridge University Press, 1992) and *A Letter to the Friars Minor and Other Writings* (Cambridge: Cambridge University Press, 1995).

87 *DP* 2.19.2–3 (pp. 384–6); 2.20.8 (pp. 397–8); 2.21.1 (pp. 402–3).

88 See H.J. Sieben, *Das Konzilsidee des lateinischen Mittelalters, 847–1378* (Paderborn: Ferdinand Schöningh, 1984), pp. 427–69.

89 See J. Canning, *The Political Thought of Baldus de Ubaldis*, Cambridge Studies in Medieval Life and Thought, fourth series, 6 (Cambridge: Cambridge University Press, 1987), pp. 79–82. But see also K. Pennington, *The Prince and the Law* (Berkeley: University of California Press, 1993), pp. 203–12, for a different interpretation of Baldus on this point, and pp. 113–16, for the opinions of Albericus de Rosciate on this question.

90 See Canning, *Political Thought of Baldus*, pp. 82–3; J. Canning, 'Law, sovereignty and corporation theory, 1300–1450', in J.H. Burns (ed.), L, *The Cambridge History of Medieval Political Thought, c. 350–c. 1450* (Cambridge: Cambridge University Press, 1988), pp. 461–2.

91 For an interpretation of the significance of the academic law of fiefs see S. Reynolds, *Fiefs and Vassals. The Medieval Evidence Reinterpreted* (Oxford: Oxford University Press, 1994), pp. 3–7.

92 See Pennington, *Prince and Law*, pp. 125–8.

93 'Deus subiecit ei leges, sed non subiecit ei contractus' (on Feud., 1.7, fol. 17v).

94 On D.1.4.4 (fol. 20v).

95 'Ecclesia debet vasallo vicem, et de suo imperio non potest eum [i.e. imperatorem] ledere. Immo papa se facit alienum a potestate si talem iusticiam non reddit imperatori qui iuravit fidelitatem … Et imperator potest se defendere cum exercitu suo' (*De pace Constantie*, to the phrase 'In nomine Christi membrum' (fol. 94v)).

96 See R.M. Johannessen, 'Cardinal Jean Lemoine's gloss to *Rem non novam* and the reinstatement of the Colonna cardinals', in S. Chodorow (ed.), *Proceedings of the Eighth International Congress of Medieval Canon Law, San Diego*, Miscellanea Iuris Canonici, Series C (Vatican City, 1992), 309–20.

97 See Pennington, *Prince and Law*, pp. 180–3.

98 See Canning, *Political Thought of Baldus*, pp. 68–9. See also G. Montagu, 'Roman Law and the emperor – the rationale of "written reason" in some *consilia* of Oldradus da Ponte', *History of Political Thought* XV (1994), pp. 1–56, where he argues that this *consilium* may not have been written in connection with this dispute.

99 See Pennington, *Prince and Law*, pp. 187–8.

100 See Pennington, *Prince and Law*, pp. 199–201.

101 See D. Maffei, *La donazione di Costantino nei giuristi medievali* (Milan: Giuffrè, 1964); and J. Canning, 'A state like any other? The fourteenth-century papal patrimony through the eyes of Roman law jurists', in D. Wood (ed.), *The Church and Sovereignty, c. 590–1918*.

Essays in Honour of Michael Wilks, Studies in Church History, Subsidia 9 (Oxford: Basil Blackwell, 1991), pp. 245–60.

102 See P.N. Riesenberg, *Inalienability of Sovereignty in Medieval Political Thought* (New York: Columbia University Press, 1956), pp. 113–44.

103 For an edition see D. Quaglioni, *Politica e diritto nel trecento italiano: il 'De tyranno' di Bartolo da Sassoferrato (1314–1357), con l'edizione critica dei trattati 'De Guelphis et Gebellinis', 'De regimine civitatis' e 'De tyranno',* Il pensiero politico, biblioteca, 11 (Florence, 1983).

104 On D.1.1.5 (fol. 7r).

105 For the juristic treatment of cities up to and including Bartolus, see Canning, *Political Thought of Baldus,* pp. 93–7. See also the classic work, C.N.S. Woolf, *Bartolus of Sassoferrato. His Position in the History of Medieval Political Thought* (Cambridge: Cambridge University Press, 1913).

106 D.1.3.32 was a major source for this interpretation of consent (see above, p. 10). For Bartolus' argument see W. Ullmann, 'De Bartoli sententia: Concilium repraesentat mentem populi', in *Bartolo da Sassoferrato-studi e documenti per il VI centenario,* 2 vols (Milan, 1962), II, pp. 711–26.

107 See *Tractatus de alveo* (third part of *Tractatus de fluminibus seu tyberiadis et alluvione*), fol. 145v. For discussion of this passage see H.G. Walther, 'Wasser in Stadt und Contado', *Mensch und Natur im Mittelalter,* Miscellanea Mediaevalia 21(2) (1992), p. 894. See also Walther, ' "Verbis Aristotelis non utar, quia ea iuristae non saperent". Legistische und aristotelische Herrschaftstheorie bei Bartolus und Baldus', in J. Miethke (ed.), *Das Publikum politischer Theorie im 14. Jahrhundert,* Schriften des Historischen Kollegs, Kolloquium 21 (Munich: R. Oldenbourg Verlag, 1992), pp. 111–26.

108 See Canning, *Political Thought of Baldus,* pp. 159–69. See also H.G. Walther, 'Die Legitimität der Herrschaftsordnung bei Bartolus von Sassoferrato und Baldus de Ubaldis', in E. Mock and G. Wieland (eds), *Rechts- und Sozialphilosophie des Mittelalters,* Salzburger Schriften zur Rechts-, Staats- und Sozialphilosophie 12 (Frankfurt-am-Main: Peter Lang, 1990), pp. 115–39.

109 See Canning, *Political Thought of Baldus,* pp. 61–3. See above, pp. 8–9.

110 On Feud., 2.56 (fol. 286r): see Canning, 'Law, sovereignty', p. 466.

111 See Canning, *Political Thought of Baldus,* pp. 68–9, and Montagu, 'Roman law and the emperor', pp. 4–23.

112 See Canning, 'Law, sovereignty', p. 467.

113 See Canning, *Political Thought of Baldus,* pp. 64–8.

114 See Canning, *Political Thought of Baldus,* pp. 221–7, and K. Pennington, 'The authority of the prince in a *consilium* of Baldus de Ubaldis', in his *Popes, Canonists and Texts, 1150–1550* (Aldershot: Variorum, 1993).

115 'Vniversitas nil aliud est nisi homines qui ibi sunt' (to D.3.4.7, fol. 63v).

116 See J. Canning, 'The corporation in the political thought of the Italian jurists of the thirteenth and fourteenth centuries', *History of Political Thought* I (1980), pp. 15–24. See also H.G. Walther, 'Die Gegner Ockhams: Zur Korporationslehre der mittelalterlichen Legisten', in

G. Göhler *et al.* (eds), *Politische Institutionen im gesellschaftlichen Umbruch. Ideengeschichtliche Beiträge zur Theorie politischer Institutionen* (Opladen: Westdeutscher Verlag, 1990), pp. 113–39.

117 For Bartolus, see especially Ullmann, 'De Bartoli sententia'.

118 'Persona regis est organum et instrumentum illius persone intellectualis et publice; et illa persona intellectualis et publica est illa que principaliter fundat actus' (*Cons.*, 1.359, ed. Brescia, 1490, fol. 109v (= *Cons.*, 3.159, ed. Venice, 1575)). For Baldus' theory of kingship see Canning, *Political Thought of Baldus*, pp. 209–21.

119 See *Tractatus contra Benedictum*, c. 8, p. 189.

120 c. 24, p. 201, and c. 25, p. 207.

121 'Papa cum concilio maior est papa solo' (c. 20, p. 185).

122 See the excellent study, C. Fasolt, *Council and Hierarchy. The Political Thought of William Durant the Younger*, Cambridge Studies in Medieval Life and Thought, fourth series, 16 (Cambridge: Cambridge University Press, 1991).

123 See K.A. Frech, *Reform an Haupt und Gliedern. Untersuchung zur Entwicklung und Verwendung der Formulierung im Hoch- und Spätmittelalter*, Europäische Hochschulschriften, Reihe 3, Series 3, vol. 510 (Frankfurt: Peter Lang, 1992), p. 366.

124 See p. 160, and *DM*, 12.5, p. 260.

125 *DM*, 12.5, p. 260.

126 For English translations of these decrees see C.M.D. Crowder, *Unity, Heresy and Reform, 1378–1460. The Conciliar Response to the Great Schism* (London: Edward Arnold, 1977), pp. 82–3 and 128–9. See also P.H. Stump, *The Reforms of the Council of Constance (1414–1418)*, Studies in the History of Christian Thought 53 (Leiden: E.J. Brill, 1994), pp. 3–21.

127 For d'Ailly see F. Oakley, *The Political Thought of Pierre d'Ailly: The Voluntarist Tradition*, Yale Historical Publications Miscellany 81 (New Haven: Yale University Press, 1964). For Gerson see J.B. Morrall, *Gerson and the Great Schism* (Manchester: Manchester University Press, 1960); and L.B. Pascoe, *Jean Gerson: Principles of Church Reform* (Leiden: E.J. Brill, 1973). For an English translation of *Ambulate* see Crowder, *Unity, Heresy and Reform*, pp. 76–82.

128 The only modern treatment of Petrus de Ancharano's political ideas is the unpublished Cornell University Ph.D. dissertation (1977) of J.J. Sawicki, 'The ecclesiological and political thought of Petrus de Ancharano (1330?–1416)'.

129 The fundamental study of the importance of canonist corporation theory in the development of conciliar ideas is B. Tierney, *Foundations of the Conciliar Theory. The Contribution of the Medieval Canonists from Gratian to the Great Schism* (Cambridge: Cambridge University Press, 1955).

130 For Zabarella's life and works see D. Girgensohn, 'Francesco Zabarella aus Padua. Gelehrsamkeit und politisches Wirken eines Rechtsprofessors während des grossen abendländischen Schismas', *Zeitschrift der Savigny-Stiftung für Rechtsgeschichte*, Kanonistische Abteilung LXXIX (1993), pp. 232–77. See also T.E. Morrissey,

'Franciscus Zabarella (1360–1417): papacy, community and limitations upon authority', in G. Fitch Lytle, *Reform and Authority in the Medieval and Renaissance Church* (Washington, DC: Catholic University of America Press, 1981), pp. 37–54; Morrissey, 'Cardinal Franciscus Zabarella (1360–1417) as a canonist and the crisis of his age: Schism and the Council of Constance', *Zeitschrift für Kirchengeschichte* XCVI (1985), pp. 196–208; Morrissey, 'Cardinal Zabarella and Nicholas of Cusa. From community authority to consent of the community', in *Mitteilungen und Forschungen der Cusanus-Gesellschaft* XVII (Mainz: Matthias-Grünewald-Verlag, 1986), pp. 157–76.

131 See T.E. Morrissey, 'The decree "Haec sancta" and Cardinal Zabarella. His role in its formulation and interpretation', *Annuarium Historiae Conciliorum* X(2) (1978), pp. 145–76.

132 The *Clementinae* were the last authentic collection of canon law included in the *Corpus iuris canonici*: they consisted of decretals of Clement V, decrees of the Council of Vienne and one decretal each by Boniface VIII and Urban IV, and were promulgated by John XXII in 1317. *Repetitiones* were repeat-lectures which sought to provide a deeper treatment of a text.

133 At X.1.6.6.

134 For John of Segovia's ideas see A. Black, *Monarchy and Community. Political Ideas in the Later Conciliar Controversy 1430–1450*, Cambridge Studies in Medieval Life and Thought, third series, 2 (Cambridge: Cambridge University Press, 1970) *passim* (with collected excerpts from John's writings, pp. 141–61); Black, *Council and Commune. The Conciliar Movement and the Fifteenth-Century Heritage* (London: Burns & Oates, 1979), pp. 118–93.

135 For an English translation, with introduction, see P.E. Sigmund, *Nicholas of Cusa. The Catholic Concordance*, Cambridge Texts in the History of Political Thought (Cambridge: Cambridge University Press, 1991).

136 See Black, *Monarchy and Community*, pp. 85–129; and J.W. Stieber, *Pope Eugenius IV, the Council of Basel and the Secular and Ecclesiastical Authorities in the Empire* (Leiden: E.J. Brill, 1978).

CONCLUSION

1 See J.H. Burns, *Lordship, Kingship and Empire. The Idea of Monarchy, 1400–1525*, The Carlyle Lectures 1988 (Oxford: Clarendon Press, 1992), pp. 146-62.

2 For the legacy of scholasticism to early modern political thought see especially Q. Skinner, *Foundations of Modern Political Thought* (Cambridge: Cambridge University Press, 1978), II, pp. 113–84. For a reassessment of Bodin's debt to scholastic jurisprudence see K. Pennington, *The Prince and the Law* (Berkeley: University of California Press, 1993), pp. 8–9 and 276–84.

3 See G. Garnett (ed. and trans.), *Vindiciae, contra tyrannos: or, Concerning the Legitimate Power of a Prince over the People, and of the People over a Prince* (Cambridge: Cambridge University Press, 1994), pp. xix–liv.

BIBLIOGRAPHY

GENERAL WORKS

Black, A. (1992) *Political Thought in Europe, 1250–1450*, Cambridge Medieval Textbooks, Cambridge: Cambridge University Press.
The Cambridge History of Medieval Political Thought, c. 350–c. 1450 (1988) J.H. Burns (ed.), Cambridge: Cambridge University Press.
Carlyle, R.W. and Carlyle, A.J. (1903–36) *A History of Medieval Political Theory in the West*, 6 vols, Edinburgh and London: W. Blackwood & Sons.
Lewis, E. (repr. 1974) *Medieval Political Ideas*, 2 vols, New York: Cooper Square.
McIlwain, C.H. (1932) *The Growth of Political Thought in the West, from the Greeks to the End of the Middle Ages*, New York: Macmillan.
Ullmann, W. (1965) *A History of Political Thought: the Middle Ages*, Harmondsworth: Penguin (reissued as *Medieval Political Thought*, Peregrine Books, 1975).

WORKS CITED
PRIMARY SOURCES

Abbo of Fleury (1853) *Collectio canonum, PL*, 139.
Accursius (1497–8) *Glossa ordinaria*, Venice.
Ambrose, St (1845) *Liber de incarnationis dominicae sacramento, PL*, 16.
Ammianus Marcellinus (1963) *Res gestae*, C.U. Clarke (ed.), Berlin: Weidmann.
Andreas de Isernia (1579) *In usus feudorum commentaria*, Lyon.
Anonymous of Hersfeld (1891) *Liber de unitate ecclesiae conservanda, MGH, Libelli de Lite*, I.
Annales regni Francorum (repr. 1950) F. Kurze (ed.), *MGH, Scriptores rerum Germanicarum in usum scholarum*, 6, Hanover: Hahn.
Aquinas, Thomas (1954) *De regimine principum ad regem Cypri [De regno]*, R.M. Spiazzi (ed.), Turin and Rome: Marietti.
Aquinas, Thomas (1964–80) *Summa theologiae*, T. Gilby *et al.* (eds), Blackfriars, 61 vols, London: Eyre & Spottiswoode.
Aquinas, Thomas (1966) *In octo libros politicorum Aristotelis expositio*, R.M. Spiazzi (ed.), Turin and Rome: Marietti.

Aquinas, Thomas (1970) *Aquinas Selected Political Writings* (Blackwell's Political Texts), A.P. d'Entrèves (ed.), J.G. Dawson (trans.), Oxford: Basil Blackwell.

Aristotle (1964) *Politica*, W.D. Ross (ed.), Oxford Classical Texts, Oxford: Oxford University Press.

Asser (1904) *Life of Alfred*, W.H. Stevenson (ed.), Oxford: Clarendon Press.

Augustine of Hippo (1957–72) *De civitate dei*, Loeb edn, 7 vols, Cambridge, Mass.: Harvard University Press.

Augustine of Hippo (1845) *De vera religione, PL*, 34.

Baldus de Ubaldis (1490) *Pars I Consiliorum*, Brescia.

Baldus de Ubaldis (1495) *Super usibus feudorum interpretatio*, Pavia.

Baldus de Ubaldis (1495) *Commentarium super Pace Constantie*, Pavia.

Baldus de Ubaldis (1498) *Super prima et secunda parte Digesti veteris*, [Lyon].

Baldus de Ubaldis (1575) *Pars III Consiliorum sive responsorum* (anastatic reproduction, Turin, 1970).

Bartolus de Sassoferrato (1577) *Tractatus de fluminibus seu tyberiadis et alluvione*, Turin.

Bartolus de Sassoferrato (1983) *De tyranno*, edn in D. Quaglioni, *Politica e diritto nel trecento italiano: il 'De tyranno' di Bartolo da Sassoferrato (1314–1357), con l'edizione critica dei trattati 'De Guelphis et Gebellinis', 'De regimine civitatis' e 'De tyranno'*, Il pensiero politico, biblioteca, 11, Florence.

Bede (repr. 1991) *Historia ecclesiastica gentis Anglorum*, B. Colgrave and R.A.B. Mynors (eds), Oxford: Clarendon Press.

Benzo of Alba (repr. 1963) *Liber ad Heinricum IV.*, MGH, *Scriptores*, XI, Hanover: Kraus.

Bernard of Clairvaux (1957–77) *Opera omnia*, J. Leclercq, H.M. Rochais and C.H. Talbot (eds), 8 vols, Rome: Editiones Cistercienses.

Bernard of Clairvaux (1963) *De consideratione*, in Vol. III of *Opera omnia*, J. Leclercq, H.M. Rochais and C.H. Talbot, Rome: Editiones Cistercienses.

Bernard of Clairvaux (1977) *Epistolae*, Vol. VIII in *Opera omnia*, J. Leclercq, H.M. Rochais and C.H. Talbot, Rome: Editiones Cistercienses.

Biblia Sacra vulgata editionis Sexti V. (1868) Paris: Garnier.

Birch, W. de G. (ed.) (1893) *Cartularium Saxonicum*, III, London: Whiting & Co.

Bonizo of Sutri (1891) *Liber ad amicum*, MGH, *Libelli de Lite*, I, 571–620.

Celestine, I (1846) *Epistolae et decreta, PL*, 50.

Cicero, Marcus Tullius (1921) *De officiis*, Loeb edn, London: Heinemann.

Cicero, Marcus Tullius (1928) *De republica*, Loeb edn, London: Heinemann.

Constitutum Constantini (1968) Horst Fuhrmann (ed.), *MGH, Fontes iuris Germanici antiqui in usum scholarum* 10, Hanover.

Continuator of Fredegar (1960) *Chronicle*, J.M. Wallace-Hadrill (ed.), London: Nelson.

Corpus iuris canonici (repr. 1959) A. Friedberg (ed.), I: *Decretum Gratiani*; II: *Decretalium Collectiones*, Graz: Akademische Druck- U. Verlagsanstalt.

Corpus iuris civilis, I: *Institutiones* (Paul Krueger, ed.) *Digesta* (Theodor Mommsen and Paul Krueger, eds), 15th edn (1928); II: *Codex* (Paul Krueger, ed.), 11th edn (1954); III: *Novellae* (Rudolf Schoell, ed.), 6th edn (1954), Berlin: Weidmann.

Dante Alighieri (1954) *Dante. Monarchy and Three Political Letters* (trans. by Donald Nicholl), London: Weidenfeld & Nicolson.

Dante Alighieri (1965) *Monarchia*, Pier Giorgio Ricci (ed.), Milan: Arnaldo Mondadori.

Dante Alighieri (1993) *The Divine Comedy* (trans. C.H. Sisson with an introduction and notes by David H. Higgins), The World's Classics, Oxford: Oxford University Press.

Disputatio inter clericum et militem, Norma N. Erikson (ed.), 'A dispute between a priest and a knight', *Proceedings of the American Philosophical Society* CXI(5) (1967), pp. 288–309.

Dubois, Pierre (1956) *Pierre Dubois. The Recovery of the Holy Land* (trans. with an introduction by W.I. Brandt), New York: Columbia University Press.

Dupuy, P. (1655) *Histoire du differend d'entre le pape Boniface VIII et Philippes le Bel roy de France*, Paris (reprint, Tucson, Arizona, 1963).

Einhard (1911) *Vita Karoli Magni*, O. Holder-Egger (ed.), *MGH, Scriptores rerum Germanicarum in usum scholarum*, 25.

Gelasius I (1868) *Epistolae*, A. Thiel (ed.), *Epistolae Romanorum pontificum genuinae et quae ad eos scriptae sunt a S. Hilaro usque ad Pelagium II*, Vol. I, Braunsberg: Edward Peter.

Giles of Rome (1961) *De ecclesiastica potestate*, R. Scholz (ed.), Böhlau Verlag, repr. Aalen: Scientia Verlag.

Giles of Rome (1967) *De regimine principum libri tres* [Rome, 1607], repr. Aalen: Scientia Verlag.

Giles of Rome (1986) *Giles of Rome on Ecclesiastical Power. The De ecclesiastica potestate of Aegidius Romanus* (trans. with an introduction by R.W. Dyson), Woodbridge, Suffolk: Boydell Press.

Gregory I (1849) *Regula pastoralis*, PL, 77.

Gregory I (1957) *Registrum, MGH, Epistolae*, II, L.M. Hartmann (ed.), Berlin: Weidmann.

Gregory I (1985) *Moralia*, Corpus Christianorum, Series latina, CXLIII B, Turnhout: Brepols.

Gregory VII (1955) *Registrum*, Erich Caspar (ed.), *MGH, Epistolae selectae in usum scholarum*, II, 1–2, 2nd edn, Berlin: Weidmann.

Gregory VII (1972) *The 'Epistolae vagantes' of Pope Gregory VII* H.E.J. Cowdrey (ed. and trans.), Oxford Medieval Texts, Oxford: Clarendon Press.

Gregory of Tours (1884) *Historia francorum, MGH, Scriptores*, I, 1, Hanover: Hahn.

Helgaud of Fleury (1965) *Epitoma vitae regis Roberti pii*, R.-H. Bautier and G. Labory (eds), Institut de recherche et d'histoire des textes, *Sources d'histoire médiévale*, I, Paris: Editions du Centre National de la Recherche Scientifique.

Henry IV, emperor (1937) *Die Briefe Heinrichs IV.*, Carl Erdmann (ed.), Leipzig: Hiersemann Verlag.

Hincmar of Rheims (1960) *De ordine palatii, MGH, Capitularia*, II, pp. 517–30 new edn., Hanover: Hahn.

Honorius Augustodunensis (1897) *Summa gloria, MGH, Libelli de Lite*, L. Dieterich (ed.), III, pp. 29–80.

Horatius Flaccus, Quintus (Horace) (1963) *Opera*, E.C. Wickham and H. Garrod (eds), Oxford: Oxford University Press.

Hugh of St Victor (1854) *De sacramentis christianae fidei*, PL, 176.

Humbert of Silva Candida (1891) *Libri III adversus simoniacos*, F. Thaner (ed.), *MGH, Libelli de Lite*, I.

Innocent III (1947) *Regestum super negotio Romani imperii*, F. Kempf (ed.), Miscellanea Historiae Pontificiae 12, Rome: Pontificia Universitas Gregoriana.

Innocent III (1964) *Die Register Innocenz' III. 1. Pontifikatsjahr, 1198/99. Texte*, O. Hageneder and A. Haidacher (eds), Publikationen der Abteilung für Historische Studien des Österreichischen Kulturinstituts in Rom: II. Abteilung – Quellen, 1. Reihe, Graz–Cologne: Herman Böhlaus Nachf.

Isidore of Seville (1850) *Differentiae*, PL, 83.

Isidore of Seville (1850) *Etymologiarum sive originum libri XX*, PL, 82.

Isidore of Seville (1850) *Sententiae*, PL, 83.

Isidore of Seville (1894) *Historia Gothorum, Wandalorum, Sueborum, MGH, Auctores Antiquissimi*, XI, 2, Berlin: Weidmann.

Ivo of Chartres (1892) *Epistolae, MGH, Libelli de Lite*, II.

James of Viterbo (1926) *Le plus ancien traité de l'Eglise, Jacques de Viterbe, De regimine christiano (1301–2), Etudes des sources et édition critique*, Critical text with an introduction by H.-X. Arquillière, Paris: Gabriel Beauchesne.

James of Viterbo (1995) *On Christian Government* (trans. with an intro. by R.W. Dyson), Woodbridge, Suffolk: Boydell & Brewer.

The Jerusalem Bible (1974) Reprint, London: Darton, Longman & Todd.

John of Mantua (1973) *In Cantica Canticorum et de sancta Maria tractatus ad Comitissam Matildam*, B. Bischoff and B. Traeger (eds), Spicilegium Friburgense 19, Freiburg, Schweiz: Universitätsverlag.

John of Paris (1969) *Johannes Quidort von Paris, Über königliche und päpstliche Gewalt (De regia potestate et papali)* F. Bleienstein (ed.), Textkritische Edition mit deutscher Übersetzung, Frankfurter Studien zur Wissenschaft von der Politik 4, Stuttgart: Ernst Klett Verlag.

John of Paris (1974) English translation of *De regia potestate et papali*, in A.P. Monahan, *John of Paris on Royal and Papal Power*, New York and London: Columbia University Press.

John of Salisbury (1909) *Policraticus* (Books V–VIII), C.C.J. Webb (ed.) 2 vols, Oxford: Clarendon Press.

John of Salisbury (1993) *Policraticus, I–IV*, K.S.B. Keats-Rohan (ed.), Corpus Christianorum, Continuatio Mediaevalis, CXVIII, Turnhout: Brepols.

Jonas of Orleans, *De institutione regia*, edn in J. Reviron (1930) *Les idées politico-religieuses d'un évêque du IXe siècle. Jonas d'Orleans et son 'De institutione regia.' Etude et texte critique*, L'Eglise et l'Etat au Moyen Age, 1, pp. 134–94, Paris: J. Vrin.

Jordanes (1961) *Romana et Getica, MGH, Auctores Antiquissimi*, V/1 (new edn).

Leo I (1846) *Sermones et epistulae*, PL, 54.

Liber pontificalis (1955) L. Duchesne (ed.), Paris: Boccard.

Manegold of Lautenbach (1891) *Liber ad Gebehardum, MGH, Libelli de Lite*, K. Francke (ed.), I, pp. 300–430.

Marculf (1886) *Formulae, MGH, Leges,* V, *Formulae,* Hanover.

Marinus da Caramanico (1957) *Super libro constitutionum,* Proem, Francesco Calasso (ed.), in his *I Glossatori e la teoria della sovranità: studio di diritto comune pubblico,* 3rd edn, Milan: Giuffrè.

Marsilius of Padua (1932–3) *Defensor pacis* Richard Scholz (ed.), *MGH, Fontes iuris Germanici antiqui in usum scholarum,* 2 vols, Hanover: Hahn.

Marsilius of Padua (1956) *The Defender of Peace* (trans. Alan Gewirth), *Marsilius of Padua,* II, New York: Columbia University Press.

Marsilius of Padua (1979) *Marsile de Padoue. Oeuvres mineures: Defensor minor, De translatione imperii,* Latin text (edited and translated into French by C. Jeudy and J. Quillet), Paris: Editions du Centre National de la Recherche Scientifique.

Marsilius of Padua (1993) *Marsiglio of Padua. Writings on the Empire. Defensor minor and the De translatione imperii,* with an English translation by Cary J. Nederman (ed.), Cambridge Texts in the History of Political Thought, Cambridge: Cambridge University Press.

MGH, Capitularia regum Francorum, I–II, Hanover: Hahn (new edn, 1960).

MGH, Concilia, I: *Concilia aevi Merovingici,* Hanover: Hahn (new edn, 1956).

MGH, Concilia, II, 1–2: *Concilia aevi Karolini I.,* Hanover and Leipzig: Hahn (repr. 1979).

MGH, Concilia, II, Suppl.: *Libri carolini,* Hanover and Leipzig: Hahn (repr. 1979).

MGH, Constitutiones et acta publica imperatorum et regum, I, Hanover: Hahn (1893).

MGH, Diplomata regum et imperatorum Germaniae, II, 2 and III, Hanover: Hahn (1926–31 and 1900–3).

MGH, Epistolae, IV: *Karolini aevi,* II, Berlin: Weidmann (repr. 1974).

MGH, Epistolae, V–VII: *Karolini aevi,* III–V, Munich: MGH (repr. 1978).

Mommsen, T.E. and Morrison, K.F. (trans.) and Benson, R.L. (ed.) (1962) *Imperial Lives and Letters of the Eleventh Century* (with an historical introduction by K.F. Morrison), The Records of Civilization Sources and Studies 67, New York and London: Columbia University Press.

Nicholas of Cusa, *De concordantia catholica* English translation, with introduction, in P.E. Sigmund, *Nicholas of Cusa. The Catholic Concordance,* Cambridge Texts in the History of Political Thought, Cambridge: Cambridge University Press, 1991.

Norman Anonymous (1966) *Die Texte des normannischen Anonymus. Neu aus des HS 415 des Corpus Christi College Cambridge,* ed. K. Pellens, Veröffentlichungen des Instituts für Europäische Geschichte, Mainz 42, Wiesbaden: Franz Steiner Verlag.

Ockham, William of (1956) *Tractatus contra Benedictum,* in J.G. Sikes, R.F. Bennett and H.S. Offler (eds), *Guilielmi de Ockham Opera Politica,* III, Manchester: Manchester University Press.

Ockham, William of (1992) *A Short Discourse on the Tyrannical Government over Things Divine and Human, but Especially over the Empire and Those Subject to the Empire, Usurped by Some who are Called Highest Pontiffs,* ed. A.S. McGrade, trans. J. Kilcullen, Cambridge Texts in the History of Political Thought, Cambridge: Cambridge University Press.

Ockham, William of (1995) *A Letter to the Friars Minor and Other Writings*, ed. A.S. McGrade, trans. J. Kilcullen, Cambridge Texts in the History of Political Thought, Cambridge: Cambridge University Press.

Orthodoxa defensio imperialis, MGH, *Libelli de Lite*, II (1892).

Peter Crassus (1891) *Defensio Heinrici IV. Regis*, MGH, *Libelli de Lite*, I.

Peter Damian (1853) *Epistolae*, PL, 144.

Quaestio in utramque partem, text in G. Vinay, 'Egidio Romano e la cosidetta "Quaestio in utramque partem" con testo critico', *Bullettino dell'Istituto Storico Italiano per il Medio Evo e Archivio Muratori*, LIII (1939), pp. 43–136.

Ptolemy of Lucca (1954) *De regno*, Printed as continuation of Aquinas, *De regimine principum ad regem Cypri* [Books 2.4–4.28], R.M. Spiazzi (ed.).

Remigio de' Girolami (1956) *De bono communi*, in L. Minio-Paluello, 'Remigio Girolami's *De bono communi*: Florence at the time of Dante's banishment and the philosopher's answer to the crisis', *Italian Studies* XI, 56–71.

Rufinus (1902) *Summa decretorum*, H. Singer (ed.), Paderborn: F. Schöningh.

Sigebert of Gembloux (1892) *Epistola Leodicensium adversus Paschalem papam*, MGH, *Libelli de Lite*, II.

Siricius (1845) *Epistolae et decreta*, PL, 13.

Smaragdus of St Mihiel (1851) *Via Regia*, PL, 102.

Tacitus, Cornelius (repr. 1962) *Opera minora. Germania et Agricola*, Henry Furneaux and J.G.C. Anderson (eds), Oxford Classical Texts, Oxford: Oxford University Press.

Venantius Fortunatus (1881) *Carmina*, MGH, *Auctores Antiquissimi*, IV/I, Berlin: Weidmann.

Victor of Vita (1879) *Historia persecutionis africanae provinciae sub Geiserico et Hunirico regibus Wandalorum*, MGH, *Auctores Antiquissimi*, III/1.

Vita Walae, MGH, *Scriptores*, II (1968) Hanover: Kraus (repr.).

Wido of Osnabruck (1891) *De controversia inter Hildebrandum et Heinricum*, MGH, *Libelli de Lite*, 1.

Widukind of Corvey (1935) *Rerum gestarum Saxonicarum libri tres*, Paul Hirsch and H.-E. Lohmann (eds), MGH, *Scriptores rerum Germanicarum in usum scholarum*, LX, Hanover.

Wipo (1915) *Gesta Chuonradi imperatoris*, H. Bresslau (ed.), MGH, *Scriptores rerum Germanicarum in usum scholarum* 61, Hanover.

SECONDARY LITERATURE

Anton, H.H. (1968) *Fürstenspiegel und Herrscherethos in der Karolingerzeit*, Bonner historische Forschungen 32, Bonn: Röhrscheid Verlag.

Arquillière, H.-X. (1955) *L'Augustinisme politique. Essai sur la formation des théories politiques du moyen-âge*, L'Eglise et l'Etat au moyen-âge, 2 (2nd edn), Paris: J. Vrin.

Bartolo da Sassoferrato – studi e documenti per il VI centenario, 2 vols, Milan (1962).

Benson, R.L. (1967) 'Plenitudo potestatis: evolution of a formula from Gregory IV to Gratian', *Collectanea Stephan Kuttner*, Studia Gratiana XIV, 195–217.

Benson, R.L. (1982) 'The Gelasian doctrine: uses and transformations', pp. 13–44 in G. Makdisi *et al.* (eds), *La notion d'autorité au Moyen Age. Islam, Byzance, Occident*, Paris: Presses universitaires de France.

Berges, W. (1938) *Die Fürstenspiegel des hohen und späten Mittelalters*, Stuttgart: Hiersemann.

Bernhardt, W. (1993) *Itinerant Kingship and Royal Monasteries in Early Medieval Germany, c. 936–1075*, Cambridge Studies in Medieval Life and Thought, fourth series, 21, Cambridge: Cambridge University Press.

Beumann, H. (1956) 'Zur Entwicklung transpersonaler Staatsvorstellungen', pp. 185–224 in T. Mayer (ed.), *Das Königtum. Seine geistigen und rechtlichen Grundlagen*, Vorträge und Forschungen III, Lindau and Constance: Jan Thorbecke Verlag.

Beumann, H. (ed.) (1968) *Karl der Grosse*, Düsseldorf: Verlag L. Schwann.

Black, A. (1970) *Monarchy and Community. Political Ideas in the Later Conciliar Controversy 1430–1450*, Cambridge Studies in Medieval Life and Thought, third series, 2, Cambridge: Cambridge University Press.

Black, A. (1979) *Council and Commune. The Conciliar Movement and the Fifteenth-Century Heritage*, London: Burns & Oates.

Blythe, J.M. (1992) *Ideal Government and the Mixed Constitution in the Middle Ages*, Princeton: Princeton University Press.

Boshof, E. (1990) 'Einheitsidee und Teilungsprinzip in der Regierungszeit Ludwigs des Frommen', pp. 161–89 in P. Godman and R. Collins, *Charlemagne's Heir. New Perspectives on the Reign of Louis the Pious (814–840)*, Oxford: Clarendon Press.

Brown, E.A.R. (1974) 'The tyranny of a construct: feudalism and historians of medieval Europe', *American Historical Review* LXXIX, 1063–88.

Bund, K. (1979) *Thronsturz und Herrscherabsetzung im Frühmittelalter*, Bonner historische Forschungen 4, Bonn: Ludwig Röhrscheid Verlag.

Burns, J.H. (1992) *Lordship, Kingship and Empire. The Idea of Monarchy, 1400–1525*, The Carlyle Lectures 1988, Oxford: Clarendon Press.

Caenegem, R. van (1988) 'Government, law and society', pp. 174–210 in J.H. Burns (ed.), *The Cambridge History of Medieval Political Thought, c. 350–c. 1450*, Cambridge: Cambridge University Press.

Cambridge History of Later Medieval Philosophy (1982) N. Kretzmann, A. Kenny and J. Pinborg (eds), Cambridge: Cambridge University Press.

Cambridge Medieval History, IV: *The Byzantine Empire* (1966–7) J.M. Hussey, D.M. Nicol and G. Cowan (eds), Cambridge: Cambridge University Press (2 vols).

Canning, J. (1980) 'The corporation in the political thought of the Italian jurists of the thirteenth and fourteenth centuries', *History of Political Thought* I, 9–32.

Canning, J. (1987) *The Political Thought of Baldus de Ubaldis*, Cambridge Studies in Medieval Life and Thought, fourth series, 6, Cambridge: Cambridge University Press.

Canning, J. (1988) 'Law, sovereignty and corporation theory, 1300–1450', pp. 454–76 in J.H. Burns (ed.), *The Cambridge History of Medieval Political Thought, c. 350–c. 1450*, Cambridge: Cambridge University Press.

Canning, J. (1991) 'A state like any other? The fourteenth-century papal patrimony through the eyes of Roman law jurists', in D. Wood (ed.),

The Church and Sovereignty, c. 590–1918. Essays in Honour of Michael Wilks, Studies in Church History, Subsidia 9, Oxford: Basil Blackwell.

Chaney, W.A. (1970) *The Cult of Kingship in Anglo-Saxon England: The Transition from Paganism to Christianity*, Manchester: Manchester University Press.

Chodorow, S. (1972) *Christian Political Theory and Church Politics in the Mid-Twelfth Century: The Ecclesiology of Gratian's Decretum*, Berkeley: University of California Press.

Classen, P. (1952) 'Romanum gubernans imperium. Zur Vorgeschichte der Kaisertitulatur Karls des Grossen', *Deutsches Archiv für die Erforschung des Mittelalters* IX, 103–21.

Classen, P. (1968) 'Karl der Grosse, das Papsttum und Byzanz. Die Begründung des Karolingischen Kaisertums', pp. 537–608 in H. Beumann (ed.), *Karl der Grosse*, Düsseldorf: Verlag L. Schwann.

Coing, H. (ed.) (1973) *Handbuch der Quellen und Literatur der neueren europäischen Privatrechtsgeschichte*, I: *Mittelalter (1100–1500)*, Munich: C.H. Beck.

Coleman, J. (1988) 'Property and poverty', pp. 607–48 in J.H. Burns (ed.), *The Cambridge History of Medieval Political Thought, c. 350–c. 1450*, Cambridge: Cambridge University Press.

Collins, R. (1977) 'Julian of Toledo and the royal succession in late seventh-century Spain', pp. 30–49 in P.H. Sawyer and I.N. Wood (eds), *Early Medieval Kingship*, Leeds: School of History, University of Leeds.

Collins, R. (1983) *Early Medieval Spain. Unity in Diversity, 400–1100*, London: Macmillan.

Crosara, F. (1953) 'Respublica e respublicae. Cenni terminologici dall' età romana all' XI secolo', in G. Moschetti (ed.), *Atti del Congresso Internazionale di Diritto Romano e di Storia del Diritto, Verona 1948*, IV, Milan: Giuffrè.

Crowder, C.M.D. (1977) *Unity, Heresy and Reform, 1378–1460. The Conciliar Response to the Great Schism*, London: Edward Arnold.

Damiatta, M. (1983) *Plenitudo potestatis e universitas civium in Marsilio da Padova*, Florence: Edizioni 'Studi Francescani'.

Davis, C.T. (1959) 'Remigio de' Girolami and Dante: a comparison of their conceptions of peace', *Studi Danteschi* XXXVI, 105–36.

Davis, C.T. (1960) 'An early Florentine political thinker: Fra Remigio de' Girolami', *Proceedings of the American Philosophical Society* CIV, 662–76.

Davis, C.T. (1974) 'Ptolemy of Lucca and the Roman Republic', *Proceedings of the American Philosophical Society* CXVIII, 30–50.

Decker, D. de and Dupuis-Masay, G. (1980) 'L'"épiscopat" et l'empereur Constantin', *Byzantion* L, 118–57.

Deshman, R. (1976) 'Christus rex et magi reges: Kingship and Christology in Ottonian and Anglo-Saxon art', *Frühmittelalterliche Studien. Jahrbuch des Instituts für Frühmittelalterforschung der Universität Münster* X, 375–405.

Devisse, J. (1976) *Hincmar, Archevêque de Reims 845–882*, 3 vols, Geneva: Droz.

Diesner, H.-J. (1973) *Isidor von Sevilla und seine Zeit*, Stuttgart: Calwer.

Dod, B.G. (1982) 'Aristoteles latinus', pp. 45–79 in N. Kretzmann *et al.* (eds), *The Cambridge History of Later Medieval Philosophy*, Cambridge: Cambridge University Press.

Dondaine, H.F. (1953) *Le Corpus Dionysien de l'Université de Paris au XIIIᵉ siècle*, Rome: Edizioni di Storia e Letteratura.

Dumville, D.N. (1977) 'Kingship, genealogies and regnal lists', pp. 72–104 in P.H. Sawyer and I.N. Wood (eds), *Early Medieval Kingship*, Leeds: School of History, University of Leeds.

Dunbabin, J. (1993) 'What's in a name? Philip, King of France', *Speculum* LXVIII(4), 949–68.

Duverger, M. (ed.) (1980) *Le concept d'empire*, Paris: Presses universitaires de France.

Dvornik, F. (1966) *Early Christian and Byzantine Political Philosophy: Origins and Background*, Dumbarton Oaks Studies 9, 2 vols, Washington, DC: Dumbarton Oaks Center for Byzantine Studies.

Eberhardt, O. (1977) *Via Regia. Der Fürstenspiegel Smaragds von St. Mihiel und seine literarische Gattung*, Münstersche Mittelalter-Schriften 28, Munich: Wilhelm Fink Verlag.

Ehlers, J. (1973) *Hugo von St. Viktor. Studien zum Geschichtsdenken und zur Geschichtsschreibung des 12. Jahrhunderts*, Frankfurter historische Abhandlungen 7, Wiesbaden: Steiner Verlag.

Erdmann, C. (1951) *Forschungen zur politischen Ideenwelt des Frühmittelalters*, Berlin: Akademie Verlag.

Fasolt, C. (1991) *Council and Hierarchy. The Political Thought of William Durant the Younger*, Cambridge Studies in Medieval Life and Thought, fourth series, 16, Cambridge: Cambridge University Press.

Feenstra, R. (1965) 'Jean de Blanot et la formule "Rex Franciae in regno suo princeps est"', in *Etudes d'histoire de droit canonique dédiées à Gabriel Le Bras*, II, Paris: Sirey.

Ferrante, J.M. (1984) *The Political Vision of the Divine Comedy*, Princeton: Princeton University Press.

Festschrift für Hermann Heimpel zum 70. Geburtstag am 19. Sep. 1971 (1972) Publ. by the Mitarbeiter des Max-Planck-Instituts für Geschichte, III, Göttingen: Vandenhoeck & Ruprecht.

Flüeler, C. (1992) *Rezeption und Interpretation der Aristotelischen Politica im späten Mittelalter*, 2 vols, Amsterdam and Philadelphia: B.R. Grüner.

Folz, R. (1969) *The Concept of Empire in Western Europe from the Fifth to the Fourteenth Century* (trans. S.A. Ogilvie), London: Edward Arnold.

Fowler-Magerl, L. (1984) *Repertorien zur Frühzeit der gelehrten Rechte: Ordo iudiciorum vel ordo iudiciarius*, Ius commune, Sonderhefte, Texte und Monographien 19, Frankfurt-am-Main: Vittorio Klostermann.

Frech, K.A. (1992) *Reform an Haupt und Gliedern. Untersuchung zur Entwicklung und Verwendung der Formulierung im Hoch- und Spätmittelalter*, Europäische Hochschulschriften, Reihe 3, Series 3, vol. 510, Frankfurt: Peter Lang.

Fried, J. (1982) 'Der Karolingische Herrschaftsverband im 9. Jh. zwischen "Kirche" und "Königshaus"', *Historische Zeitschrift* CCXXXV, 1–43.

Fuhrmann, H. (1966) 'Konstantinische Schenkung und abendländisches Kaisertum. Ein Beitrag zur Überlieferungsgeschichte des Constitutum

Constantini', *Deutsches Archiv für die Erforschung des Mittelalters* XXII, 63–178.

Fuhrmann, H. (1972–4) *Einfluss und Verbreitung der pseudoisidorischen Fälschungen*, 3 vols, Schriften der MGH 24, Stuttgart: Hiersemann.

Fuhrmann, H. (1975) '"Volkssouveränität" und "Herrschaftsvertrag" bei Manegold von Lautenbach', pp. 21–42 in S. Gagnér *et al.* (eds), *Festschrift für Hermann Krause*, Cologne and Vienna: Böhlau Verlag.

Gagnér, S., Schlosser, H., and Wiegand, W., (eds) (1975) *Festschrift für Her-mann Krause*, Cologne and Vienna: Böhlau Verlag.

Ganshof, F.L. (1955) 'Wat waren de capitularia?' *Verhandelingen van de Koninklijke Vlaamse Academie voor Wetenschappen, Letteren en shone Kunsten van Belgie*, Kl Letteren XXII, Brussels (with French résumé).

Garnett, G. (1994) *Vindiciae, contra tyrannos: or, Concerning the Legitimate Power of a Prince over the People, and of the People over a Prince*, Cambridge: Cambridge University Press.

Geary, P. (1983) 'Capitulary', in J. Strayer, *Dictionary of the Middle Ages*, New York: Charles Scribners' Sons.

Gersh, S. (1978) *From Iamblichus to Eriugena. An Investigation of the Prehistory and Evolution of the Pseudo-Dionysian Tradition*, Studien zur Problemgeschichte der Antiken und Mittelalterlichen Philosophie 8, Leiden: E.J. Brill.

Gewirth, A. (1951–6) *Marsilius of Padua: The Defender of Peace*, 2 vols, New York: Columbia University Press.

Gierke, O. von (1881) *Das deutsche Genossenschaftsrecht*, III: *Die Staats- und Korporationslehre des Altertums und des Mittelalters und ihre Aufnahme in Deutschland*, Berlin: Weidmann.

Gillingham, J. (1971) *The Kingdom of Germany in the High Middle Ages (900–1200)*, Historical Association Pamphlet 77, London.

Gillmann, F. (1924) 'Zur scholastischen Auslegung von Mt 16, 18', *Archiv für katholisches Kirchenrecht* CIV, 41–53.

Girgensohn, D. (1993) 'Francesco Zabarella aus Padua. Gelehrsamkeit und politisches Wirken eines Rechtsprofessors während des grossen abendländischen Schismas', *Zeitschrift der Savigny-Stiftung für Rechtsgeschichte*, Kanonistische Abteilung LXXIX, 232–77.

Godman, P. (1987) *Poets and Emperors. Frankish Politics and Carolingian Poetry*, Oxford: Clarendon Press.

Godman, P. and Collins, R. (1990) *Charlemagne's Heir. New Perspectives on the Reign of Louis the Pious (814–840)*, Oxford: Clarendon Press.

Grabmann, M. (1934) 'Studien über den Einfluss der aristotelischen Philosophie auf die mittelalterlichen Theorien über das Verhältnis von Kirche und Staat'. *Sitzungsberichte der Bayerische Akademie der Wissenschaften*, Phil.-hist,. Abteilung II, 41–60.

Graus, F. (1959) 'Über die sogennante germanische Treue', *Historia* I, 71–121.

Graus, F. (1966) 'Herrschaft und Treue. Betrachtungen zur Lehre von der germanischen Kontinuität', *Historia* XII, 5–44.

Grégoire, H. (1966) 'The Amorians and Macedonians 842–1025', in *Cambridge Medieval History*, IV, 1, Cambridge: Cambridge University Press.

Gregory, T. (1966) 'L'idea di natura nella filosofia medievale prima dell' ingresso della fisica di Aristotele – il secolo XII', pp. 27–65 in *La filosofia della natura nel medioevo. Atti del Terzo Congresso internazionale di filosofia medioevale* (Passo della Mendola, Trento, 31 agosto – 5 settembre, 1964), Milan: Società editrice Vita e Pensiero.

Gregory, T. (1975) 'La nouvelle idée de nature et de savoir scientifique au XIIᵉ siècle', pp. 193–218 in J.E. Murdoch and E.D. Sylla (eds), *The Cultural Context of Medieval Learning* (Proceedings of the First International Colloquium on Philosophy, Science and Theology in the Middle Ages, September, 1973), Boston Studies in the Philosophy of Science 26, Dordrecht and Boston: D. Reidel Publishing Co.

Grignaschi, M. (1970) 'L'ideologia marsiliana si spiega con l'adesione dell'autore all'uno o all'altro dei grandi sistemi filosofici dell'inizio del trecento?', *Medioevo. Rivista di storia della filosofia medievale* V, 201–22.

Haendler, G. (1993) 'Die drei grossen nordafrikanischen Kirchenväter über Mt 16, 18–19', in G. Haendler, *Die Rolle des Papsttums in der Kirchengeschichte bis 1200. Ein Überblick und achtzehn Untersuchungen*, Göttingen, Vandenhoeck & Ruprecht.

Hannig, J. (1982) *Consensus fidelium. Frühfeudale Interpretationen des Verhältnisses von Königtum und Adel am Beispiel des Frankenreiches*, Monographien zur Geschichte des Mittelalters 27, Stuttgart: Hiersemann.

Herman, E. (1967) 'The secular church', pp. 105–33 in *Cambridge Medieval History*, IV, 2, Cambridge: Cambridge University Press.

Herrin, J. (1987) *The Formation of Christendom*, Oxford: Basil Blackwell.

Hibst, P. (1991) *Utilitas publica – Gemeiner Nutz – Gemeinwohl. Untersuchungen zur Idee eines politischen Leitbegriffs von der Antike bis zum späten Mittelalter*, Europäische Hochschulschriften, Reihe III, Geschichte und ihre Hilfswissenschaften, Series III, vol. 497, Frankfurt, Bern, New York, Paris: Peter Lang.

Hoffmann, H. (1964) 'Die beiden Schwerter im hohen Mittelalter', *Deutsches Archiv für die Erforschung des Mittelalters* XX, 78–114.

Höfler, O. (1956) 'Der sakralcharakter des germanischen Königtums', pp. 75–104 in T. Mayer (ed.), *Das Königtum. Seine geistigen und rechtlichen Grundlagen*, Vorträge und Forschungen III. Constance: Jan Thorbecke.

Imkamp, W. (1983) *Das Kirchenbild Innocenz' III. (1198–1216)*, Päpste und Papsttum 22, Stuttgart: Anton Hiersemann Verlag.

Johannessen, R.M. (1992) 'Cardinal Jean Lemoine's gloss to *Rem non novam* and the reinstatement of the Colonna cardinals', pp. 309–20 in S. Chodorow (ed.), *Proceedings of the Eighth International Congress of Medieval Canon Law, San Diego*, Miscellanea Iuris Canonici, Series C, Vatican City: Biblioteca Apostolica Vaticana.

Kantorowicz, E.H. (1957) *The King's Two Bodies: A Study in Medieval Political Theology*, Princeton: Princeton University Press.

Keller, H. (1989) 'Zum Charakter der "Staatlichkeit" zwischen karolingischer Reichsreform und hochmittelalterlichen Herrschaftsausbau', *Frühmittelalterliche Studien* XXIII, 248–64.

Kennan, E. (1967) 'The "De consideratione" of St Bernard and the papacy in the mid-twelfth century: a review of scholarship', *Traditio* XXIII, 73–115.

Kern, F. (1939) *Kingship and Law in the Middle Ages* (trans. S.B. Chrimes), Oxford: Basil Blackwell.

Kerner, M. (1977) *Johannes von Salisbury und die logische Struktur seines Policraticus*, Wiesbaden: Franz Steiner Verlag.

King, P.D. (1972) *Law and Society in the Visigothic Kingdom*, Cambridge Studies in Medieval Life and Thought, third series, 5, Cambridge: Cambridge University Press.

King, P.D. (1980) 'The alleged territoriality of Visigothic law', pp. 1–11 in B. Tierney and P. Linehan, *Authority and Power. Studies on Medieval Law and Government Presented to Walter Ullmann on his Seventieth Birthday*, Cambridge: Cambridge University Press.

King, P.D. (1988) 'The barbarian kingdoms', pp. 123–53 in J.H. Burns (ed.), *The Cambridge History of Medieval Political Thought, c. 350–c. 1450*, Cambridge: Cambridge University Press.

Kretzmann, N., Kenny, A., and Pinborg, J., (eds) (1982) *The Cambridge History of Later Medieval Philosophy*, Cambridge: Cambridge University Press.

Kroeschell, K. (1972) ' "Rechtsfindung." Die mittelalterlichen Grundlagen einer modernen Vorstellung', pp. 498–517 in *Festschrift für Hermann Heimpel* III, Göttingen: Vandenhoeck & Ruprecht.

Kuttner, S. (1936) 'Sur les origines du terme "droit positif"', *Revue historique de droit français et étranger*, 4ième série, XV, 728–40.

Levison, W. (1952) 'Die mittelalterliche Lehre von den beiden Schwertern', *Deutsches Archiv für die Erforschung des Mittelalters* IX, 14–42.

Lewis, E. (1963) 'The "positivism" of Marsiglio of Padua', *Speculum* XXXVIII, 541–82.

Leyser, K.J. (1979) *Rule and Conflict in an Early Medieval Society: Ottonian Saxony*, London: Edward Arnold.

Leyser, K.J. (1982) *Medieval Germany and its Neighbours, 900–1250*, London: Hambledon Press.

Lieber, H.J. (ed.) (1991) *Politische Theorien von der Antike bis zur Gegenwart*, Munich: Olzog Verlag.

Löwe, H. (1963) 'Kaisertum und Abendland in Ottonischer und Frühsalischer Zeit', *Historische Zeitschrift* CXCVI, 529–62.

Lucrezi, F. (1982) *Leges super principem: la 'monarchia costituzionale' di Vespasiano*, Naples: Jovene.

Luscombe, D.E. (1979) 'Conceptions of hierarchy before the thirteenth century', pp. 1–19 in A. Zimmermann (ed.), *Soziale Ordnungen im Selbstverständnis des Mittelalters*, Berlin and New York: Walter de Gruyter.

Luscombe, D.E. (1984) 'John of Salisbury in recent scholarship', pp. 21–37 in M. Wilks (ed.), *The World of John of Salisbury*, Studies in Church History, Subsidia 3, Oxford: Basil Blackwell.

Luscombe, D.E. (1988) 'Thomas Aquinas and conceptions of hierarchy in the thirteenth century', pp. 261–77 in A. Zimmermann (ed.), *Thomas von Aquin. Werke und Wirkung im Licht neuerer Forschungen*, Berlin and New York: Walter de Gruyter.

Luscombe, D.E. (1988) 'Introduction: the formation of political thought in the west (c. 750–c. 1150)', pp. 157–73 in J.H. Burns (ed.), *The Cambridge History of Medieval Political Thought, c. 350–c. 1450*, Cambridge: Cambridge University Press.

Maccarrone, M. (1952) *Vicarius Christi. Storia del titolo papale*, Rome: Facultas Theologica Pontificii Athenaei Lateranensis.

Maccarrone, M. (1954) '"Potestas directa" e "potestas indirecta" nei teologi del XII e XIII secolo', in *Sacerdozio e regno da Gregorio VII a Bonifacio VIII*, Miscellanea Historiae Pontificiae XVIII, 27–47.

Maccarrone, M. (1959) 'Il sovrano "vicarius dei" nell'alto medio evo', pp. 581–94 in *The Sacral Kingship*, Contributions to the Central Theme of the VIIIth International Congress for the History of Religions, Rome, April, 1955, Leiden: E.J. Brill.

McGrade, A.S. (1974) *The Political Thought of William of Ockham*, Cambridge Studies in Medieval Life and Thought, third series, 7, Cambridge: Cambridge University Press.

Maffei, D. (1964) *La donazione di Costantino nei giuristi medievali*, Milan: Giuffrè.

Magnou-Nortier, E. (1976) *Foi et fidélité. Recherches sur l'évolution des liens personnels chez les Francs du VIIe au IXe siècle*, Publications de l'Université de Toulouse-Le Mirail, série A, 28, Association des publications de l'Université de Toulouse-Le Mirail.

Makdisi, G., Sourdel, D. and Sourdel-Thomine, J. (eds) (1982) *La notion d'autorité au Moyen Age. Islam, Byzance, Occident*, Paris: Presses universitaires de France.

Markus, R.A. (1965) 'Two conceptions of political authority: Augustine, *De civitate dei*, XIX.14–15, and some thirteenth-century interpretations', *The Journal of Theological Studies*, new series, XVI, 68–100.

Markus, R.A. (1970) *Saeculum: History and Society in the Theology of St Augustine*, Cambridge: Cambridge University Press.

Markus, R.A. (1981) 'Gregory the Great's Europe', *Transactions of the Royal Historical Society*, 5th Series, XXXI, 21–36.

Mayer, T. (ed.) (1956) *Das Königtum. Seine geistigen und rechtlichen Grundlagen*, Vorträge und Forschungen, III, Lindau and Constance: Jan Thorbecke Verlag.

Mayer, T. (1956) 'Staatsauffassung in der Karolingerzeit', pp. 169–83 in T. Mayer, *Das Königtum. Seine geistigen und rechtlichen Grundlagen*, Lindau and Constance: Jan Thorbecke Verlag.

Meijers, E.M. (1959) *Etudes d'histoire du droit*, R. Feenstra and H.F.W.D. Fischer (eds), Vol. III, Leiden: Universitaire Pers.

Melloni, A. (1990) *Innocenzo IV. La concezione e l'esperienza della christianità come regimen unius personae*, Genoa: Marietti.

Merzbacher, F. (1958) 'Recht und Gewaltenlehre bei Hugo von St. Viktor', *Zeitschrift der Savigny Stiftung für Rechtsgeschichte*, Kan. Abt. XLIV, 181–208.

Micza, G. (1970) *Das Bild der Kirche bei Johannes von Salisbury*, Bonner historische Forschungen 34, Bonn: Ludwig Röhrscheid Verlag.

Miethke, J. (1989) 'Marsilius von Padua. Die politische Philosophie eines lateinischen Aristotelikers des 14. Jahrhunderts', pp. 52–76 in H. Boockmann, B. Moeller, K. Stackmann and L. Grenzmann (eds),

Lebenslehren und Weltentwürfe im Übergang vom Mittelalter zur Neuzeit, Abhandlungen der Akademie der Wissenschaften in Göttingen, Phil.-Hist. Klasse, Dritte Folge, CLXXIX, Göttingen: Vandenhoeck & Ruprecht.

Miethke, J. (1991) 'Politische Theorien im Mittelalter', pp. 47–156 in H.J. Lieber (ed.), *Politische Theorien von der Antike bis zur Gegenwart*, Munich: Olzog Verlag.

Minio-Paluello, L. (1956) 'Remigio Girolami's *De bono communi*: Florence at the time of Dante's banishment and the philosopher's answer to the crisis', *Italian Studies* XI, 56–71.

Mochi Onory, S. (1951) *Fonti canonistiche dell'idea moderna dello stato – imperium spirituale, iurisdictio divina, sovranità*, Publ. dell'Università Cattolica del Sacro Cuore, n.s., 38, Milan: Società editrice 'Vita e Pensiero'.

Mommsen, T. (1887) *Römisches Staatsrecht*, 3rd edn, Leipzig: S. Hirzel.

Mommsen, T.E. and Morrison, K.F. (trans.) and Benson, R.L. (ed.) (1962) *Imperial Lives and Letters of the Eleventh Century* (with a historical introduction by K.F. Morrison), The Records of Civilization Series 67, New York and London: Columbia University Press.

Montagu, G. (1994) 'Roman law and the emperor – the rationale of "written reason" in some *consilia* of Oldradus da Ponte', *History of Political Thought* XV, 1–56.

Morral, J.B. (1960) *Gerson and the Great Schism*, Manchester: Manchester University Press.

Morris, C. (1991) *The Papal Monarchy. The Western Church from 1050 to 1250*, Oxford: Clarendon Press.

Morrissey, T.E. (1978) 'The decree "Haec sancta" and Cardinal Zabarella. His role in its formulation and interpretation', *Annuarium Historiae Conciliorum* X(2) 145–76.

Morrissey, T.E. (1981) 'Franciscus Zabarella (1360–1417): papacy, community and limitations upon authority', in G. Fitch Lytle, *Reform and Authority in the Medieval and Renaissance Church*, Washington, DC: Catholic University of America Press.

Morrissey, T.E. (1985) 'Cardinal Franciscus Zabarella (1360–1417) as a canonist and the crisis of his age: schism and the Council of Constance', *Zeitschrift für Kirchengeschichte* XCVI, 196–208.

Morrissey, T.E. (1986) 'Cardinal Zabarella and Nicholas of Cusa. From community authority to consent of the community', pp. 157–76 in *Mitteilungen und Forschungen der Cusanus-Gesellschaft* XVII, Mainz: Matthias-Grünewald-Verlag.

Mostert, M. (1987) *The Political Theology of Abbo of Fleury. A Study of the Ideas about Society and Law of the Tenth-Century Monastic Reform Movement*, Medieval Studies and Sources 2, Hilversum: Verloren Publishers.

Muldoon, J. (1971) 'Boniface VIII's forty years of experience in the law', *The Jurist* XXXI, 449–77.

Muldoon, J. (1979) *Popes, Lawyers and Infidels: The Church and the Non-Christian World, 1250–1500*, Philadelphia: University of Pennsylvania Press.

Müller, W.P. (1994) *Huguccio: The Life, Works and Thought of a Twelfth-Century Jurist*, Studies in Medieval and Early Modern Canon Law 3, Washington, DC: Catholic University of America Press.

Nederman, C.J. (1988) 'A duty to kill: John of Salisbury's theory of tyrannicide', *Review of Politics* L, 365–89.

Nederman, C.J. (1988) 'Nature, sin and the origins of society: the Ciceronian tradition in medieval political thought', *Journal of the History of Ideas* XLIX, 3–26

Nederman, C.J. (1995) *Community and Consent. The Secular Political Theory of Marsiglio of Padua's Defensor Pacis*, Lanham, Md.: Rowman & Littlefield.

Nelson, J.L. (1980) 'The earliest surviving royal *Ordo*: some liturgical and historical aspects', pp. 29–48 in B. Tierney and P. Linehan (eds), *Authority and Power. Studies on Medieval Law and Government Presented to Walter Ullmann on his Seventieth Birthday*, Cambridge: Cambridge University Press.

Nelson, J.L. (1986) 'On the limits of the Carolingian Renaissance', pp. 49–67 in J.L. Nelson, *Politics and Ritual in Early Medieval Europe*, London: Hambledon Press.

Nelson, J.L. (1986) 'National synods, kingship as office, and royal anointing: an early medieval syndrome', pp. 239–57 in J.L. Nelson, *Politics and Ritual in Early Medieval Europe*, London: Hambledon Press.

Nelson, J.L. (1986) 'Kingship, law and liturgy in the political thought of Hincmar of Rheims', pp. 133–71 in J.L. Nelson, *Politics and Ritual in Early Medieval Europe*, London: Hambledon Press.

Nelson, J.L. (1986) 'Inauguration rituals', pp. 283–307 in J.L. Nelson, *Politics and Ritual in Early Medieval Europe*, London: Hambledon Press.

Nelson, J.L. (1986) *Politics and Ritual in Early Medieval Europe*, London: Hambledon Press.

Nelson, J.L. (1988) 'Kingship and Empire', pp. 211–51 in J.H. Burns (ed.), *The Cambridge History of Medieval Political Thought, c. 350–c. 1450*, Cambridge: Cambridge University Press.

Nicol, D.M. (1988) 'Byzantine political thought', pp. 51–79 in J.H. Burns (ed.), *The Cambridge History of Medieval Political Thought, c. 350–c. 1450*, Cambridge: Cambridge University Press.

Oakley, F. (1964) *The Political Thought of Pierre d'Ailly: The Voluntarist Tradition*, Yale Historical Publications Miscellany 81, New Haven: Yale University Press.

O'Callaghan, J.F. (1975) *A History of Medieval Spain*, Ithaca, N.Y.: Cornell University Press.

O'Collins, G. (1973) *The Easter Jesus*, London: Darton, Longman & Todd.

Ostrogorsky, G. (1956) *History of the Byzantine State* (trans. J. Hussey), Oxford: Basil Blackwell.

Paradisi, B. (1987) 'Formule di sovranità e tradizione biblica', pp. 447–511 in Vol. I, *Studi sul Medioevo giuridico*, Istituto storico italiano per il medio evo, Studi storici, fasc. 163–73, 2 vols, Rome.

Pascoe, L.B. (1973) *Jean Gerson: Principles of Church Reform*, Leiden: E.J. Brill.

Pennington, K. (1970) 'Bartholomé de Las Casas and the tradition of medieval law', *Church History* XXXIX, 149–61.

Pennington, K. (1984) *Popes and Bishops. The Papal Monarchy in the Twelfth and Thirteenth Centuries*, Philadelphia: University of Pennsylvania Press.

Pennington, K. (1988) 'Law, legislative authority, and theories of government, 1150–1300', pp. 424–53 in J.H. Burns (ed.), *The Cambridge History of Medieval Political Thought, c. 350–c. 1450*, Cambridge: Cambridge University Press.

Pennington, K. (1993) *Popes, Canonists and Texts, 1150–1550*, Aldershot: Variorum.

Pennington, K. (1993) 'Further thoughts on Pope Innocent III's knowledge of law', in K. Pennington, *Popes, Canonists and Texts, 1150–1550*, Aldershot: Variorum.

Pennington, K. (1993) 'The legal education of Pope Innocent III', in K. Pennington, *Popes, Canonists and Texts, 1150–1550*, Aldershot: Variorum.

Pennington, K. (1993) 'The authority of the prince in a *consilium* of Baldus de Ubaldis', in K. Pennington, *Popes, Canonists and Texts, 1150–1550*, Aldershot: Variorum.

Pennington, K. (1993) *The Prince and the Law 1200–1600*, Berkeley: University of California Press.

Post, G. (1946) 'A Romano-canonical maxim, "Quod omnes tangit", in Bracton', *Traditio* IV, 197–251.

Post, G. (1964) *Studies in Medieval Thought, Public Law and the State, 1100–1322*, Princeton: Princeton University Press.

Quillet, J. (1970) *La philosophie politique de Marsile de Padoue*, Paris: Vrin.

Quillet, J. (1979) 'L'Aristotelisme de Marsile de Padoue et ses rapports avec l'Averroisme', *Medioevo. Rivista di storia della filosofia medievale* V, 81–123.

Renna, T. (1974) 'The populus in John of Paris' theory of monarchy', *Tijdschrift voor Rechtsgeschiedenis* XLII, 243–68.

Renna, T. (1978) 'Aristotle and the French monarchy, 1260–1303', *Viator* IX, 309–24.

Reviron, J. (1930) *Les idées politico-religieuses d'un évêque du IXe siècle. Jonas d'Orleans et son 'De institutione regia'. Etude et texte critique*, L'Eglise et l'Etat au Moyen Age 1, Paris: J. Vrin.

Reydellet, M. (1981) *La royauté dans la littérature latine de Sidonie Apollinaire à Isidore de Seville*, Ecole française de Rome.

Reynolds, S. (1994) *Fiefs and Vassals. The Medieval Evidence Reinterpreted*, Oxford: Oxford University Press.

Richards, J. (1980) *Consul of God: The Life and Times of Gregory the Great*, London: Routledge.

Riesenberg, P.N. (1956) *Inalienability of Sovereignty in Medieval Political Thought*, New York: Columbia University Press.

Rivière, J. (1926) *Le problème de l'Eglise et de l'Etat au temps de Philippe le Bel*, Etudes et documents 8, Louvain: Spicilegium sacrum Lovaniense.

Robinson, I.S. (1978) *Authority and Resistance in the Investiture Contest. The Polemical Literature of the Late Eleventh Century*, Manchester: Manchester University Press.

Robinson, I.S. (1990) *The Papacy 1073–1198. Continuity and Innovation*, Cambridge Medieval Textbooks, Cambridge: Cambridge University Press.

Rouse, R.H. and Rouse, M.A. (1967) 'John of Salisbury and the doctrine of tyrannicide', *Speculum* XLII, 693–709.

Rubinstein, N. (1965) 'Marsilius of Padua and Italian Political thought of his time', pp. 44–75 in J.R. Hale, J.R.L. Highfield and B. Smalley (eds), *Europe in the Late Middle Ages*, London: Faber & Faber.

Rubinstein, N. (1987) 'The history of the word *politicus* in early-modern Europe', in A. Pagden (ed.), *The Languages of Political Theory in Early-Modern Europe*, Cambridge: Cambridge University Press.

Sawicki, J.J. (1977) 'The ecclesiological and political thought of Petrus de Ancharano (1330?–1416)', Unpublished Ph.D. dissertation, Cornell University.

Sawyer, P.H. (1968) *Anglo-Saxon Charters: An Annotated Guide and Bibliography*, Royal Historical Society Guides and Handbooks, London: Royal Historical Society.

Sawyer, P.H. and Wood, I.N. (eds) (1977) *Early Medieval Kingship*, Leeds: School of History, University of Leeds.

Scheltema, H.J. (1967) 'Byzantine law', in *Cambridge Medieval History*, Vol. IV: *The Byzantine Empire*, Part 2, pp. 55–77, Cambridge: Cambridge University Press.

Schieffer, R. (1981) *Die Entstehung des päpstlichen Investiturverbots für den deutschen König*, Schriften der MGH 28, Stuttgart: Anton Hiersemann Verlag.

Schmugge, L. (1966) *Johannes von Jandun (1285/89). Untersuchungen zur Biographie und Sozialtheorie eines lateinischen Averroisten*, Pariser Historische Studien, Herausgegeben vom Deutschen Historischen Institut in Paris, 5, Stuttgart: Hiersemann.

Schneidmüller, B. (1979) *Karolingische Tradition und frühes französisches Königtum. Untersuchungen zur Herrschaftslegitimation der westfränkisch-französischen Monarchie im 10. Jahrhundert*, Frankfurter historische Abhandlungen 22, Wiesbaden: Franz Steiner Verlag.

Scholz, R. (1903) *Die Publizistik zur Zeit Philipps des Schönen und Bonifaz' VIII. Ein Beitrag zur Geschichte der politischen Ausschauungen des Mittelalters*, Kirchenrechtliche Abhandlungen 6/8, Stuttgart: Ferdinand Enke.

Schramm, P. (1968) *Kaiser, Könige und Päpste*, 4 vols, Stuttgart: Hiersemann.

Sieben, H.J. (1984) *Das Konzilsidee des lateinischen Mittelalters, 847–1378*, Paderborn: Ferdinand Schöningh.

Skinner, Q. (1978) *Foundations of Modern Political Thought*, 2 vols, Cambridge: Cambridge University Press.

Steinwenter, A. (1946) 'Νόμος ἔμψυχος: zur Geschichte einer politischen Theorie', *Anzeiger der Akademie der Wissenschaften in Wien*, phil.–hist. Kl., CXXXIII, 250–68.

Stengel, E.E. (1960) 'Imperator und imperium bei den Angelsachsen. Eine wort- und begriffsgeschichtliche Untersuchung', *Deutsches Archiv für die Erforschung des Mittelalters* XVI, 15–72.

Sternberger, D. (1981) 'Die Stadt und das Reich in der Verfassungslehre des Marsilius von Padua', pp. 89–149 in *Sitzungsberichte der Wissenschaftlichen Gesellschaft an der Johann Wolfgang Goethe-Universität, Frankfurt-am-Main* XVIII, Wiesbaden: Franz Steiner Verlag.

Stickler, A.M. (1954) 'Sacerdozio e regno nelle nuove ricerche attorno ai secoli XII e XIII nei Decretisti e Decretalisti fino alle decretali di Gregorio IX', *Sacerdozio e regno da Gregorio VII a Bonifacio VIII,* Miscellanea Historiae Pontificiae XVIII, 1–26.

Stickler, A.M. (1959) 'Alanus Anglicus als Verteidiger des monarchischen Papsttums', *Salesianum* XXI, 346–406.

Stieber, J.W. (1978) *Pope Eugenius IV, the Council of Basel and the Secular and Ecclesiastical Authorities in the Empire,* Leiden: E.J. Brill.

Strayer, J.R. (1980) *The Reign of Philip the Fair,* Princeton: Princeton University Press.

Struve, T. (1978) *Die Entwicklung der organologischen Staatsauffassung im Mittelalter,* Monographien zur Geschichte des Mittelalters 16, Stuttgart: Hiersemann.

Struve, T. (1988) 'Kaisertum und Romgedanke in salischer Zeit', *Deutsches Archiv für die Erforschung des Mittelalters* XLIV, 424–54.

Stump, P.H. (1994) *The Reforms of the Council of Constance (1414–1418),* Studies in the History of Christian Thought 53, Leiden: E.J. Brill.

Stürner, W. (1987) *Peccatum und potestas. Der Sündenfall und die Entstehung der herrscherlichen Gewalt im mittelalterlichen Staatsdenken,* Beiträge zur Geschichte und Quellenkunde des Mittelalters (ed. H. Fuhrmann), Sigmaringen: Jan Thorbecke Verlag.

Suerbaum, W. (1977) *Vom antiken zum frühmittelalterlichen Staatsbegriff: über Verwendung und Bedeutung von Res publica, regnum, imperium und status von Cicero bis Jordanis,* Orbis antiquus 16/17, Münster: Aschendorff.

Szabó-Bechstein, B. (1985) 'Libertas ecclesiae: ein Schlüsselbegriff des Investiturstreits und seine Vorgeschichte, 4.–11. Jahrhundert', *Studi Gregoriani* XII, Rome.

Tierney, B. (1954) 'Some recent works on the political theories of the medieval canonists', *Traditio* X, 594–625.

Tierney, B. (1955) *Foundations of the Conciliar Theory. The Contribution of the Medieval Canonists from Gratian to the Great Schism,* Cambridge: Cambridge University Press.

Tierney, B. (1963) '*Natura id est deus*: a case of juristic pantheism', *Journal of the History of Ideas* XXIV, 307–22.

Tierney, B. (1963) ' "The prince is not bound by the laws." Accursius and the origins of the modern state', *Comparative Studies in Society and History* V(4) (July), 378–400.

Tierney, B. (1964) *The Crisis of Church and State, 1050–1300,* Englewood Cliffs, N.J.: Prentice-Hall.

Tierney, B. (1965) 'The continuity of papal political theory in the thirteenth century. Some methodological considerations', *Mediaeval Studies* XXVII, 227–45.

Tierney, B. (1983) 'Tuck on rights: some medieval problems', *History of Political Thought* IV(3) (Winter), 429–41.

Tierney, B. (1989) 'Origins of natural rights language: texts and contexts, 1150–1250', *History of Political Thought* X(4) (Winter), 615–46.

Tierney, B. and Linehan, P. (eds) (1980) *Authority and Power. Studies on Medieval Law and Government Presented to Walter Ullmann on his Seventieth Birthday,* Cambridge: Cambridge University Press.

Ullmann, W. (1952) 'The origins of the *Ottonianum*', *The Cambridge Historical Journal* XI(1), 114–28.

Ullmann, W. (1960) 'Leo I and the theme of papal primacy', *Journal of Theological Studies*, new series XI, 25–51.

Ullmann, W. (1960) 'The significance of the *Epistola Clementis* in the Pseudo-Clementines', *Journal of Theological Studies*, new series XI, 295–317.

Ullmann, W. (1961) *Principles of Government and Politics in the Middle Ages*, London: Methuen.

Ullmann, W. (1962) 'De Bartoli sententia: Concilium repraesentat mentem populi', pp. 707–33 in Vol. II, *Bartolo da Sassoferrato-studi e documenti per il VI centenario*, 2 vols, Milan.

Ullmann, W. (1965) *A History of Political Thought: The Middle Ages*, Harmondsworth: Penguin Books.

Ullmann, W. (1967) *The Individual and Society in the Middle Ages*, London: Methuen.

Ullmann, W. (1968–9) 'Juristic obstacles to the emergence of the concept of the state in the Middle Ages', *Annali di storia del diritto – rassegna internazionale* XII–XIII, 43–64.

Ullmann, W. (1969) *The Carolingian Renaissance and the Idea of Kingship*, London: Methuen.

Ullmann, W. (1970) *The Growth of Papal Government in the Middle Ages*, 3rd edn, London: Methuen.

Ullmann, W. (1972) 'A note on inalienability in Gregory VII', *Studi Gregoriani* IX, 117–40.

Ullmann, W. (1972) *A Short History of the Papacy in the Middle Ages*, London: Methuen.

Ullmann, W. (1975) *Law and Politics in the Middle Ages: An Introduction to the Sources of Medieval Political Ideas*, London: The Sources of History.

Ullmann, W. (1976) 'Boniface VIII and his contemporary scholarship', *Journal of Theological Studies*, new series XXVII, 58–87.

Ullmann, W. (1979) 'Arthur's homage to King John', *English Historical Review* XCIV, 356–64.

Ullmann, W. (1981) *Gelasius I. (492–496): Das Papsttum an der Wende der Spätantike zum Mittelalter*, Päpste und Papsttum 18, Stuttgart: Hiersemann.

Vacca, S. (1993) *Prima sedes a nemine iudicatur: genesi e sviluppo storico dell'assioma fino al Decreto di Graziano*, Miscellanea historiae pontificiae 61, Rome: Editrice Pontificia Università Gregoriana.

Verbeke, G. (1989) 'Moerbeke, traducteur et interprète; un texte et une pensée', in J. Brams and W. Vanhamel (eds), *Guillaume de Moerbeke. Recueil d'Etudes à l'occasion du 700ᵉ anniversaire de sa mort (1286)*, Louvain: University Press.

Wallace-Hadrill, J.M. (1971) *Early Germanic Kingship in England and on the Continent*, Oxford: Clarendon Press.

Wallace-Hadrill, J.M. (1988) *Bede's Ecclesiastical History of the English People. An Historical Commentary*, Oxford: Clarendon Press.

Walther, H.G. (1976) *Imperiales Königtum, Konziliarismus und Volkssouveränität. Studien zu den Grenzen des mittelalterlichen Souveränitätsgedankens*, Munich: Wilhelm Fink Verlag.

Walther, H.G. (1990) 'Die Gegner Ockhams: zur Korporationslehre der mittelalterlichen Legisten', in G. Göhler, K. Lenk, H. Münkler and M. Walther (eds), *Politische Institutionen im gesellschaftlichen Umbruch. Ideengeschichtliche Beiträge zur Theorie politischer Institutionen*, Opladen: Westdeutscher Verlag.

Walther, H.G. (1990) 'Die Legitimität der Herrschaftsordnung bei Bartolus von Sassoferrato und Baldus de Ubaldis', in E. Mock and G. Wieland (eds), *Rechts- und Sozialphilosophie des Mittelalters*, Salzburger Schriften zur Rechts-, Staats- und Sozialphilosophie 12, Frankfurt-am-Main: Peter Lang.

Walther, H.G. (1992) '"Verbis Aristotelis non utar, quia ea iuristae non saperent." Legistische und aristotelische Herrschaftstheorie bei Bartolus und Baldus', in J. Miethke (ed.), *Das Publikum politischer Theorie im 14. Jahrhundert*, Schriften des Historischen Kollegs, Kolloquium 21, Munich: R. Oldenbourg Verlag.

Walther, H.G. (1992) 'Wasser in Stadt und Contado. Perugias Sorge um Wasser und der Flusstraktat *tyberiadis* des Perusiner Juristen Bartolus von Sassoferrato', in *Mensch und Natur im Mittelalter*, Miscellanea Mediaevalia 21(2), 882–97.

Watt, J.A. (1965) *The Theory of Papal Monarchy in the Thirteenth Century. The Contribution of the Canonists*, London: Burns & Oates.

Watt, J.A. (1965) 'The use of the term "plenitudo potestatis" by Hostiensis', pp. 161–87 in S. Kuttner and J.J. Ryan (eds), Proceedings of the Second International Congress of Medieval Canon Law (Boston College, 12–16 August, 1963), *Monumenta Iuris Canonici*, Series C, Subsidia I, Vatican City.

Watt, J.A. (1967) 'The "Quaestio in utramque partem" reconsidered', *Studia Gratiana* XIII, 411–53.

Watt, J.A. (1988) 'Spiritual and temporal powers', pp. 367–423 in J.H. Burns (ed.), *The Cambridge History of Medieval Political Thought, c. 350–c. 1450*, Cambridge: Cambridge University Press.

Wehlen, W. (1970) *Geschichtsschreibung und Staatsauffassung im Zeitalter Ludwigs des Frommen*, Historische Studien 418, Lübeck and Hamburg: Matthiesen Verlag.

Weigand, R. (1967) *Die Naturrechtslehre der Legisten und Dekretisten von Irnerius bis Accursius und von Gratian bis Johannes Teutonicus*, Münchener Theologische Studien III, Kanonistische Abteilung 26, Munich: Max Huebler Verlag.

Werner, K.F. (1965) 'Das hochmittelalterliche imperium im politischen Bewusstsein Frankreichs (10.–12. Jahrhundert)', *Historische Zeitschrift* CC, 1–60.

Werner, K.F. (1980) 'L'empire carolingien et le Saint Empire', pp. 151–98 in M. Duverger, *Le concept d'empire*, Paris: Presses universitaires de France.

Werner, K.F. (1990) 'Hludowicus augustus: gouverner l'empire chrétien – idées et réalités', pp. 3–123 in P. Godman and R. Collins, *Charlemagne's Heir. New Perspectives on the Reign of Louis the Pious (814–840)*, Oxford: Clarendon Press.

Wilks, M.J. (1963) *The Problem of Sovereignty in the Later Middle Ages. The Papal Monarchy with Augustinus Triumphus and the Publicists*,

Cambridge Studies in Medieval Life and Thought, second series, 9, Cambridge: Cambridge University Press.

Wilks, M.J. (1971) '*Ecclesiastica* and *Regalia*: Papal investiture policy from the Council of Guastalla to the First Lateran Council, 1106–23', *Studies in Church History* VII, 69–85.

Wilks, M.J. (1972) 'Corporation and representation in the Defensor Pacis', *Studia Gratiana* XV, 253–92.

Williams, G.H. (1951) *The Norman Anonymous of 1100 A.D. Toward the Identification and Evaluation of the So-Called Anonymous of York*, Harvard Theological Studies 18, Cambridge, Mass.: Harvard University Press.

Witte, F.-W. (1957) 'Die Staats- und Rechtsphilosophie des Hugo von St Viktor', *Archiv für Rechts- und Sozialphilosophie* XLIII, 555–74.

Wolf, A. (1973) 'Die Gesetzgebung der entstehenden Territorialstaaten', pp. 505–800 in H. Coing, *Handbuch der Quellen und Literatur der neueren europäischen Privatrechtsgeschichte*, I: *Mittelalter (1100–1500)*, Munich: C.H. Beck.

Wolfram, H. (1967) *Intitulatio*, I: *Lateinische Königs- und Fürstentitel bis zum Ende des 8. Jahrhunderts*, Mitteilungen des Instituts für Österreichische Geschichtsforschung 21, Graz–Vienna–Cologne: Böhlau Verlag.

Wood, I.N. (1977) 'Kings, kingdoms and consent', pp. 6–29 in P.H. Sawyer and I.N. Wood (eds), *Early Medieval Kingship*, Leeds: School of History, University of Leeds.

Woolf, C.N.S. (1913) *Bartolus of Sassoferrato. His Position in the History of Medieval Political Thought*, Cambridge: Cambridge University Press.

Wormald, P. (1977) '*Lex scripta* and *Verbum regis*: legislation and Germanic kingship from Euric to Cnut', pp. 105–38 in P.H. Sawyer and I.N. Wood, *Early Medieval Kingship*, Leeds: School of History, University of Leeds.

Zimmermann, A. (ed.) (1979) *Soziale Ordnungen im Selbstverständnis des Mittelalters*, Berlin and New York: Walter de Gruyter.

Zimmermann, A. (ed.) (1988) *Thomas von Aquin. Werke und Wirkung im Licht neuerer Forschungen*, Berlin and New York: Walter de Gruyter.

INDEX